Across Time and Tundra

Across Time and Tundra

The Inuvialuit of the Western Arctic

Ishmael Alunik, Eddie D. Kolausok and David Morrison

Raincoast Books
Vancouver

University of Washington Press
Seattle

Canadian Museum of Civilization
Gatineau

This book is dedicated to the elders and the children.

CANADIAN MUSEUM MUSÉE CANADIEN
OF CIVILIZATION DES CIVILISATIONS

(*Page ii–iii*) ROBERT SEMENIUK

Raincoast Books
9050 Shaughnessy Street
Vancouver, British Columbia
Canada v6p 6e5
www.raincoast.com

University of Washington Press
PO Box 50096
Seattle, Washington
U.S.A.   98145-5096
www.washington.edu/uwpress

Canadian Museum of Civilization
100 Laurier Street
Gatineau, Quebec
Canada j8x 4h2
www.civilization.ca

The story "How Tulugak, the Raven, Stole the Sun" is retold from a version first published in a collection of stories by Simon Bennettin in the magazine *Inuvialuit* (Summer 1981: 13–15).

Raincoast Books acknowledges the ongoing financial support of the Government of Canada through The Canada Council for the Arts and the Book Publishing Industry Development Program (BPIDP); and the Government of British Columbia through the BC Arts Council.

Edited by David Morrison and Scott Steedman
Design by Val Speidel

Photo credits appear below the individual captions. The NWT Archives is divided into a number of donor collections. Catalogue prefixes cited in this work can be associated with the following collections: N-1979-050 (Archibald Fleming/NWT Archives); N-1979-062 (Terrance Hunt/NWT Archives); N-1991-068 (Charles Rowan/NWT Archives); N-1990-004 (Holman Photohistorical and Oral History Research Committee/NWT Archives); N-1993-002 (Robert C. Knignts/NWT Archives); N-1979-051 (Douglas Wilkinson/NWT Archives); G-1979-023 (Northwest Territories Dept. of Information/NWT Archives). All photos from the Anglican Archives are from the General Synod of the Anglican Church. The objects on page 74 from the Department of Anthropology, Smithsonian Institution, photos by D.E. Hurlbert, catalogue numbers E001635 (above) and E001630 (below).

NATIONAL LIBRARY OF CANADA
CATALOGUING IN PUBLICATION DATA
Alunik, Ishmael, 1923–
  Across time and tundra : the Inuvialuit of the Western Arctic / Ishmael Alunik, Eddie Dean Kolausok and David Morrison.

  Co-published by: Canadian Museum of Civilization.
  Issued also in French under title: À travers temps et toundra.

  Includes index.
  ISBN 1-55192-645-8

  1. Inuvialuit. 2. Inuvialuit—Pictorial works. I. Morrison, David A. II. Kolausok, Eddie D. III. Canadian Museum of Civilization. IV. Title.
  E99.E7A478 2003   971.9'0049712   C2003-910295-5

LIBRARY OF CONGRESS
CATALOGING-IN-PUBLICATION DATA
Alunik, Ishmael, 1923–
  Across time and tundra : the Inuvialuit of the western Arctic/ Ishmael Alunik, Eddie D. Kolausok, and David Morrison.
    p. cm.
    Includes bibliographical references and index.
    ISBN 0-295-983345 (alk. paper)
  1. Inuvialuit Eskimos—Northwest Territories—Mackenzie River Delta—History. 2. Inuvialuit Eskimos—Northwest Territories—Mackenzie River Delta—Social life and customs. 3. Mackenzie River Delta (N.W.T.)—History. 4. Mackenzie River Delta (N.W.T.)—Social life and customs. I. Kolausok, Eddie E. II. Morrison, David A.

  E99.E7.A492 2003
  971.9'3—dc21   2003047037

Printed in Hong Kong, China by Book Art Inc., Toronto
10 9 8 7 6 5 4 3 2 1

Contents

Acknowledgements

The authors wish to thank the following people for their assistance: Nellie Cournoyea, Beverly Amos, Elisa Hart, Pat Winfield and all the staff at the Inuvialuit Regional Corporation; Wendy Smith and the staff of the Inuvialuit Communications Society; Derek Smith; Dick Hill; Rita Carpenter; and Renie Arey.

EDK would like to thank the following people for their encouragement, support and friendship: Bertha Allen; Ishmael and Ruth Alunik; Walter Gardlund; Danny and Velma; George Edwards; both Peter Smiths; Vivian Smith; Dave and Myrna; Clive and Vivian; Kimberly and Altaf Staples-Lakhani; Jarvis Gray; Randy and Stephanie; O.D.; Jerry Lennie, Emmanuel Atiomo; Michael Walsh; Janet Pound; Clarissa Richardson; Edward Wright; Billy Getz; John Robson; Dennis Allen; Mabel Chicksi; Elenor Firth, Aunt Rosalie; Violet, Dorie, Joey and Robert Firth; Pete Fraser; Bob Overvold; Cece MaCauly; James Lawrence; Lorne T.; Winston, keep laughing; Robert and Richard; Ernest and Mary, Zeek, Doodles; Martin and Ruth Carroll, Don Hunter, Bruce and Ruth Ann, Bernadette and Leo Norwegian, Herb and Albertine Rohd, Dennis and Snookie, George K., Paul H., Shannon, Bill Megill, Caroline Davis, Michael G., Robin Aitken, Wayne Walsh, Phil Maracle, Donna Mousley, Suzanne Grenier, Barry Dewar, David Gowans, Tony Rabesca, Dick Hill, Daniel Watson, Gary V, Tim Christian, Larry and Susan, Eli and Kelly. Derek Morfitt, thanks for the music and laughter. My brothers: Noah gone but never forgotten; John; Brian, my foundation from childhood; Hugh; Darrel; Dennis; Rodney; Michael; and sweet sister Ann Marie, I love you all so much and understand fully the challenges you all went through and thank you for still caring. Keep on moving forward. To my dad George and sister Gabriel who carry the traditional knowledge of our ancestors, thank you for your support. Nellie Cournoyea, *quyannini* for the encouragement and support, you are a great leader and beautiful soul. Eunice and William in Tuk, thanks for the good food. Thank you Robert Gibson for your wisdom, advice and friendship. Kiviaq, David Ward, *mahsi* for the great times. Dr. James & Dorothy Battle; Dr. Charles Catto; Don Hunter; Stanley MacDonald, Kenny and Karen, Bones, Jimmy and Brian. To my son Travis, you were part of an incredible journey and are still a part of a bigger better journey. To my partner Karen who is as solid as any soul steeped in kindness and love, I thank you for the support, caring, encouragement and love. Gigi John Greenland, grandson of Arviuna, I will always cherish your love. I also want to thank all those people who have been there for me during the residential schools, group homes and no home times. To my co-authors, David and Ishmael, thank you. To all my friends that I have missed, *mahsi cho*, *quyannini*, *merci*, *ayay*, thank you.

Foreword

Across Time and Tundra is the first book that attempts to present an overview of Inuvialuit history. Through the perspective of the authors, we are fortunate to see both the outsider and insiders' view of Inuvialuit history.

The book reflects the work of three co-authors. David Morrison is an archaeologist from the Canadian Museum of Civilization who has conducted numerous archaeological studies in the Inuvialuit Settlement Region. Ishmael Alunik is an Inuvialuit elder who has patterned his life to promoting Inuvialuit culture, language and traditions — and who has recently published under the title *Call Me Ishmael: Memories of an Inuvialuit Elder*. Eddie Kolausok is an author and publisher. His most recent publication is *Aurora Shining*, a collection of short stories and poems. Ishmael and Eddie are two of the few Inuvialuit who have put their knowledge into print.

No one book can tell the entire history of a people, but *Across Time and Tundra* provides us with a broad overview of our history and some of the key factors that have shaped who we are today.

Nellie Cournoyea
Chairman, Inuvialuit Regional Corporation

Ingilraqpaaluk
(A Very Long Time Ago)

David Morrison

INTRODUCTION: THE LAND

The western Canadian Arctic is far from world centres of commerce and the bustling cities of southern Canada and the United States. It is cold and remote, a seemingly barren wilderness incapable of supporting agriculture and barely capable of supporting life. Yet for a thousand years it has been the homeland of a rich and accomplished people called Inuvialuit, "the real people." Throughout their history they have been hunters and fishermen, depending for their livelihood not on agriculture but on the rich fish and animal resources of the land.

The Inuvialuit are Inuit ("Eskimos"), biologically and culturally related to other Inuit living across the roof of North America, from Bering Strait to eastern Greenland. Yet they have long nurtured a separate identity. In modern times, this has meant following a political path different from that of other Canadian Inuit. In 1984 they signed their own land claim, the Inuvialuit Final Agreement, and in 1999 were unable to join the new "Inuit" territory of Nunavut.

Their distinctiveness has a basis in geography. The western Canadian Arctic is a relatively rich land bounded by poorer lands, a well-occupied oasis bordered by deserts. At the time of European contact in the early 19th cen-

**An Inuvialuit family,
about 1900**
A hundred and fifty years ago, the Inuvialuit were the largest and most prosperous Inuit group in Canada.
NATIONAL ARCHIVES OF CANADA, C5107

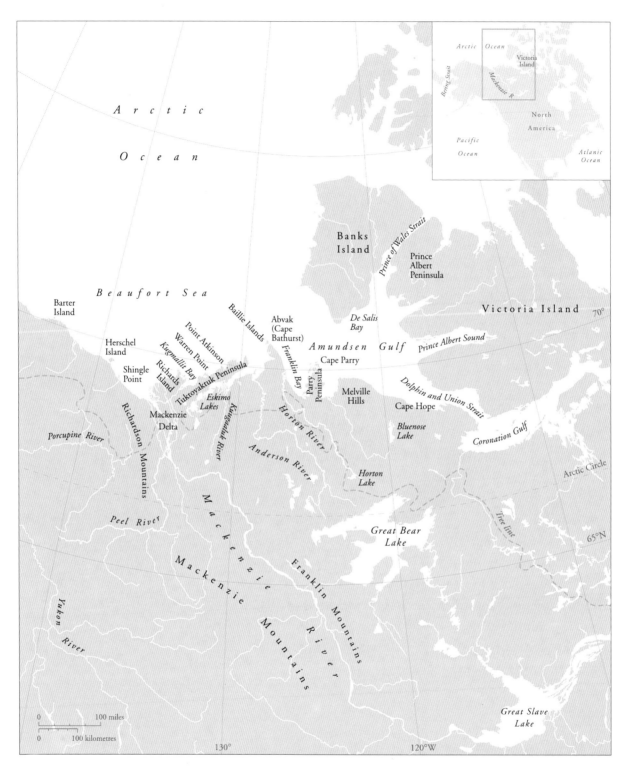

MAP I Northwest Canada: before the arrival of Europeans, Inuvialuit territory stretched along the Arctic coast from Barter Island to Franklin Bay.

ACROSS TIME AND TUNDRA

tury, eastern Arctic Alaska was too resource-poor to support a long-term resident population, as was the area to the east of the Inuvialuit, between Cape Parry and Dolphin and Union Strait. In between, the Inuvialuit homeland supported perhaps the richest and densest knot of humanity in all of Arctic Canada. Although never completely isolated, the Inuvialuit were — and in many ways remain — a world unto themselves.

The Inuvialuit homeland is centred on the great delta of the Mackenzie River, Canada's longest river (in North America, only the Mississippi is longer). In traditional times, their lands stretched from Barter Island just over the Alaskan border to Franklin Bay, and inland to the tree line and sometimes beyond. West of the Mackenzie River — called the Kuukpak or "Great River" — and south of the Yukon coastal plain are the Richardson Mountains, stretching west into Alaska. Otherwise, the western Arctic is low and flat, a northern extension of the interior plains of North America. Huge ice hills, called "pingos," provide the only topographic relief.

The coastline is complex and the waters off shore are shallow. East of the Mackenzie are the Eskimo Lakes (also known as the Husky Lakes), a series of lake-like basins which are actually shallow inlets of the sea. The land is also slowly sinking. Every year erosion pushes the coastline back — in some areas as much as 10 metres (33 feet) in a single season — and places that were once important settlement areas now flood with every storm tide.

By Arctic standards the region is well vegetated. A few spruce trees straggle northwards as far as tidewater in the Mackenzie Delta and the upper Eskimo Lakes. Immense windrows of Mackenzie River driftwood clothe the beaches. In summer, the Tuktoyaktuk Peninsula and the Yukon north slope are verdant with grass, willow and brush, often too dense to walk through, and aswarm with mosquitoes. Only to the far northeast, around Cape Bathurst, does the traveller encounter the lingering summer snowdrifts and sparse vegetation characteristic of, for instance, the central Arctic. Winters are cold, averaging between about −25 and −35°C (−13 to −31°F) in January or February, but summers tend to be a month longer than in the central Arctic, with a break-up in late June rather than July or August. Most seas are entirely ice-free by mid-July and do not begin to freeze again until October.

The sea is richer than the land and the coastline has always been the focus of human life. The western Arctic supports four important sea mammal species.[1] The ringed seal and bearded seal are both able to make breathing

The Mackenzie Delta

The immense delta is a maze
of oxbow channels and kettle
lakes.

DAVID MORRISON, CANADIAN
MUSEUM OF CIVILIZATION

ACROSS TIME AND TUNDRA

holes through the thick winter ice, and are found in the area all year round. Both are widespread, and for many Inuvialuit the ringed seal, in particular, was a mainstay of winter life in ancient times. Neither seal is a small animal. The bearded seal can reach a weight of almost 400 kilograms (nearly half a ton!), while the smaller ringed seal still averages almost 100 kilograms (220 pounds) for an adult male.

Two important whale species spend the summer in the area: the 15-metre-long (50-foot) bowhead and the four-metre (13-foot) beluga. Less able than the seals to deal with thick winter ice, both are migratory. They winter in the warmer waters of the north Pacific, then move north and east around Alaska with the summer melt, entering the eastern Beaufort Sea and Amundsen Gulf in late spring or early summer and leaving before freeze-up. Belugas are found as far east as Banks and Victoria islands, but congregate in large numbers off the mouth of the Mackenzie River, where they feed on the abundant herring crop. By contrast, bowheads are deep-sea feeders best hunted from large promontories such as Point Atkinson and Cape Bathurst. Killer whales are sometimes seen off the northern Yukon coast. Walrus are occasional visitors only, strays from Arctic Alaska.

In times past, sea mammals were a crucial source of meat and fat and an important basis for much of the prosperity enjoyed by the Inuvialuit. The Dene Indian groups in the forests to the south lived much harder, more meagre lives without the rich bounty which sea mammals could yield. Even in the central Arctic, where seals but no whales are found, life was much more impoverished and hand-to-mouth than among the Inuvialuit. Today the beluga hunt in particular is still of great cultural and social importance.

The western Canadian Arctic has important terrestrial resources as well. It is home to two great caribou herds: the Porcupine herd, which roams the lands west of the Mackenzie River, and the Bluenose herd to the east. Both herds winter in the northern forests and migrate each spring onto the Arctic tundra, where the females give birth in late May or early June, generally to a single calf. The calving grounds are located along the Yukon coast in the west and around the Cape Bathurst peninsula to the east. Traditionally the Inuvialuit depended upon caribou for their meat and particularly for their hides, which produce the warmest winter clothing.

Driftwood

The Mackenzie River deposits enormous quantities of driftwood on western Arctic beaches, giving the Inuvialuit far easier access to wood than most other Canadian Inuit. They use it to make tools and frames for houses, sleds and boats, and even as a source of fuel.

CLAIRE ALIX

Caribou on the shoreline

Caribou were (and are) the most important land animal to the Inuvialuit. The meat is esteemed, and the antler was useful for making tools. Perhaps most important are the hides, which are warmer and lighter than those of almost any other animal, and a near necessity for making warm winter clothing.

DAVID MORRISON, CANADIAN

MUSEUM OF CIVILIZATION

Muskoxen are found along the Yukon Arctic coast and in the Horton River valley, and are very abundant on both Banks and Victoria islands. Moose are creatures of the forested river valleys, but in summer often range north to the Arctic coast, while Dall or big-horned sheep can be found in the Richardson Mountains. All have been hunted since earliest times, but none are as abundant or as important to the Inuvialuit as caribou.

Two species of bears are the largest local carnivores. Polar bears and brown or grizzly bears are very closely related, but have quite different habits. Polar bears are semi-aquatic, hunting seals and other sea mammals in the icy waters of the Arctic Ocean. Grizzly bears live inland, where they feed on ground squirrels, roots, fish, carrion and the occasional ambushed caribou or moose. Both are dangerous animals and are treated with great caution and respect.

Fur-bearers include red and Arctic fox, wolves, wolverines and muskrats. Before the arrival of European fur traders, these species were used mainly to provide trim for fur clothing. Wolverine fur was used to make ruffs for parka hoods, and muskrat skins as trim on gloves or boots, or for undergarments. Men sometimes wore the "mask" of a wolf or wolverine as a frontlet or forehead ornament, and attached fox or wolf tails to the backs of their belts. As furs acquired a commercial value, they became far more important in the Inuvialuit economy, especially foxes along the Arctic coast and muskrats in the Mackenzie Delta.

Kettle lakes and sloughs dot the western Arctic landscape, and nesting waterfowl abound during the brief Arctic summer. Particularly in the Mackenzie Delta, around the Eskimo Lakes, and on Banks and northern Victoria islands, tundra swans, geese, loons and ducks gather in the tens of thousands. They too were avidly hunted.

Fish resources in the Inuvialuit homeland are by far the richest in Arctic Canada, with at least 20 economically significant species. Major fresh-water and anadromous species include Arctic char, burbot, inconnu, lake trout and five species of cisco and whitefish. Marine species include Arctic cod and

Names of Mammals, Birds and Fishes in Inuvialuktun, English and Latin

	Inuvialuktun*	English	Latin
MAMMALS	*aarlu*	killer whale	*Orcinus orca*
	aklaq	brown or grizzly bear	*Ursus arctos*
	amaruq	wolf	*Canis lupus*
	arviq	bowhead whale	*Balaena mysticetus*
	aukpilaqtaq	red fox	*Vulpes vulpes*
	imnaiq	Dall or mountain sheep	*Ovis dalli*
	kivgaluk	muskrat	*Ondatra zibethicus*
	nanuq	polar bear	*Ursus maritimus*
	natchiq	ringed seal	*Phoca hispida*
	qavvik	wolverine	*Gulo gulo*
	qilalugaq	beluga	*Delphinapterus leucas*
	tiriganniaq	Arctic fox	*Alopex lagopus*
	tuktu	caribou	*Rangifer tarandus*
	tuktuvak	moose	*Alces alces*
	ugyuk	bearded seal	*Erignathus barbatus*
	umingmak	muskox	*Ovibos moschatus*
BIRDS	*agidjgivik*	willow ptarmigan	*Lagopus lagopus*
	ivugaq	pintail duck	*Anas acuta*
	qaqsuaq	red-throated loon	*Gavia stellata*
	qaugaq	eider duck	*Somateria mollisima*
	qugyuk	tundra swan	*Cygnus columbianus*
	tingmiaq	white-fronted goose	*Anser albifrons*
	uluagullik	Canada goose	*Branta canadensis*
FISHES	*anaakliq*	broad whitefish	*Coregonus nasus*
	iqalukpik	Arctic char	*Salvelinus alpinus*
	iqalusaaq	least cisco ("big-eyed herring")	*Coregonus sardinella*
	pikuktuuq	humpback whitefish	*Coregonus clupeaformis*
	qaaktaq	herring	*Clupea haerengus*
	salukpaugaq	Arctic grayling	*Thymallus arcticus*
	singayuriaq	lake trout	*Salvelinus namaycush*
	siiraq	inconnu	*Stenodus leucichthys*
	tiktaalik	burbot	*Lota lota*
	uugaq	Arctic cod	*Boreogadus saida*

* Siglit dialect, spellings from Lowe 1984a

Lone muskox
These shaggy, horned herbivores are members of the cattle family. Big bulls can weigh 270 kg (600 pounds).
DAVID MORRISON, CANADIAN MUSEUM OF CIVILIZATION

herring. With so diverse a resource, the Inuvialuit fishery was — and is — productive nearly all year round, and fish may have been the single most important element in the traditional diet.

What kind of people did such a land produce? First and foremost, an Arctic people: hunters, trappers and fishermen; people hardy enough to cope with the extremes of climate and fortune, and skilled enough to make a living under difficult conditions. But also people a little richer, a little more settled, than many of their neighbours. And finally, a people living far from the main centres of world civilization, with its dense populations, its commerce and its infectious diseases. The Inuvialuit and their history, as they met and were challenged by this civilization, are the subjects of this book.

THE INUVIALUIT ARRIVE

Biologically and culturally, the Inuvialuit are closely related to all other Inuit living across the roof of North America from Bering Strait to eastern Greenland.[2] This is a distance of over 6,000 kilometres (3,700 miles), making the Inuit the most widespread aboriginal people on earth. Occupying so vast an area, they go by a variety of regional and local names, including Inupiat in north Alaska, Inuvialuit around the Mackenzie Delta, Inuit in most of Arctic Canada and Kalaallit in Greenland. Until recently, all were commonly called "Eskimos" by the outside world, a term of Algonquian Indian origin said to mean "eaters of raw meat." Many Inuvialuit elders still prefer this word, although it is sometimes considered offensive in the eastern Arctic.

All modern Inuit — or their immediate ancestors — share a common language, sometimes called Inuit-Inupiaq by linguists. It consists of a continuum of dialects spoken by small, local communities across the top of North America. These local dialects are easily understood by their neighbours in adjacent communities, but the greater the geographic distance, the greater the degree of mutual incomprehension. Speech communities separated by half a continent are understood only with difficulty. The ends of the continuum would normally be classed by linguists as different languages — that is, they are not mutually intelligible — were it not for the absence of a clear geographic dividing line. Major regional dialects include Inupiaq in northern Alaska, the Inuvialuktun of the Inuvialuit, Innuinaqtun in the central Arctic and Inuktitut in the Baffin region.

Polar bear
Both polar bears and brown or grizzly bears live in the western Arctic, the former in and around the ocean, the latter inland. Both are dangerous animals treated with great respect by the Inuvialuit. Even today a wise hunter is careful about what he thinks or says about bears, lest the spirit of the animal overhear him.
DAVID MORRISON, CANADIAN MUSEUM OF CIVILIZATION

The shared language of the Inuit reflects a common origin. Archaeological research[3] indicates that all Inuit can trace their history to an archaeological culture known as Thule (pronounced *too-lee*), first recognized by the archaeologist Therkel Mathiassen in the 1920s. Eighty years of subsequent research make it clear that this Thule culture arose from local antecedents in northwestern Alaska about a thousand years ago. Over the course of the next few centuries, Thule pioneers spread rapidly east in a series of migrations which changed the ethnic map of the North American Arctic. The earliest well-attested Thule site in Canada, dated to about AD 1000, is located on southern Banks Island in what is now the Inuvialuit Settlement Region. Within less than two centuries Thule hunters had spread as far as northern Greenland, bringing their language and culture with them.

They were not entering an unoccupied land. Most of Arctic Canada and Greenland was already the home of an Arctic people known to archaeologists as Palaeoeskimos and remembered by the Inuit as *Tunit*. Within a few decades, or at most a few centuries, they had disappeared, apparently pushed into oblivion by the more vigorous and accomplished newcomers. Late Palaeoeskimo archaeological sites, however, are unknown in the Inuvialuit region, so we have no clear idea who — if anyone — the first Thule immigrants met there. Inuvialuit oral tradition seems to be silent on the subject.

The traditional Inuvialuit appear to have shared a number of important traits and practices with their Thule ancestors. Like the Inuvialuit, Thule people enjoyed an elaborate hunting culture, with permanent sod-house winter villages and a relatively complex social organization.

There are also clear differences. The Thule population seems to have been significantly smaller, and did not benefit from the efficient fish-netting and beluga-hunting techniques on which the Inuvialuit depended. The Inuvialuit seem to have adopted these between about 1300 and 1400, probably from western Arctic Alaska. There are a number of strong stylistic parallels between the two areas, and it seems likely that the development of Inuvialuit culture in the western Canadian Arctic owed much to communication with early Alaskan Inupiat, probably including significant population movement.

Inuvialuit culture proved remarkably successful and stable, apparently much better adapted to the shallow seas and river-mouth environments of the western Canadian Arctic than its Thule predecessor. From its origins seven centuries ago to the time of European contact five hundred years later, the archaeological record shows little significant change in Inuvialuit culture.

The Inuvialuit have their own stories about their origins and the creation of the world they live in. One tells the tale of an argument between two brothers, one of whom was the ancestor of the Inuvialuit, the other of the Alaskan Inupiat.[4] It reflects the common origin and close ongoing relationship which the Inuvialuit have always shared with their Alaskan neighbours.

Another story tells of the richness of the Inuvialuit lands and how the modern world — and the Inuvialuit — were born out of a great flood. Similar stories are widespread in aboriginal North America and despite parallels with the Noah's ark story, this one is almost certainly — as Inuvialuit elders insist — pre-Christian and pre-European in its inspiration. Slightly different versions of the story have been told by elders Ishmael Alunik and Kenneth Peelolook, under titles such as "The Great Flood" and "Beginnings of the Eskimo People."[5] The following version is based mainly on Herbert Schwarz's story "The Mackenzie Land," in *Elik and other Stories of the Mackenzie Eskimos.*[6]

The Great Flood

Long ago, the Inuvialuit lands were not as they are today. Instead of countless rivers and lakes, the land was barren and mountainous, and game was very scarce. But the pingo or ice hill called Ibyuk, which today stands overlooking the town of Tuktoyaktuk, was already in existence, and on its top lived an Inuvialuit hunter and his wife and son. This son was the spirit of the Raven. And with them lived an orphan girl.

It happened one day that the hunter went out to check his traps and was greatly surprised to find a large sealskin bag, which was filled with water. Day by day as he watched, the bag grew larger and larger, and the hunter was filled with misgivings. He warned his neighbours, but they laughed at him. Helped by his family, the hunter began hauling heavy driftwood logs up to the top of his pingo, where he built a large raft, and on top of it a cabin. And still the sealskin bag grew larger. The man's neighbours laughed even harder at his ridiculous efforts.

And it happened one day that the sealskin bag burst, and water poured from it continuously for days and weeks and months. Soon all the land beneath the pingo was flooded and all the people who had laughed at the hunter had drowned. Eventually the flood over-topped even Ibyuk, and the man and his family were left floating on their raft. All around them was a vast expanse of water. And after days and weeks and months, the water still did not go down.

One day the boy, who was the spirit of the Raven, asked his father for the use of his kayak and hunting equipment. He wanted to get some food and check for dry land. His father let him go, and the boy, who was the spirit of the Raven, set off to explore the great waters all around him.

He paddled his kayak for many days until he found a small island bobbing up and down in the waves. He approached it cautiously, but as he did so, the island disappeared. So the boy, who was the spirit of the Raven, threw his harpoon at the island and caught it on its very top. Now the island could not sink again and the boy pulled it up out of the waves. It was Ibyuk, the pingo. The boy, who was the spirit of the Raven, got his father and the others and returned with them to the pingo. Gradually the waters receded.

The land was transformed. Where before it had been sterile, now it was filled with lakes and rivers and fish and game of all kinds. The boy, who was the spirit of the Raven, married the orphan girl, and they had many children. And these children — the Inuvialuit — grew and prospered.

THE TRADITIONAL CULTURE

The traditional culture of the Inuvialuit before it was changed forever by contact with European and Euro-American society is now beyond living memory. Inevitably, some information has been lost forever. But a great deal can be salvaged from the family stories and memories of recent Inuvialuit elders,[7] written accounts of 19th- and early 20th-century explorers, fur traders and missionaries, especially the explorer Vilhjalmur Stefansson,[8] and the results of modern archaeological investigations.[9] Unfortunately, no single source presents a detailed and coherent picture, so information has to be pieced together. Although a great and formidable people, the Inuvialuit were nearly destroyed by infectious disease epidemics before a coherent account of their traditional life could be written.

Even their name, Inuvialuit, is of recent origin. In traditional times there is evidence that at least some of the ancestors of the modern Inuvialuit called themselves "Siglit" or "Chiglit," a word first recorded by a missionary in the 19th century.[10] Present-day elders confirm its use, but no one knows the exact

meaning of the word. The modern term Inuvialuit is used throughout this book. It means, literally, "the real people." The singular form is Inuvialuk.

REGIONAL GROUPS

When they first came into contact with Europeans in the early 19th century, the Inuvialuit appear to have been divided into a number of distinct territorial groups. Most had a main village which was the focus of an annual summer sea-mammal hunt lasting for several weeks or even months. The group took its name from this village, tacking on the suffix "miut," meaning "the people of." Thus the Kitigaaryungmiut were the "people of Kitigaaryuit," a major village on the Arctic coast.

We know little about the structure of these groups, or of relationships between them. There seem to have been frequent tensions or outright hostility, and members of one community were barred from hunting in another's territory unless they formed a partnership with a resident hunter. On the other hand, intermarriage seems to have been relatively common, so that many individuals had relatives in a number of communities. Trade was also an important link. In total, the different Inuvialuit communities may have embraced about 2,500 people at any one time.[11]

A young kayaker, about 1900
The Inuvialuit are a coastal people whose lives revolved around the sea mammal hunt. Boys learned to handle a kayak at a very young age, and delighted in races and feats of bravado.

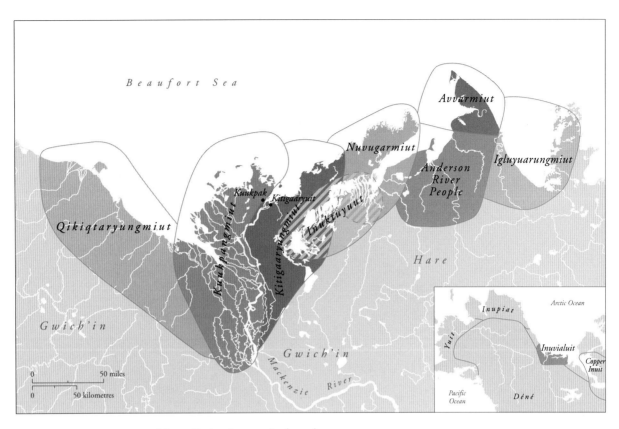

MAP 2 **Regional groups in the 19th century**

The **Qikiqtaryungmiut** were the westernmost Inuvialuit, named for Qikiqtaryuk, or Herschel Island. Their territory seems to have included the north Yukon coast from Shingle Point to Barter Island, and they may have numbered a few hundred people in the mid-19th century. Sometimes called Tuyurmiat ("strangers"), the Qikiqtaryungmiut seem to have been seen by their eastern neighbours as somehow different. They may also have spoken a slightly different dialect of Inuvialuktun. Unfortunately the northern Yukon coast was the first area to be disrupted by the arrival of European and American traders, and much of the traditional culture remains poorly understood.mmm

The **Kuukpangmiut** were named for the village of Kuukpak (also Gupuk, Kopuk, et cetera), situated on the western shore of Kugmallit Bay at the mouth of the East Channel of the Mackenzie River. Kuupak means "Great River," and the range of this group seems to have focused on Richards Island and the western half of the Mackenzie Delta. It also seems to have been common for small groups of Kuukpangmiut to travel each summer to the

ACROSS TIME AND TUNDRA

Anderson River area via the Eskimo Lakes, to hunt caribou and to trade. The economy seems to have been based mainly on fishing and the communal hunting of beluga whales during the open-water season.

While the Kuukpangmiut were clearly one of the larger Inuvialuit groups, it is — as always — difficult to arrive at a definitive population estimate. When the English explorer John Franklin passed through the Delta in 1826, he met an estimated 250 men in kayaks off Tent Island,[12] in what was most likely Kuukpangmiut territory (see page 60). Assuming one adult man for every three women and children, this might suggest a total population of at least a thousand people. However, Franklin's count may have been exaggerated — the people he met were quite aggressive — and his expedition may have attracted many non-Kuukpangmiut to the area. An estimate of a thousand people is probably most safely applied to the entire Mackenzie Delta area, including Kitigaaryungmiut as well as Kuukpangmiut.

According to Inuvialuit testimony, Kuukpak itself was abandoned in the 18th or early 19th century, apparently because channel silting had ruined the beluga hunting. People moved across Kugmallit Bay to Tsannirak (also spelled Tsaunrak or Tchenerark), a village that has not yet been located, but which is said to be only a mile from Kitigaaryuit. The missionary Emile Petitot translated Tsannirak as "the workshop," and describes it, rather than Kitigaaryuit, as the chief "place of rendezvous of the Chiglit Eskimos."[13] The Kuukpangmiut seem to have retained their group name and distinct identity even after this move.

The **Kitigaaryungmiut**, or "people of Kitigaaryuit," were named after their chief village on the eastern shore of Kugmallit Bay, directly facing Kuukpak. Their territory seems to have included the western portion of the Tuktoyaktuk Peninsula and much of the East Channel, and they shared with the Kuukpangmiut the rich beluga-hunting waters of Kugmallit Bay. By the 19th century they also controlled the upper half of the Eskimo Lakes, which earlier may have belonged to a different people (see below). Like their close neighbours the Kuukpangmiut, the "people of Kitigaaryuit" depended on fishing and beluga hunting in the Mackenzie Delta, especially around the mouth of the East Channel.

Kuukpangmiut and Kitigaaryungmiut were often lumped together as "Mackenzie River Esquimaux" by the early traders and explorers, and it is clear that they had a close if sometimes acrimonious relationship. On a cultural level they were described as being "all the same" and were sometimes difficult to distinguish, even socially. For instance, Mimurana ("Roxy"), Stefansson's Inuvialuit informant, describes a man known as Kax'alik (also Kakilik, Kokhlik, et cetera) as a "chief" or leader among the Kuukpangmiut until his death in about 1900 (see photo, page 22).[14] From other sources, he appears to have been strongly associated instead, or as well, with Kitigaaryuit. The close proximity of the villages must have increased the possibilities for social friction. "Roxy tells me," Stefansson writes, "that when he was a boy about twelve years of age fights with weapons were frequent between Kitigaru and Kopuk. . . . He says that men of one village often picked up things which men of another claimed belonged to them, and fights resulted. In these spears, clubs, snow knives, or anything else, were used and men were often killed."[15] The Kitigaaryungmiut elder Nuligak tells a story about a long and bloody feud which began over the theft of a steel-bladed knife, between a Kitigaaryungmiut man and the "Kukpakmeut, people-of-the-great-river."[16]

By the later 19th century, if not earlier, Kitigaaryuit was the largest and most important Inuvialuit village. It still occupies a central place in the cultural memory of the Inuvialuit people.

The **Inuktuyuut** have a punning name with two possible translations: "the gentle people" or "the cannibals." Stefansson[17] says that they were the original inhabitants of the Eskimo Lakes and they seem to be identical to the **Imaryungmiut** or "Eskimo Lake people" remembered in modern oral tradition.[18] In traditional stories they are described as peace-loving and inoffensive people who were always being harassed by their coastal neighbours. One day the son of an Inuktuyuut leader, rankled by insults, murdered a young coastal man whom he found hunting caribou without permission on Inuktuyuut lands. After confessing to his father, he was forced to ritually eat a part of the body of the murdered youth as a punishment since, as his father told him, "we kill only to eat." Filled with guilt and fearing reprisals, the Inuktuyuut then fled the area and did not stop until they got to Greenland.

The Inuktuyuut appear to have been mainly fishermen and caribou hunters. Their major village, if they had one, is unknown, although several archaeological sites in the Eskimo Lakes area are associated with them in modern oral tradition. It is impossible to estimate their numbers accurately, but they were probably one of the smaller Inuvialuit societies.

The **Nuvugarmiut**, or "the people of Nuvugaq," were named for their main village at Point Atkinson. Their territory included the eastern portion of the Tuktoyaktuk Peninsula and the lower or eastern part of the Eskimo Lakes, to as far south as the lower Kuugaaluk River. In 1826 there were 17 multi-family sod houses in Nuvugaq, suggesting a population of several hundred people.[19] The people of Nuvugaq hunted seals and even bowhead whales from the village itself and from Warren Point to the west, and fished and hunted caribou in the interior. They reported that they "dreaded their turbulent countrymen" living around the mouth of the Mackenzie River, while their relations with the Avvarmiut at Cape Bathurst do not seem to have been much better.[20] Their total population was probably somewhere between three hundred and five hundred people.

The **Avvarmiut** ("the people of Avvaq," at Cape Bathurst) and the **Anderson River people** lived still farther east. In the 19th century there were two major population centres between Nuvugaq and Franklin Bay. One was located around Cape Bathurst, where there were two large villages, one at the tip of the cape and the other on Baillie Island, just offshore. People from these villages lived and hunted at least as far south as Harrowby Bay, and were collectively referred to as Avvarmiut.

To the south lived the "Anderson River people," who may have formed their own distinct community. Emile Petitot, a 19th-century missionary, distinguished them, referring to the Cape Bathurst people as "Kragmaliveit" and the Anderson River people as "Kragmalit."[21] While Petitot probably learned both names from Mackenzie Delta Inuvialuit (both are based on a word meaning "easterner"), the notion of a separate identity is supported by Avvarmiut testimony that they did not normally travel as far as Anderson River (although they knew of it), and even thought that Cape Bathurst was an island (!).

These two groups survived by hunting bowhead whales from Cape Bathurst and Baillie Island and caribou and perhaps seals elsewhere. Their total population was probably between five hundred and a thousand people.

Archaeological research and oral history indicate that the Franklin Bay area was also occupied by Inuvialuit until the early 19th century.[22] The people who lived there, **Igluyuaryungmiut**, took their name from their main village, Iglulualuit, "the place of many houses," located near the mouth of the Horton River on Franklin Bay. They hunted seals from the village in spring, and bowhead whales and caribou elsewhere. Suffering from starvation and disease, they seem to have abandoned the area in about 1840; the survivors moved to Cape Bathurst. No precise population estimate is possible, but like the Inuktuiut, this group may have numbered a few hundred people at most.

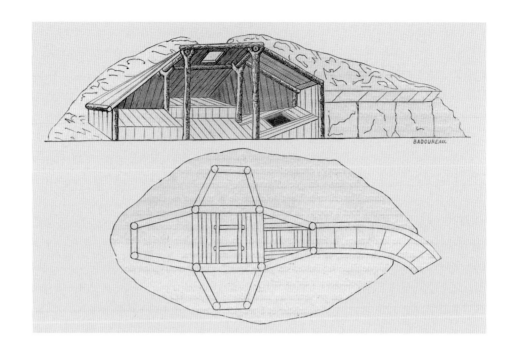

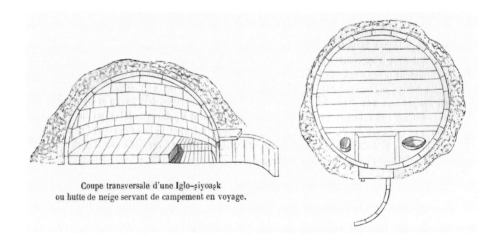

Coupe transversale d'une Iglo-ρiyoaρk
ou hutte de neige servant de campement en voyage.

Floor plans and diagrams of an Inuvialuit sod and driftwood house (*above*) and snow house (*below*), about 1870

The Inuvialuit spent most of the winter in comfortable, well-insulated houses made of sod and driftwood, only resorting to snow houses while travelling or camped on the sea ice. Certain architectural principles were common to both, including a *katak*, or cold-trap entrance passage, and a recessed floor flanked by raised sleeping platforms.

EMILE PETITOT

Villages

A typical traditional Inuvialuit village was a group of sod and driftwood houses, each accompanied by various storage facilities such as cache pits and racks or stages. Built to a cruciform pattern, the dwellings often housed several families, with one or two occupying each sleeping alcove and everyone sharing a common central living space. Single families also lived in smaller houses. At Kitigaaryuit, and possibly other villages as well, individual houses had traditional names that persisted for generations.

The traditional Inuvialuit house was called an *igluyuaryuk*.[23] Whether built for one or many families, it was framed in driftwood using a four-post construction technique and had vertical log walls. These walls were slanted in slightly towards the top, so that sods stacked on the outside as insulation remained in place. Floors were recessed below ground level to conserve warmth and were paved with split logs or adzed boards. The doorway was through a *katak* or entrance tunnel set below the level of the house. Because cold air sinks, warm air from the house interior could not escape through the door. The *katak* also served as a pantry and storage area. Each house had a window made of whale or bearded seal intestine, while further light and heat were supplied by oil lamps and interior hearths.

These were primarily winter houses, although modern elders say[24] that the better-drained ones were sometimes used in summer as well, when they offered a cool, dark respite from the mosquitoes and the endless midnight sun. But most people coming to a major village for the summer hunt had to live in tents, since their winter houses were located elsewhere. As Stefansson described it, "Kittegaryuit [sic] was a large village only in summer. In winter the people scattered."[25] An important village like Kitigaaryuit thus had two zones: an interior area back from the beach where the winter sod houses stood and a coastal strip where summer residents pitched their tents. In either season, there is evidence that different areas of the village were occupied by different extended families, so that there were a number of distinct family "neighbourhoods." Kitigaaryuit probably had a winter population of several hundred people, which in summer would swell to two or three times that number.

During the winter, when houses were banked high with snow, they must have appeared from the outside like little more than bumps on the ground. But inside they were snug and comfortable and far warmer than snow houses. The explorer Stefansson, who lived with the Inuvialuit for several winters, suggests that inside temperatures fluctuated between about 24 and 29°C (75–85°F) during even the coldest weather.[26] The houses were ventilated by a hole in the roof.

Houses were simply furnished. There were no chairs, and people sat on the edge of the sleeping platform or lounged behind it. Platforms were covered with sleeping skins of caribou hide or some other soft fur, and mattresses made from musk ox robes or woven heather. Houses were well stocked with food dishes and cooking pots, hunting weapons, wooden toolboxes, bundles of clothing, children's playthings and all of the inevitable paraphernalia of life.[27]

On the floor in front of the platform sat the focal point of the house: the lamp or *qulliq*. It burned sea-mammal oil and took the form of an elongated D-shaped saucer, with a pinched-up wick along one edge. The residents used the *qulliq* for cooking meals and as a heat source for a drying rack, on which they suspended damp articles of clothing to be dried overnight. Many houses also had a large central hearth where an open driftwood fire burned, its smoke escaping through an expanded hole in the roof. Sometimes open hearths were placed in a separate kitchen built on to the main house, often a conical tipi-shaped structure.[28] This allowed the Inuvialuit to generate enough heat to keep warm without suffocating in the smoke.

Major villages also included one or more "dance houses" or *qatdjgit*. Kitigaaryuit had three and Tsannirak two; others have been reported for Tuktoyaktuk, Qikiqtaryuk and Nuvugaq. Like winter dwellings, these were normally made of logs and sod. Up to 20 metres (60 feet) long, they had a doorway covered by a beluga skin, a large central hearth and a bench which ran around the inside wall.[29] *Qatdjgit* were the preferred location for drum dances, and other important ceremonies, including many events of the winter solstice festival Kaivitjvik (see below), were held in the *qatdjgi*. Men also congregated here to talk and to make and repair tools. The Avvarmiut of Cape Bathurst used a snow-block structure which may have functioned more like the dance houses of the central Arctic (also *karigi*, *qalgi*, et cetera).

The snow house or *iglu* had a similar layout to the sod house. Built of snow blocks arranged in a spiral fashion to form a dome, it had a raised sleeping platform at the back, a *katak* or cold-trap entrance and a small window, often made of clear ice, set in the roof. Unlike their neighbours in the central Arctic, the Inuvialuit spent most of the winter in the much more comfortable sod houses and only made *iglus* when they had to. Snow houses were used primarily when travelling or late in the winter when food was running low and people left their sod-house villages to hunt seals on the frozen ocean.[30]

Summer tents were simple affairs, conical arrangements of driftwood poles covered with caribou, moose or seal skins. Just outside the doorway was a hearth for cooking. Individual family tents were sometimes connected to a central skin lodge, recalling the shape of the cruciform winter houses.[31] Families sharing summer tents or winter houses were probably closely related by blood, marriage or friendship.

Another kind of tent-like structure, the *qaluurvik*, was dome-shaped and framed with willow branches. It was primarily an autumn dwelling, apparently adopted from Alaska during the late 19th century.

Social Organization

Evidence is less than complete, but it seems likely that traditional Inuvialuit societies operated much like their better-documented counterparts in northern Alaska.[32] Here each dance house or *qatdjgi* was built and operated by a single large extended family, often numbering fifty or more people. Each had a family head or leader known as an *ataniq* ("boss" or "leader") or, more commonly, *umialik* ("rich man"), terms also used by the Inuvialuit. The literal meaning of *umialik* is "*umiaq* owner," a reference to the large skin boat — the *umiaq* — needed to transport a wealthy household.

Among both the Alaskan Inupiat and the Inuvialuit such leadership positions depended very much on the skill, generosity and family connections of the individual involved. There was a tendency for the office to be hereditary, since a capable oldest son could sometimes step into his father's shoes. On

Inside a sod and driftwood house, 1865
A man and his two wives sit on the edge of the sleeping platform, with other family members and guests behind. Each woman has her own lamp, above which is suspended a rack used for drying damp clothing. The floor and sleeping platform are paved with adzed planks, while the walls and roof consist of tightly spaced vertical driftwood posts. The Inuvialuit kept their houses very warm and wore few clothes indoors.
EMILE PETITOT

the other hand, an unsuccessful *umialik* could lose his following or even be assassinated by rivals. There is indirect evidence of a successful coup at Kitigaaryuit during the late 1880s, and such events may not have been rare.[33]

Umialit (the plural form) controlled several important sources of wealth and power. As family leaders they had first call on family productivity, and also controlled regional trade. In areas where bowhead whaling was important, the *umialik* was both the sponsor and the captain of the whaling boat (normally his *umiaq*), and benefited from a large share of the proceeds. But he had no advantages in beluga hunting, where the position of hunt coordinator rotated day by day or hunt by hunt.[34]

Kax'alik and his wife, 1890s
Kax'alik was a powerful chief or *umialik*. Like other *umialit,* he depended on the support of his followers to maintain his position. A successful *umialik* was generous, wise, a successful hunter, and the oldest man in a large and prosperous family, with many younger brothers, cousins and brothers-in-law.

Some *umialit* were very powerful men. As the Inuvialuit elder Bertram Pokiak remembers, "Each tribe in those days had a leader or chief and what he said went."[35] But these powers did not extend into all aspects of Inuvialuit life. Theft and murder, for instance, were normally regarded as private matters, and were dealt with by individuals or their families. Close relatives were obliged to avenge insults and wrongs, leading to what were essentially blood feuds. Nuligak, born in about 1895, tells the story of one such feud which began in about 1860 and played itself out over the next 25 years. It began with the theft of a steel-bladed knife and led to the death of at least a dozen individuals. "In the olden days the Inuit slew those who killed their kinsmen," he explained. "One vengeance followed another like links in a chain."[36]

Family and Partnerships

Inuvialuit life revolved around the nuclear family. Families enjoyed considerable social and economic independence, although some now poorly understood duties were owed the *umialik,* and there were strict rules concerning the sharing of food. Both polygyny (the taking of more than one wife) and, very occasionally, polyandry (the taking of more than one husband) were practised, although neither could have been common. In families with more than one wife, it was usual for each to keep her own lamp as a symbol of her role in the household. The first wife normally had authority over any subsequent wives.

According to one early visitor, the Inuvialuit "tend to choose among strangers a friend whom they call their double (*illoua-laralou*) … This friendship, once recognized and sanctioned, becomes inviolable. It constitutes a sort of relationship between the two friends and links them in a form of communism."[37] Such alliances between non-kin were often cemented by the short-term exchange of spouses. Close friends and partners often shared a house or tent.

As among Inuit nearly everywhere, children were named for a deceased relative who was believed to be somehow reincarnated in the child. The relative's soul found a new home and helped protect the child. A girl named after her grandmother, for instance, might often be called "my mother" by her own mother (much to the confusion of foreign visitors!). Because it could damage their souls, children were rarely if ever struck, and there were strong prohibitions against scolding. It was considered better to risk injury by letting a child play with a sharp knife, for instance, rather than certainly damage his soul — and offend his namesake — by scolding.[38]

Within the family, work was clearly divided between men and women. Although not foolishly strict, this allowed each sex to specialize in a suite of skills that were often difficult to master. Men made most of the tools and weapons and were responsible for most of the hunting. Women helped with the fishing, did much of the snaring and other small-game hunting, helped with caribou drives and sometimes took an oar on bowhead hunts. But a woman's major tasks were domestic.

Along with child-rearing, sewing was an Inuvialuit woman's most important and most time-consuming responsibility. She looked after all stages of the process, skinning the animals her husband brought home, working and softening the hides, cutting the patterns and then doing the actual sewing. Her tool kit consisted of a semi-lunar knife or *ulu* — normally slate-bladed in the days before European metal became widely available — and various kinds of hide scrapers and bone or copper needles. Sinew was split and twisted to make thread. As well as clothes, women sewed boat covers, tents, sleeping robes and many other vital items.

Women also butchered game animals, processed the meat for drying or

Avumnuk and his wife, 1890s
Before the adoption of Christianity, marriage involved no particular ceremony; the couple simply began living together.

Mamayauk sewing,

1915 or 1916

Sewing was by far the
most time-consuming of
a woman's many tasks,
particularly during the
autumn. Whenever possible,
women tried to sew out-
doors, where the light
was better.

NATIONAL ARCHIVES OF CANADA,

C23641

other storage and did most of the cooking. Food
was boiled or roasted or eaten raw, fermented or
half-frozen. When different families shared the
same house, each one cooked and ate separately.

Religion and Ritual

What is known of the pre-Christian religion
indicates a system of belief similar to that of
other Inuit. The spirit world of the Inuvialuit
was inhabited by a multitude of often malignant
spirits, and much of their spiritual life was
aimed at placating these beings so that people
could live in health and comfort. People too had
souls or spirits (*nappan*), and as we have seen the
Inuvialuit believed in reincarnation through naming. At the same time they
shared with many other Inuit an apparently contradictory belief in a kind of
heaven and hell, where souls went after death depending on their behaviour
in life.[39]

Religious practitioners or shamans were known as *angatkuq.* Like
shamans everywhere they were both respected and feared. Central to the
shamanic experience was the ability to enter an ecstatic, trance-like state in
which the shaman communicated with spirit beings. With the assistance of
spirit helpers, shamans could transform themselves into animals, undertake
magical journeys, heal the sick and perform other miracles. In times of
scarcity they could use magic or their link to the spirit world to help find
food. Hostile sorcery was also practised. One recurring motif is of attack by
a magic bear, made by a hostile shaman and recognized because its intestines
were made of seal skin.[40] Shamans were only part-time religious specialists
and often charged for their services.

As with other Inuit, an important part of Inuvialuit spiritual beliefs was
respect towards the animals they hunted. Animals had souls or spirits, which
were offended if not treated properly. They could become dangerous mon-
sters or, less dramatically, could refuse to be killed so that people would
starve. Every hunter knew that animals allowed themselves to be killed, and
for this reason the hunt was rife with taboos and rituals. For instance,
caribou bones could not be cracked for marrow until the hunting season was

over, lest the animals be offended, nor could seal bones be gnawed by dogs. Hunters collected and dried the nose skin and bladders of seals, then ritually returned them to the water at the end of the season to be reborn. When a bear was killed, its skin had to be hung with gifts offered to its soul, and slain seals and whales were offered a drink of water. The strict division of land and sea observed by central Arctic Inuit had its reflection in rules which forbade the sewing of caribou skins when an unbutchered seal was in the house, and vice versa.

The most important ceremony was the drum dance. It was often held in the *qatdjgi,* but any suitable location would do. Drummers beat large, tambourine-like drums, producing compelling, often complex rhythms. Others danced while the onlookers sang an accompaniment. People took turns dancing and drumming, dancers in particular sometimes achieving a state of ecstatic frenzy. Dances were sometimes held simply for enjoyment or to mark an important event such as a visit. Drum dancing was — and still is — a major creative outlet for the Inuvialuit, and the best dancers, drummers and song composers were highly respected members of the community.[41]

Drum dances could be held at any time. But other rituals were associated with the seasons of the traditional year. The elder Nuligak remembered from his childhood that the central event of the year was the Polar Nights Festival, Kaivitjvik. It took place in December, when the sun disappeared and was reborn. People would congregate at Kitigaaryuit and probably other large villages as well. The *umialik* (leader) presided over rituals and games held in the *qatdjgi* (dance house). Events included acrobatic contests, wrestling matches, feasts, songs and stories. There were also mime and other shows in which people were chased by realistic stuffed bears, and animal puppets were exhibited as if alive. People dispersed with the return of the sun.[42]

A little girl and her brother, about 1900

Appearance, Clothing and Ornaments

Early visitors were unanimous in describing the Inuvialuit as a striking-looking people, tall and well built. The missionary Petitot described the wife of one of his hosts as a "fine, plump girl with good, almost distinguished features … a majestic bosom … [and] the fine hands and feet of a duchess."[43] Her husband, seen in the engraving to the right, was even more impressive:

> He was a very good-looking, tall man with a pleasant face. He was dressed in an elegant caribou skin costume, hair on the outside, which had been pieced together with great care. I can compare its shape only to that of the doublets of our ancestors of the time of Henry IV [of France]. His parka, breeches and tight-fitting boots of brown summer caribou skin were edged with a triple strip of otter, white wolf, and wolverine fur, the long reddish hairs of the latter on his hooded collar forming a sort of fiery halo about his head … Nowhere but on the shores of the Arctic Ocean do fine clothes give such aplomb and confidence to those who wear them.[44]

In cold weather, the Inuvialuit wore two layers of caribou-skin clothing, the inner layer worn hair side in, the outer layer hair side out. Sometimes inner garments were made of muskrat skin. A man's pullover parka or *atigi* was ornamented with inset bands of different-coloured hide, including a characteristic V-shaped gore on either side of the chest. Trousers were worn to about calf length, tucked into knee-high boots. Men's clothing in particular involved considerable animal imagery. Many men hung wolf tails from their belts and occasionally wore a wolf or wolverine mask on their foreheads.

Women's *atigis* were cut longer than men's, coming almost to the knee, with a deep, rounded hem and a very large hood to accommodate the hairstyle, an elaborate double bun or chignon. Characteristically, women also wore a single one-piece boot and trouser combination. In summer, both sexes wore a single layer of clothing, normally the previous winter's inner clothes turned hair-side out. [45]

Men wore labrets or lip ornaments, called *tuutak*. These were button-like knobs or flat plates of stone or ivory, worn through small holes cut through the cheeks, one on either side just below the corners of the mouth. Similar ornaments were worn in Alaska.

Noulloumallok-Innonarana, 1865
This is the leader who so impressed Petitot.
EMILE PETITOT

(*Facing page*)
An Inuvialuit woman in all her finery, about 1900
Women took pride in their skill as seamstresses. The patterns were achieved by inlaying different coloured hides and fur from animals, including muskrat, wolverine, wolf, mink and caribou.
NATIONAL ARCHIVES OF CANADA, C5109

Both men and women sometimes wore nose pendants and earrings and both were tattooed, the women almost always so, with tattooed lines radiating below their mouths and marks on the backs of their hands. These were meant to enhance a woman's beauty. Men's tattoos consisted of crosses on the shoulder, marking a successful whaler, or transverse lines on the cheek, which identified a murderer or "man-killer."

Beluga Hunters by Rex Kangoak and Elsie Anaginak, 1988

Beluga whales were hunted from kayaks. If they could, hunters grounded the whales in shallow water. In deeper water, they hunted using harpoons and floats, as shown here.

HOLMAN, STENCIL, 66 × 56.5 CM (26 × 22 INCHES), HI 1988-18

LIFE ON THE LAND

The Inuvialuit lived almost solely by hunting and fishing, using boats and dogsleds to move from place to place as different resources became available in different locations. Skillful sea-mammal hunters, they had two kinds of boat: the fleet single-man kayak and the roomy *umiaq*. Both were built around a light wooden frame covered with beluga, seal or caribou skin, and were propelled with oars or paddles. *Umiaqs* were large flat bottomed boats up to 10 metres (33 feet) long that could accommodate a whole family on their summer travels.

Kayaks were more impressive. As one early visitor described it: "With the short double paddle with its thick heavy shaft in hand, the Eskimo can make his kayak fly over the surface of the sea like a sort of water locomotive ... Man and kayak have become one ... One can see that Eskimo men are as proud and as much in love with these boats as the Sioux are with the horses they use for hunting."[46] Bertram Pokiak remembers that a good hunter had two kayaks, one for hunting sea mammals and a sleeker, narrower one for racing and hunting caribou.[47]

Beluga hunting was done from a kayak, often with dozens of men forming a line across the mouth of a bay, driving a pod of beluga before them. The frightened animals would ground themselves in the shallows, where it was a simple matter to lance them to death. The shape of Kugmallit Bay was particularly well suited for this kind of hunting, described in some detail by Nuligak, who witnessed the hunt from Kitigaaryuit as a child.

The very first among my early memories is of the white whale hunt. In the spring, families from all the surrounding camps came to Kitigaaryuit for the hunt. Lots of people — lots of kayaks. I was too young to be able to count them; I only know the long sandbank of the Kitigaaryuit beach was hardly large enough for all the kayaks drawn up there. And the beach was a good eight

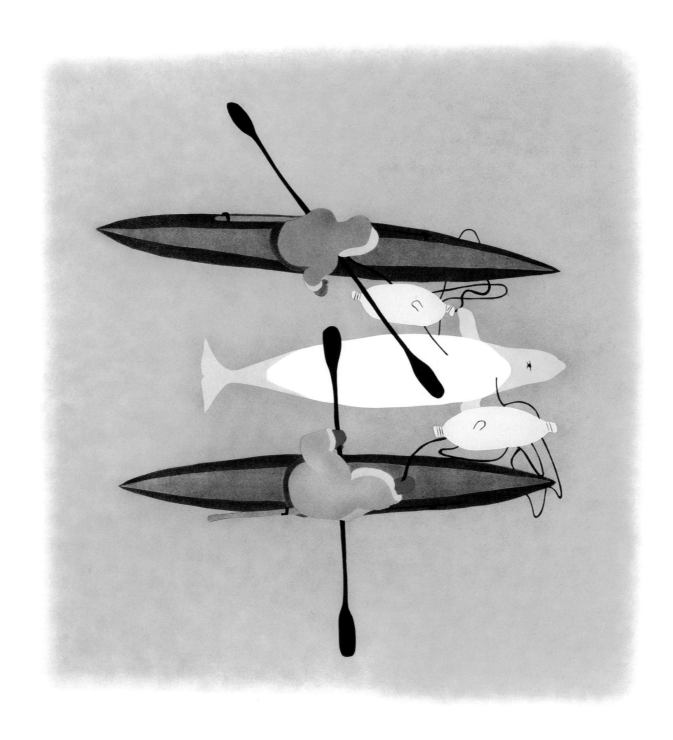

or nine hundred yards long. The sight of all those kayaks putting out to sea was a spectacle we children never tired of.

The kayak paddles bore designs in red, and the hunters' weapons were red as well. Each kayak was furnished with two harpoons of very slender wood, eight or nine feet long. To one of the harpoons was attached a kind of skin bottle, rather small and inflated with air. A long string was tied to the end of the second harpoon. A wooden disc, *illivciark*, was fastened to the middle of the string, and at the end was another skin bag, larger than that of the first harpoon, and embellished by eagle feathers. The kayak itself was sixteen or eighteen feet long, eighteen or nineteen inches wide, and about fourteen inches deep. The two harpoons were in their place on the foredeck.

When the kayak fleet first assembled, a file leader was chosen by the hunters. The file leader was singled out, whatever his age, by yelling his name. He it was who launched the first kayak in pursuit of the whales once they were among the shoals. The chosen hunter's kayak would be followed by a second, a third, and the others in succession. At the great whale hunts I remember there was such a large number of kayaks that when the first had long disappeared from view, more and more were just setting out.

During the season of the whale hunt, the men of Kitigaaryuit were always on the watch. They rose early, observing signs of fair weather and consulting over them. Some would stay on watch, eyes turned to the open sea until they discovered the belugas approaching the sandbars and shallows. Once the whales had disappeared among the shoals, the sentinels awoke their companions. Immediately a swarm of kayaks was launched. The hunters, paddling with all their might, drove their craft in pursuit of the whales.

Then, on the seaward side of the shallows, they faced the belugas and paddled forward all abreast. With loud shouts they struck the water with their paddles, splashing it in great cascades. Panic-stricken at the noise, the whales threw themselves on the sandbanks in their efforts to flee. The largest soon had but two feet of water beneath them, and found it impossible to escape. The Inuit called, then, at the top of their voices, the name of the oldest hunter. The first shot was reserved for him. The old man chose a very large beluga, snatched a harpoon from its place on the foredeck of the kayak, and hurled it at his prey. Then all the hunters joined the slaughter. The trapped whales thrashed and lunged in the shallows, hurling spray that often nearly blinded the men in the kayaks.[48]

Two Inuvialuit in their kayaks, about 1900
Elders recall that hunters often had two kayaks: a broader, more stable vessel for hunting on the ocean and a narrower, sleeker boat for racing or hunting caribou. The sharply upturned prow is characteristic of traditional Inuvialuit kayaks.
NATIONAL ARCHIVES OF CANADA, C5106

INGILRAQPAALUK (A VERY LONG TIME AGO)

Eskimo Western Arctic 1972   Fishing through the Ice   1/30

ALIKVAK

Beluga hunting was most important around the mouth of the Mackenzie River. But the blubber, meat and *maktak* (or *muktuk;* the edible skin) were then transported widely. As Stefansson described it, "The white whale caches were drawn upon when needed, hauled by sleds to where the owners were wintering."[49] *Maktak* and *mipku* (dried whale meat) were often stored in sealskin containers along with rendered whale oil. The head and tail were stored in deep, cold cache pits until winter, when they were moved to above-ground stages or meat racks.

Bowhead whaling involved deeper waters and larger boats. Bowheads are usually slow, peaceful animals, easily approached as they sleep on the surface of the sea. But they are huge animals, up to 15 or even 20 metres (50–65 feet) in length, and very difficult to kill. The Inuvialuit usually hunted them from *umiaqs* propelled by six or eight paddlers, often women. In the bow stood the harpooner with his weapon in hand, a heavy, powerful harpoon at least two metres (six feet) long, too heavy to be thrown any distance but meant for stabbing. It had a sharp, slate-bladed head designed to detach when it was thrust into the whale. This head was attached in turn to a long line of walrus hide with a bundle of floats at the end. These were thrown overboard when the animal was struck. Dragged through the water, they helped tire the whale as it swam and marked its location when it dove. This is how one witness described the hunt:

> The harpooner singles out a fish [whale], and drives into its flesh this weapon [the harpoon], to which an inflated seal-skin is attached by means of a walrus-hide thong. The wounded fish is then incessantly harassed by men in kayaks with weapons of a similar description, a number of which, when attached to the whale, baffle its efforts to escape, and wear out its strength, until in the course of a day, the whale dies from sheer exhaustion and loss of blood.[50]

The Inuvialuit had a magic song which they sang as they towed the dead whale home, asking its spirit to send them good weather:

Ah, ya ah e ya,
Big whale, big whale,
Stir up the sea with your tail
E ya ah e ya
Give us fair weather today

Fishing Through the Ice by Peter Aliknak Banksland, 1972
Jiggling through the ice was an important fishing technique, particularly during the early winter.
HOLMAN, STONE CUT, 46 × 61 CM (18 × 24 INCHES), HI 1972-25

So we arrive safe and sound on shore
E ya ah e ya
Tug — tug along hard
E ya ah e ya
Row — row[51]

As a productive, predictable activity, bowhead whaling seems to have been limited to coastal promontories such as Point Atkinson, Cape Bathurst and various points along the Yukon coast, where two or three whales might be killed each year. It was a high-status activity marked with considerable ritual. The whaling captain or *umialik*, normally the sternsman of the whaling boat, celebrated a successful hunt by hosting a great feast. Successful whalers were allowed to wear fully plumed raven skins across their backs and were rewarded with tattoo lines on their shoulders. "These," bragged one, "are glorious marks. They commemorate whales that I killed and brought ashore on the coast."[52]

Seal hunting was a more hand-to-mouth activity. The hunter used a number of techniques, such as harpooning the seal from a kayak in open water or at breathing holes in the sea ice during the winter. Seals were also taken with nets set under the ice, as the Inuvialuit elder Ishmael Alunik remembers:

> My grandfather, my mother's father, was named Charlie Koruguk. He taught me how to set net under the ice only four miles from where he lived. He used five-inch net bought from the Hudson Bay Company. But he said in the time of his grandfather they would use nets made of twisted sinews. They used chisels made of hard animal bone. He made four holes about two feet apart with the seal hole in the middle of the four holes. They put the net under the seal hole about three feet down and attached it to the four corner holes. The seal would come up to breathe, or crawl along the ice, getting warm in the sun, and dive straight down getting caught in the seal net. My grandfather said he learned that from before twine net came around.[53]

Nets were also used for fishing. Made of baleen, willow bark or sinew, they were set under the winter ice, or in open water during summer, suspended between bark floats and stone sinkers. In warm weather, fishermen used special poles 20 or 30 metres (65–100 feet) or more in length to set the nets from shore. "In some places the fish would be so plentiful that the net would have to be pulled out after ten minutes," Ishmael Alunik remembers. "Over 80 fish could be caught in a single check during good fishing seasons. The Inuvialuit would continue to set the net, pull it in to check it and set it again as long as there were lots of fish."[54]

Fish were probably the single most important item in the Inuvialuit diet. They were also often caught with hooks through the ice, a technique known as jigging or jiggling. In the summer, fish were smoked and dried or preserved in oil or in deep cache pits. In the winter they were simply frozen.

Caribou were the most important land animals, valued for their meat but even more for their hides, which could be made into warm winter clothing. The bow used for caribou hunting was a powerful weapon made of spruce backed with braided caribou sinew, quite capable of propelling an arrow right through a caribou. But to make a successful kill, most Inuvialuit depended more on their consummate skill in getting close to the animal than on their abilities as archers.

Caribou hunters used a variety of techniques. The most productive was probably the communal drive. A line of shouting and howling women and children would drive a herd of caribou towards an ambush, where the hunters lay in wait. The hunters might conceal themselves in a line of shooting pits, their bows at the ready, or wait at a narrow water crossing where the caribou could be speared from kayaks.

A successful drive could employ a whole summer community of several dozen people, but they were often employed even on a small scale. Two men out hunting might split up upon seeing a small herd or even a single animal. While one got into position downwind, the other would show himself and try to startle the caribou into bow range of his companion. A more passive technique involved watching a herd as it leisurely grazed its way across the tundra. With their intimate knowledge of caribou behaviour and local topography and wind conditions, the hunters could often anticipate the direction the herd would move in and prepare an ambush. Great patience was often as important as skill.

Caribou were most intensively hunted during late summer and early autumn, when animals are fattest and their skins are in the best condition for making warm clothing. According to the elders, "The skins and meat were dried, the marrow from the legbone was stored in a sack made from the outer skin of the caribou heart. All the bones, including the leg joints, were pounded and boiled down into tallow. Nothing was wasted."[55]

Tough Times

. . . .

Ishmael Alunik (as told to Eddie D. Kolausok)

Cold and Hungry by Stanley Klengenberg, 1986

Although more prosperous than many of their neighbours, the Inuvialuit still often went cold and hungry. By modern standards, traditional life was sometimes hard and precarious.

HOLMAN, STENCIL, 66 × 50.4 CM (26 × 20 INCHES), HI 1986-24

Tough times in the Arctic often meant that people had to resort to other methods of gathering food. Some winters were tough right up to springtime before the ground squirrels came out of their seven-month-long hibernation. This harsh weather would continue during the summer when the ice conditions would not let up. With lots of ice around the shore it was almost impossible to use nets to fish or to hunt seals and whales. Sometimes killer whales would hang around close to shore and keep everything away, such as fish, seals and whales. When this occurred, the Inuvialuit would never get enough food for the long, dark months of winter.

A shortage of land animals would also hurt hunters. When caribou became scarce or did not migrate close to where people lived, the Inuvialuit would go to the mountain areas where there were ptarmigan and other small game. In the mountains live some moose that are hard to get. To save the lives of hungry people, hunters would set snares for moose. But sometimes there were no moose around too.

If people could not get game inland and their seal oil or whale oil ran out, they would starve to death. If they had seal skins or whale skins, they would have to eat them to keep alive longer. In tough times they would have to kill their dogs to keep alive. Some people located on different parts of the coast would get enough to eat because ice conditions were not as harsh where they lived. They would share their food with others and this helped to keep the poor people alive until springtime came. When spring arrived, ground squirrels and ptarmigan along with returning migratory birds were hunted and this helped the starving people. My grandfathers told me that a lot of people starved during some hard winters.

HOLMAN '86   "COLD AND HUNGRY"   39/50   MARY OKHEENA

Small game was not neglected. In spring and fall, hunters brought down geese and swans with bola balls and bird spears and snared ptarmigan or caught them in recycled fishing nets. They speared muskrats, wolves and wolverines, and even killed bears with deadfalls and with coils of sharpened baleen, wrapped in blubber or meat and left where they would be eaten. As the blubber or meat softened, the baleen uncoiled, piercing the animal's stomach. The elders remember that a good leader saw to it that there was no overhunting of any kind of animal.

The Seasonal Round

A people who live by hunting and fishing cannot stay in one place all year round. Food sources are available at different times in different places, and the people have to keep on the move to make the most of the available resources. Not all Inuvialuit shared the same seasonal round, but certain generalities can be made. Perhaps the earliest information comes from the account of Dr. John Richardson of the British Royal Navy, who visited the village of Nuvugaq on the Tuktoyaktuk Peninsula in the summer of 1848.

> This small community does not wander far from their winter station on Point Atkinson. The hunters pursue rein-deer and water-fowl on the neighbouring flats in summer, chase the whale during one month or six weeks of autumn, live with their families in the village during the dark winter months, and in spring travel sea-ward on the ice to kill seals, at which time they dwell in snow-houses.[56]

The "whale" which Richardson refers to was the bowhead; many other Inuvialuit depended instead on beluga hunting during the open-water season. Not all of them hunted seals during the late winter and spring, either. People living around the Mackenzie Delta or on the Eskimo Lakes, for instance, were mostly jigging through the ice for fish at this time of year. And even at the height of the whaling season, some Inuvialuit were off hunting caribou in interior locations like the Eskimo Lakes.

Richardson probably underestimated the degree of mobility enjoyed by most Inuvialuit. Travel and visiting were social pleasures as well as economic necessities. In the open-water season, most travel was by boat, particularly the large, roomy *umiaq*, which could be filled with children, dogs, tents and all the paraphernalia necessary for comfort. The women normally did the paddling, while the men kept pace alongside in their kayaks.

Dogsleds made for relatively easy travel during the winter. The Inuvialuit had several styles of sled, including the Alaskan-style basket sled and the eastern Arctic *komatik,* ladder-shaped and shoed with ice or frozen moss. Because of the cost of maintaining them, dog teams were small, so that adults (at least) normally walked alongside, or even helped pull the sleigh in harness. "Fortunately," as one visitor remarked, "the Eskimos are patient and don't try to make racing units out of their teams." Nor did they travel light. In the words of the same visitor:

> These polar sybarites need comforts such as the northern Indians can easily do without. They travel with all their kitchen utensils, with a veritable store of fur robes, with pots and cauldrons, seal oil lamps, spare boots and clothes, with playthings for the children, food, and above all, with a certain vessel

Summer village, about 1870
During the summer, people lived in small tent villages. In the foreground, an *umiaq* can be seen rigged for laying fishnets; beside it a kayak is stored on stumps to keep it off the ground. Notice the trees; the camp is located south of the treeline.
EMILE PETITOT

NANOGAK

The "Months" of the Inuvialuit Year

. . . .

Inuvialuit elder Nuligak[57] was taught the names for the months of the Inuvialuit year by his adopted grandfather Naoyavak. Even a hundred years ago, when Nuligak was a boy, the traditional calendar was already almost forgotten.

Avunniviayuk corresponded roughly to January. According to Nuligak, "It was during this month that the dwarf seals produce their little ones. Premature young of the ordinary seals freeze and do not survive."

Avunnivik, or February, was the season when "true seals bring forth their young. These develop and become the seals we hunt."

Amaolikkervik, or March, was the month that "the little snowbirds (*amaolikat*) arrive from the south."

April is called Kriblalikvik, "because the sun has melted the top of the snow, and as we stare at it, it sparkles with whiteness."

Tigmiyikvik, or May, is "the time when ducks and geese return from the south" (*tingmiluk* means "waterfowl" or "duck").

June is called Nuertorvik, the month when "in our kayaks we go after muskrats swimming in the rivers and lakes — we hurl harpoons."

According to Nuligak, July is called Padlersersivik, "because everything dries up during this month, even the earth."

Nuligak equates Krugyuat Tingiviat with August, when "the young swans take their flight" (cf. modern *qugyuk:* "swan").

In September, the Inuit "leave in the kayaks to harpoon seals, using a special harpoon, the *aklikat*. Therefore the moon is called Aklikarniarvik."

Nuligak writes that "in October thin sheets of ice form on the shores of the ocean. This ice is called *tuglu*, and the moon Tugluvik" (cf. modern *tuglu:* "land-fast ice").

"In November," Nuligak remembered, "it is cold and when we open the door white mist fills the igloo; this is the mist of the freezing days. That is the reason why this moon is called *Itartoryuk*."

December is called Kaitvitjvik, "because during this month of darkness the Inuit assemble, forget their worries, rejoice, dance, perform with puppets, and the like" (cf. modern *katidjvik:* "meeting place," "gathering place").

Sorcerer's Powers by Agnes Nanogak, 1973
"This sorcerer shows his magic power in the shape of two owls," explains the artist. Like shamans elsewhere, the Inuvialuit *angatkuq* often employed spirit helpers.
HOLMAN, STONE CUT, 61 × 46 CM (24 × 18 INCHES), HI 1973-20

without a lid, a *vade-mecum*, for them the highest necessity, as indispensable as if they ate from it.[58]

(The last reference is to a chamber pot.)

Easy transportation didn't just allow the Inuvialuit to travel around; it also helped them move heavy and bulky materials such as food over long distances. Stefansson writes of people based at Nuvugaq hunting caribou in the Eskimo Lakes area, "Large quantities of dried meat were made; *umiaqs* used to return deep loaded with dry meat, fat, and skins from the hunt in the fall."[59] And of course, easy transportation also facilitated trade.

TRADE

The Inuvialuit were extraordinarily self-sufficient by modern standards. Each family made almost everything that it needed itself: tools, weapons, clothing, houses, boats and sleds. They hunted their own food, or received it according to the rules of sharing from close relatives and neighbours. Yet trade was by no means unimportant. As everywhere, it achieved an importance far beyond its merely "commercial" value.

Small durable items were sometimes traded over long distances. It is likely, for instance, that all of the ivory and walrus hide used by the Inuvialuit came from Alaska, as did nephrite, a jade-like stone used primarily for adze blades. Copper and soapstone — used for pots and lamps — came from the Copper Inuit to the east. And smelted iron was available in small quantities, from Alaska and ultimately Siberia.[60]

Most early trade, however, was regional in scope and based on bulk perishables. Some Inuvialuit, such as the Kitigaaryungmiut, had a surplus of sea-mammal products, notably skins and blubber, but few caribou hides. So they traded in these items with other groups, such as the neighbouring Nuvugarmiut, where the situation was reversed. Coastal groups did not have to neglect the summer sea-mammal hunt to obtain the caribou hides they needed for winter clothing, while interior groups could hunt caribou and still have access to the blubber they needed for fuel. In many other parts of the Arctic, economies were simpler and regional trade less active, and people lived far more impoverished, precarious lives as a result. Trade raised the general living standard in the western Arctic, and helped tie the region together as a single cultural area.

NEIGHBOURS

While in many ways the Inuvialuit were a world unto themselves, they did have neighbours who were important to them. To the west lived the Alaskan Inupiat, fellow Inuit and trading partners. Relations between the two people seem to have been relatively cordial, fostered by strong cultural similarities and a lack of close physical proximity, since the Arctic coast between the mouth of the Colville River in Alaska and the westernmost settlements of the Inuvialuit seems to have been largely unoccupied.

The Inuvialuit distinguished several distinct groups of Inupiat. As compiled and interpreted by Petitot,[61] not all of these can be easily matched against present knowledge. However, the list does include the "Nuna-tag-meut," or inland people (i.e., Nunataarmiut) and the "Nuvung-meut" of Point Barrow (i.e., Nuvungmiut). In turn, the Inuvialuit were known collectively by their

A group of Inuvialuit men and boys, about 1900
Note the snow house, barely visible in the background to the right.
ANGLICAN ARCHIVES, STRINGER COLLECTION, 376

Alaskan neighbours as "Kang-ma-lee"[62] (Kugmallit or Kogmullick), a term meaning "Easterner." The Kuukpangmiut were also known by name ("Ko-pan'g-meun"), as was the village of Kitigaaryuit ("Kit-te-ga'-ru").[63] The Inuvialuit believed that they shared a common origin with the Inupiat, who were said to be the source of many stylistic innovations, such as the wearing of labrets and the elaborate hair style worn by Inuvialuit women.[64]

To the east of the Inuvialuit and separated from them by several hundred kilometres of uninhabited coastline were the Copper Inuit or *Inuinnait* of the central Arctic. The Inuvialuit seem to have had little contact with them before the mid-19th century. Franklin reports that Inuvialuit people told him their neighbours "were very far off, and ... they had no intercourse with them." The Copper Inuit were known collectively as the Nagyuktogmiut, or "Deer Horn Esquimaux,"[65] after a single small group that lived on the southern coast of Victoria Island. According to Petitot, the Inuvialuit described their eastern countrymen as "mere savages,"[66] and it was believed that they "kill all strangers."[67]

Their closest neighbours were Indians, members of the great Athapaskan or Dene language family, divided into many different bands and nations. To the south and west of the Mackenzie Delta lived the Mackenzie Flats, Peel River and Upper Porcupine Gwich'in bands, with a total population of roughly 1,500 people.[68] Like Inuvialuit, Gwich'in is a self-designation, meaning simply "the people." However, the Inuvialuit called them Itqilit, or "louse eggs." In return, the Gwich'in called the Inuvialuit Anakren, meaning "enemy feet," but erroneously interpreted by the Inuvialuit as *anakrae*, meaning "excrementer."[69] As these terms suggest, relations between Inuvialuit and Gwich'in were not cordial, and there was a long tradition of sporadic violence. Relations with the Peel River band were particularly bad, described by one visitor as "war to the knife."[70]

Yet it would be easy to over-emphasize the bad relations between Inuvialuit and Gwich'in. While hostilities could break out at any moment, so too could peaceful interaction. In 1829, for instance, the Gwich'in reported that a few Inuvialuit had spent part of the winter with them "apparently on very good terms."[71] Trade was common, and there were Gwich'in who were bilingual in Inuvialuktun.

Living to the east of the Mackenzie River, and directly south of the more easterly Inuvialuit, were the Hare or Hareskin Dene. Unlike the Gwich'in, the Hare had a reputation for being timid, and perhaps as a consequence seem to have enjoyed better relations with the Inuvialuit than did their western neighbours. There were Hare individuals who were fluent in both Inuvialuktun and Gwich'in, and there are even stories of a Hare–Inuvialuit marriage, or at least a Hare man whose father was said to have been Inuvialuit.[72]

The Hare were actively involved in trade with the Inuvialuit, and there are no historical accounts of killings between the two peoples. One Hare party, however, was said to have had "a rather narrow escape with their lives" when they met a group of Mackenzie River Inuvialuit, and were saved only by their local eastern Inuvialuit hosts, "whom they found very friendly."[73] Descriptions like this can only hint at the complexity of inter-ethnic relations between Inuivialuit and their southern neighbours.

Inupiat (Alaskan Inuit) couple

The Inuvialuit had much in common with their Alaskan Inupiat relatives, including clothing, hairstyles and the wearing of labrets (lip ornaments) by the men.

LOUIS CHORIS, 1822

Legends from Long Ago

Ishmael Alunik (as told to Eddie D. Kolausok)

HOW TULUGAK, THE RAVEN, STOLE THE SUN

Tulugak is the word for Raven in the Inuvialuit language. This is the story of how the Raven was born and how he stole the sun.

. . . .

The Raven woke up all alone one day. He flew a little and then walked around and saw that he was on a very good piece of land, with lots of plants and berries to eat. But soon he was restless and said to himself, "How can I live alone? Am I the only Raven? I wonder if I dig in the ground, what might I find down there?"

So he began to dig and dig, and at last he was through the ground. He felt a rush of cold air and looked down the hole. Everything was pitch black. He was afraid. Then he remembered that he was a Raven and could fly. So he said to himself, "I'll just go down a little way and look around. I can always come back up." He took off and glided down. Soon he looked back and could still see light through the hole, so he thought, "I'll just go a little farther."

But when he next looked back, the hole was gone and all around him was nothing but water and darkness and no land. "So what," he thought. "I can fly until I find a place to rest." He flew on and on, and soon he was getting really tired. But there was still no place to land because there was

Tulugak **by Agnes Nanogak and Mabel Nigiyok, 1983**
Tulugak, the Raven, is an important cultural hero, appearing in many traditional Inuvialuit stories.
HOLMAN, STENCIL, 50 × 65.5 CM
(19.5 × 26 INCHES), HI 1983-13

only water. Finally he saw a light and went to it and landed. Someone said to him, "You might as well have some lunch and get some rest, but you can only stay with us overnight. We know you are searching for land, and in the morning you must continue your journey."

After lunch he went to sleep, but it seemed that he slept only a little before the voice woke him up again and said, "You must be on your way because we can't stay here any longer ourselves. But we ask you to look back after you've gone a little way so you will remember us." Tulugak flew away, and when he looked back, there was no land in sight, only a school of beluga whales swimming gracefully along and blowing puffs of water. He had spent the night among whales.

He flew on and on and still there was no land. It was getting darker and darker and he was more and more tired and hungry. Finally he again saw a light ahead and flew to it and landed. Again someone came out and said to him, "We know who you are and what you're looking for, but you must have a rest and spend the night with us." After eating lunch, it seemed he'd just fallen asleep again when they woke him up, saying, "You must go now, for we cannot stay here. But look back after you leave so you will remember us." And when Tulugak looked back, there was no land in sight but only a school of bowhead whales, moving slowly through the water.

He flew on and on and had gone very far when he could just make out a little strip of land. He stopped there and came upon a Snowbird. "Are there any other people living on this island?" asked Tulagak. "There used to be quite a few of us," said the Snowbird, "but the others were all killed by a tribe of people from far away."

Tulugak felt sorry for the Snowbird. He seemed to be alone and lonely. Tulugak stopped asking the Snowbird questions and began to walk along the beach. Soon he came to a dead seal that had drifted ashore and quickly began to eat, as he was very hungry. After a short rest, he went back to the Snowbird and asked him if there was any other land around besides this little island. To his surprise, the bird replied, "Yes, there is a big island, but the people who live there are very dangerous. Their chief is a man who owns a bright light that he uses when he goes out hunting with his men. He also has a smaller light that he uses at home. He is the only man who has these lights. It is also said that he has a beautiful daughter who has sworn never to get married."

The Snowbird gave Tulugak directions to the island, but he warned him, "Don't go directly to the village when you get there. Every morning the people go down to the river to drink the water. They only have one pitcher and that belongs to the chief. The last person to go down is always the leader's daughter."

Tulugak flew off in the direction he was told, and soon he came to the island and found a hiding place down by the water. He waited for the people to come. The next morning it was just as the Snowbird had said. All the people came to drink. Everything went well, except that when the leader came, he looked right at the place where Tulugak was hiding and an ugly grin crossed his face.

Then came the leader's daughter, carrying the pitcher. Feeling alarmed and unsure, Tulugak turned himself into a seed and fell into the water. "If only she'll dip me up with her pitcher," thought Tulugak, "then I might get into her home and be safe until the men go out to hunt."

When the leader's daughter dipped her pitcher into the water, Tulugak found himself floating into it. But when she took a deep drink, try as he might, he couldn't keep away from her mouth, and suddenly he was swallowed. What was he to do now? "I am a seed," he thought, " so I must find some place to grow."

Presently he was in her womb, and in a few months he heard the leader ask his daughter if she was pregnant. She said, "How can you speak to me like that? You know I've never even looked at a man, and never could be and never will be pregnant, so stop teasing."

Tulugak could hear the leader laugh out loud.

It wasn't long before the daughter's time came and Tulugak was born as a baby boy. "The newborn," the leader said. "What a big baby boy for a newborn. I'm sure one day he will be a great hunter." His daughter said, "I don't understand at all how this happened because I've never known a man, but just the same I am proud to be a mother."

The boy grew fast and when he was almost ready to walk, he made a move towards the small light that the Snowbird had told him about. "That's not to play with," the leader said. But the boy began to scream as loud as he could and his mother said to her father, "You're always so stingy with your lights. You know you don't have a son, and one day your grandson will have them." So the leader gave in and the boy played with the small light.

Time went by fast, and soon the boy was reaching for the bright light. Again his grandfather told him that it was not to play with, and again the boy screamed, and again his grandfather gave in.

Now everybody loved the boy, but he always remembered his friend the Snowbird. Every day he played with the bright light, and said to himself, "Soon I will steal this light and return to my little friend."

One day he kept playing with the light until he got to the door of the house and slipped out. His grandfather ran after him, but the boy was already in the air with the light. He still had the power to turn himself into a Raven, for after all, he was a Raven in the first place. His grandfather tried to follow him, but he couldn't. Tulugak flew higher and higher. At last he heard his grandfather yell, "Grandson, you can have the light. But promise at least to let me see it once a day."

Now Tulugak realized he could fly no higher with the light, so he threw it with all his strength, and it went up and up and grew brighter and brighter. But he kept his promise and now the sun goes down every evening and comes up again each morning. Tulugak flew back to his friend the Snowbird, who was very glad to see him. Now they could both hunt for food in the daylight.

He asked his friend if there was any other land around. The Snowbird said there was a land nearby that kept disappearing into the ocean. It would appear at a certain time of day and almost immediately disappear under the water again before anyone could land on it. Tulugak thought for a long time. Then he made himself a harpoon and started out. He had not gone far when he saw the water moving away in all directions below him. What luck! Soon a piece of land came up, and he threw his harpoon with all his strength and might. When it struck, the land shuddered and shook as if trying to throw the harpoon off. Tulugak held the line as tight as he could. The land shivered and finally became still.

He flew down to it and rested. As he rested, he noticed that plants were already growing where the sun was shining on the ground. Now his friend the Snowbird joined him as more and more land appeared. Tulugak found a kayak and he and the Snowbird started to paddle together. The land and the sun provided a home for many other animals and Tulugak and the Snowbird talked to many newcomers who were finding sanctuary on the new land.

TULUGAK AND HIS COUSIN

. . . .

It was very hot and Tulugak was flying along above the trees following a river. He was looking for a place to stop and drink. He was also getting hungry, as he had eaten only a little food earlier in the morning, and he'd had only a little then. He was on a journey to visit his cousin on the coast.

He said to himself, "There's a small creek going into the river." He swooped down and landed on the beach and went to the water and had a good drink. As he backed away, he almost fell over an old seal-skin (mukluk) kayak. He said aloud, "How stupid of someone to leave such a nice kayak." Looking around, he saw a place where some people had long ago made a campfire. Soon he found a stick that had been used for poking up the fire. He said, "Here's a good paddle. I will cross the creek in this kayak."

He got into the mukluk kayak and started paddling across the creek. The kayak was very easy to handle. When he got across, he looked up the bank and saw a house. He went up and started making some noise and calling to see if anyone was home. He went in. No one was home. But it was a neat little home and on the table were some freshly cooked ground squirrels, still steaming. He was very hungry, and oh, he just could not resist the smell, so he said, "I'll have a little piece and wait for the owner of this house to come home. Then I will have a good meal before I go on, because I have a long way to go to visit my cousin on the coast."

The next thing he knew, he'd eaten all the meat, and now he was a little afraid and was about to leave when he heard someone outside say, "Oh, a kayak is on the bank. I must have a visitor." As the speaker came in, he saw Tulugak and said, "Oh, a distant cousin of mine, otherwise known as the Devourer."

Tulugak said, "I was very tired and stopped to rest, and then I found a kayak and came across the creek and saw your house. When I came in, I saw some freshly cooked meat. I had not eaten since early this morning. I was going to have just a little piece, but I got carried away and ate it all. I can repay you in any way. I'd be glad to, as I am on my way to the coast to visit my cousin."

"No trouble at all," replied the Owl. "You may stay here overnight, and I'll go out now and bring in my catch. I was very lucky and caught a rabbit. You may look at all my tools if you like, and have a look around my place, but whatever you do, don't look in the small box up on the shelf, as I keep my good luck charm in it."

And then he was off. Now Tulugak was very curious, and said aloud, "I wonder why he doesn't want me to look in that box. What's a good luck charm?" He reached up for the box, but when he opened it and saw a big sea bug in it, he suddenly got so ticklish that he snatched up the bug with his beak and swallowed it. Then he heard the Owl coming back. Before he could move or say a word, the Owl came in and saw the empty box and said, "What have you done with my good luck charm?"

Tulugak replied, "I suddenly got so ticklish I busted it and ate it." Before he could say any more, the Owl picked up a big club and chased him out of the house, shouting, "Don't you ever come into my house again, you devouring fool!" So Tulugak was flying once more, but he was still tired, and he thought to himself, "What an old grouch that Owl is." Finally he had to stop and rest for the night.

The next morning he was up early and on his way, but he needed food, and soon he was really hungry. In a little while, he saw another small creek. Someone was fishing there and doing very well. Tulugak came down and asked, "Can you spare some food for a poor hungry traveller?" To his surprise, the fisherman said he could eat all he wanted. At last Tulugak was full and said, "I don't even know who you are." The fisherman looked at him and laughed. "But I know who you are. I know almost everyone. You're called the Devourer, and I am the Fisherman of the North." He was a Fish Duck.

Thanking him, Tulugak was on his way again. Soon the distant land of his cousin came in sight. If he could find his cousin, he'd be there in time for supper. But he didn't worry, because he suddenly remembered he had not a cousin but many "Issungnak" cousins (for they were Long-Tailed Jaegers), and he knew what kind of surroundings they liked. So when he saw a fair-sized lake with a creek running out of it, he followed the creek, and he was about to land on the seashore where it ran into the ocean when he heard a cry. "Eeeeow!" He was so surprised that he almost fell over as he landed. It was the call of his cousin, and there his cousin was. What a time they had, telling each other stories! They talked and talked and laughed and laughed for many hours.

I learned most of the old stories I know from the three old men you can see drumming here [*from left to right, in the foreground*]: Bennet Ningagsik, Tommy Goose and Kenneth Peeloolook.

At last night began to fall, and he said to his cousin, "Don't you think it's time we went and had supper?"

"It's a bit early yet. Wait until everyone is asleep before we eat their dry fish and muktuk." He was speaking of the whale hunters along the coast. But when everyone was asleep, Tulugak and his cousin ate until the early hours of the morning. Tulugak thought again of the Owl, and laughed and said, "Cousin, if only you could come back with me and visit me at home." But he knew his cousin wouldn't, because he was from the coast and liked to stay where he was, safe in his home territory. But what a tale of his adventures Tulugak would have to tell his children and friends when he got back. And what other adventures would he have before he got there? "Kow-kow, kow-kow," Tulugak cried as he flew back towards his home.

The Arrival of Strangers, 1789–1889

David Morrison

PREMONITIONS

Inuvialuit man with kayak, *umiaq,* and domed skin tents, about 1900

NATIONAL ARCHIVES OF CANADA, PA13582

For hundreds of years before the arrival of Europeans, the Inuvialuit lived stable and prosperous lives. Their society was no impossible utopia. It had its internal stresses and strains, its competing great men and its unfriendly neighbours. But it was self-reliant and accomplished, built to a human scale and based on a profound knowledge of the land. In Inuvialuit tradition, the arrival of Europeans was foretold by prophets, who said they would appear to be friendly but would bring much pain, as indeed they did. With their arrival, the world of the Inuvialuit began to change forever.

The Europeans were preceded by their reputation. In the 19th century, the Inuvialuit called Europeans or whites Kabloonacht or Krablounet,[1] variants of the term used by Inuit throughout Arctic Canada (Kabloona, Qallunaaq, etc.), meaning "heavy eyebrows." It must have been from their eastern neighbours, then, that the Inuvialuit first learned of these strange foreigners, for in Alaska they were called Tan'ngit,[2] a word that has now replaced "Kabloonacht" in modern Inuvialuktun. The stories and descriptions that must have accompanied these terms have not been recorded. However, their central Arctic neighbours long believed that Europeans were semi-fabulous beings, with no chins and other strange characteristics.[3]

Inuvialuit woman, 1826

The Inuvialuit first met outsiders in 1826, with the arrival of a British Royal Navy expedition under the command of John Franklin. This drawing and the four opposite are by George Back, an officer on the expedition.

GEORGE BACK, 1828

Europeans were also preceded by their commerce. Long before face-to-face contact, European trade goods were already widely available in the western Arctic.[4] The first and most important source was from the west. Since ancient times, the western Canadian Arctic had been linked with Alaska by a small-scale, long-distance trade in low-bulk luxury items such as iron and ivory. This trade was greatly increased by events in Siberia, conquered by the burgeoning Russian empire over the course of the 16th, 17th and 18th centuries.[5] In 1649 a small Russian trading post was built at the mouth of the Anadyr River in eastern Siberia. In 1742 Steller, a member of the Bering Expedition, described a well-organized trade across Bering Strait to Alaska, already several generations old and mainly in the hands of the Siberian Chukchi, who were trading Alaskan furs for Russian metal goods obtained at the Anadyr post. By the 1780s at the very latest, some of this material was reaching the Inuvialuit, along with reports of strange white men in large canoes,[6] likely a reference to the Alaskan voyage of Captain James Cook in 1778. mmmmmm

In 1788 the Russians signed a peace treaty with the easternmost Chukchi, and the following year established the important Anyui Fort on the Kolymya River in Siberia. It became the site of an annual trade fair which vastly increased the volume of Russian goods entering the New World, through both Chukchi and Alaskan Inupiat middlemen. These Russian goods now included tobacco as well as glass beads and ironware such as knives, spear points and cooking pots, which were traded along with native Siberian products such as spotted reindeer hides. In return the Asian shore received Alaskan and Inuvialuit goods such as oil, ivory, carved wooden implements and, above all, furs.

In Alaska, the Inupiat created new and bigger trade fairs to redistribute their new-found wealth. Trade with the Inuvialuit centred on an annual gathering at Barter Island, at the western edge of Inuvialuit territory. In 1826 two Inuvialuit men told the British explorer John Franklin that trade with Alaskans at Barter Island had begun within their lifetime,[7] while from the other end, Alaskan Inupiat testified 25 years later that the trade had begun "within the memory of people recently dead."[8] In the Inuvialuit heartland, Kitigaaryuit became an important secondary trading centre.

Metal goods, particularly knives, seem to have been an early staple of this trade. The first tobacco did not reach the Inuvialuit until the mid-19th century,[9] although Alaskan Inupiat had begun smoking by about 1815, using pipe styles and tobacco from Asia. By the 1850s, the Inuvialuit had become thoroughly addicted too, adopting both the Asian-style pipe and the distinctive smoking habits of their western neighbours. "The Esquimaux, both men and women, are immoderately fond of tobacco, which they smoke differently from other people," wrote one observer. "The bowl of their pipe is less than half the size of a thimble, and two or three whiffs are all they use on each occasion. This smoke, however, they swallow, which produces a transient intoxication or even unconsciousness."[10] The missionary Petitot remarked that their pipes were of the same shape as those "found throughout Alaska and among the Ingaliks, the Kamtchatkans, the Chukchee, the Siberian Eskimos, the Kurile islanders, the Chinese and the Malays. However," he notes, "here tobacco replaces opium; it is introduced with a pinch of caribou hairs torn from the parka, with which the bowl is first partly filled."[11]

A second indirect source of European goods opened up in the 1820s. Since the late 1700s the Hudson's Bay Company, led by its rival the North West Company, had been expanding its operations into the Canadian Northwest. In 1821 the two companies merged, and five years later Fort Good Hope was established just south of the Arctic Circle in the Mackenzie valley. Hare Indian middlemen immediately began trading Hudson's Bay Company goods downriver to the Gwich'in and eventually the Inuvialuit. Until then, trade had flowed the other way, with Mackenzie valley Indian groups receiving Russian goods from the Inuvialuit or directly from Alaskan Inupiat.[12]

This protohistoric trade network eventually expanded even farther east to include the Copper Inuit, the source of much-coveted soapstone lamps and cooking pots. But it was short-lived. Local middlemen were soon undercut with the arrival of European traders and the beginnings of direct face-to-face trading. Two pivotal events in this process were the appearance in north Alaska of the American whaling fleet after 1848 and the start of direct trading between the Hudson's Bay Company and the Inuvialuit in the early 1850s. Native trade fairs and networks continued throughout the 19th century, but they soon dwindled in scale and importance.

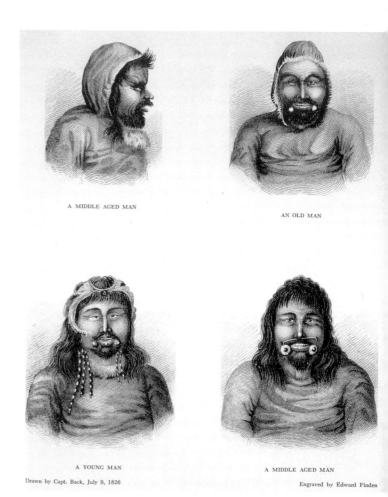

A MIDDLE AGED MAN

AN OLD MAN

A YOUNG MAN

A MIDDLE AGED MAN

Drawn by Capt. Back, July 9, 1826

Engraved by Edward Finden

Inuvialuit men, 1826
These drawings and the one opposite may not be perfectly accurate, but they do capture the wearing of labrets and nose ornaments, and the woman's distinctive hairstyle.

GEORGE BACK, 1828

FIRST CONTACT AND
EUROPEAN EXPLORATION, 1789–1850

The first European to visit Inuvialuit territory was the Scottish fur trader and explorer Alexander Mackenzie. In 1789 he journeyed down the Mackenzie River (which now bears his name) all the way to the sea. His Dene Indian guides were careful not to meet any Inuvialuit, though he did see some abandoned camps. The Dene and Inuvialuit were traditional enemies, and his guides became very cautious once in Inuvialuit lands (which began at Point Separation at the upper end of the Mackenzie Delta), steering Mackenzie clear of the well-populated East Channel of the river towards the maze of the middle Delta.[13] If they did not know of it at the time, the Inuvialuit must have soon learned of this visit.

The next visitor did not do even this well. A Mr. Clarke of the North West Company attempted to reach the sea via the Mackenzie River in 1809. He was able to travel as far as the Delta, but here "in the various channels of which Sir Alexander Mackenzie speaks," he came upon a "numerous party of Eskimaux, occupying both banks of the river, [who] put themselves in such a menacing attitude, that it was deemed prudent to return."[14]

ACROSS TIME AND TUNDRA

In 1826 the British Royal Navy, intent upon finding a Northwest Passage, sent a much larger and more resolute party under the command of Lieutenant John Franklin down the Mackenzie River in several small boats. At Point Separation they split into two groups. One, under Franklin himself, took the West Channel of the river to Shallow Bay and then coasted west in an attempt to reach Point Barrow, Alaska. The second party under Dr. John Richardson travelled east to the Coppermine River. We owe our earliest documentary information on the Inuvialuit to this second Franklin expedition[15] and especially to Dr. Richardson, who was an intelligent and sometimes sympathetic observer. Both were aided by Central Arctic Inuit interpreters, who had been brought along for this purpose.

The Inuvialuit were already skilled traders. Richardson records that "they were particularly cautious not to glut the market by too great a display of their stock in trade; producing only one article at a time, and not attempting to out-bid each other." When the interpreter Ooligbuk lit a pipe and began to smoke, "they shouted '*ookah, ookah,*' (fire, fire); and demanded to be told what he was doing. He replied with the greatest gravity, '*poo-yoo-al-letchee-raw mah*' (I smoke); and this answer sufficed." (The Inuvialuit would not take up smoking themselves for another generation.) Seeing Richardson use his pocket telescope, "they speedily comprehended its use, and called it '*eetee-yawgah*' (far eyes), the name that they give to the wooden shade which is used to protect their eyes from the glare of the snow."[16]

It is from Richardson that we first hear of the Kitigaaryungmiut or "people of Kitigaaryuit," probably the largest Inuvialuit village. Travelling down the East Channel of the Mackenzie on July 7, 1826, Richardson writes, "We learned, in the course of the day, from the Natives, that they called themselves *Kitte-garroe-oot* (inhabitants of the land near the mountains), and that they were now on their way to a place favourable for the capture of white whales."[17] Unfortunately, he did not visit or even see the village itself.

Continuing along the coast of the Tuktoyaktuk Peninsula, the British explorers did visit the village of Nuvugaq at Point Atkinson. At that time of year it was abandoned save for one old woman, but it was speedily re-occupied during their visit by people congregating for the summer whale hunt. It was a village of 17 multi-family winter houses and a large *qatdjgi,* the latter surrounded by the skulls of 21 whales. As Richardson carefully noted, "The general attention to comfort in the construction of the village, and the erection of a building of such magnitude [the *qatdjgi*], requiring an union of

A camp on Richards Island, 1826
Arriving uninvited, the British were often met with hostility and suspicion. The men at this small camp on the outer coast of the Mackenzie Delta can be seen arming themselves in preparation for any attack.
FRANKLIN EXPEDITION, 1828

purpose in a considerable number of people, are evidence of no small progress towards civilization." Richardson was told that while these people had heard of Europeans, they had never before seen any.[18]

While Richardson's reception was occasionally hostile, the most dramatic encounter occurred between Franklin's party and a group of Inuvialuit in Shallow Bay, just west of the Delta.[19] Franklin found himself with both of his boats — the *Lion* and the *Reliance* — aground on an ebb tide, surrounded by a large group of "at least" two hundred and fifty Inuvialuit men in their kayaks. They were eager to trade, offering their bows, arrows and whatever else they had when one of their number, accidentally overset by an oar, was taken aboard the *Lion*. Once there he was awestruck when he saw the wealth of European goods it contained. "He soon began to ask for every thing he saw, and expressed much displeasure on our refusing to comply with his demands; he also, as we afterwards learned, excited the cupidity of others by his account of the inexhaustible riches in the *Lion*, and several of the younger men endeavored to get into both our boats, but we resisted all their attempts."

Several "chiefs" were invited onboard to help defuse the situation, but to no avail. The upset kayaker was discovered with a stolen pistol and fled the *Lion*, which was now in water less than knee deep. The vessel was quickly surrounded by a crowd of younger men intent on pilfering everything within reach, "slyly, however, and with so much dexterity, as almost to escape detection." Both boats were dragged towards shore. Two Inuvialuit jumped aboard the *Lion* and seized Franklin himself, still offering reassurances: "The whole way to the shore, they kept repeating the word '*teyma*' [*taima*: "don't" or "that's all"], beating gently on my left breast with their hands, and pressing mine against their breasts."

Once ashore, the pillaging became more forceful, the Inuvialuit stripping to the waist and drawing their knives. Some, including a young "chief," attempted to restore order and protect the English party. Soon, in the words of Franklin, "I found the sides of the boat [*Lion*] lined with men as thick as they could stand, brandishing their knives in the most furious manner, and attempting to seize every thing that was movable." The crew attempted to hold them off, "the self-possession of our men was not more conspicuous than the coolness with which the Esquimaux received the heavy blows dealt to them with the butts of the muskets." As events hovered on the brink of disaster, the *Reliance* managed to get itself afloat, and Lieutenant Back directed the men to level their muskets. This threat finally made the Inuvialuit flee.

In the end, bloodshed was avoided on both sides, although several crew members had their clothing cut, and Franklin was just able to prevent one sailor "from discharging the contents of his musket into the body of an Esquimaux." In so doing, Franklin was motivated by the belief that "the first blood we had shed would have been instantly revenged by the sacrifice of all our lives."

Over the next fifty years the Inuvialuit were visited by several other British expeditions. In the 1830s, Thomas Simpson of the Hudson's Bay Company crossed Inuvialuit territory several times in the continuing exploration of the Northwest Passage. He met Inuvialuit on a number of occasions, mainly along the northern Yukon coast, and like Franklin was sometimes harassed and menaced.[20]

The third Franklin expedition, launched in 1845 and considered missing by 1848, led to a major flurry of exploration. We now know that Franklin himself died in 1847, probably of natural causes, while his two ships were frozen in near King William Island in the central Arctic. Disaster struck the following year, when the ships were abandoned. There were no survivors, but the fate of the expedition was not known in detail until 1859.[21]

"The Esquimaux pillaging the Boats"
In the most violent episode, the British were pillaged by a large party of kayakers. Looking at this scene it is difficult to believe that bloodshed was avoided by both sides.
FRANKLIN EXPEDITION, 1828

In the meantime, literally dozens of expeditions were launched in search of Franklin and his men, in what was possibly the largest rescue attempt in history. In 1848, Dr. Richardson returned to the western Arctic in a vain attempt to find his former commander, descending the Mackenzie River and travelling east to the Coppermine River, on the same route he had taken in 1826. He was followed by expeditions led by captains M'Clure, Pullen and McClintock, all travelling by ship from the Pacific. All met Inuvialuit in the Mackenzie area and left published journals.[22]

One of the most colourful accounts is that of Johann Miertsching, a Moravian missionary from Labrador, who shipped as a translator with Captain M'Clure aboard HMS *Investigator*. Travelling in a ship's boat, they visited the Avvarmiut at Cape Bathurst on the last day of August 1850:

> Through my glass I noticed on the flat cape near by a few humps, veiled in a light mist … The captain and doctor called them ant-hills, because they did not move. In the twinkling of an eye the mist disappeard, and to our joy we counted thirty tents and nine winter huts; thereupon we quickly perceived farther down the beach thirteen *umiaqs* or skin-boats and a multitude of *kayaks* … We had barely got out of the boat when a swarm of Eskimos came pouring down towards us with long spears, knives, harpoons, and bows ready drawn; they let fly several arrows and set up a hideous outcry. The women were following behind them with more weapons … I drew my pistol from my pocket, discharged it in the air before their eyes, and shouted to them to throw down their weapons. But they only shouted all the louder … I took my stand before them with my pistol in my hand … and told them that we were friends, brought gifts, and intended to do them no harm whatsoever; whereupon they became more quiet and peaceful; the captain came forward to join me, and finally, after much debate and giving of pledges, they laid down their weapons, but left their knives within easy reach on the ground. I marked a line on the snow between them and us which no one was to cross, and this also impressed them. They became more friendly, and finally all fear vanished, and they brought wives, children, and sucklings, and laid their little ones in our arms that we might observe them more closely.[23]

Miertsching discovered that his Labrador dialect of Inuktitut was of some service: "The dialect of these people is somewhat different from that of other Eskimos along this coast; they understand me very well; but to me, especially at the first, it was difficult to understand them." Despite these limitations, he held a theological discussion with a group including an elder named Kanalualik: "These people know nothing of a Divine Being on high, and have apparently never thought that the sun, moon, rocks, and water were created by anyone, and were much astonished when I told them of a great, good Spirit, Who can do whatsoever He wills." It was, he writes, a "most interesting conversation with these Eskimos whom I was beginning to love."[24]

By the end of the Franklin search, the Inuvialuit coastlines were well explored and radical cultural change was just over the horizon.

DIRECT TRADE, 1850–1890

In 1840 the Hudson's Bay Company established Peel's River Post (later called Fort McPherson) on the lower Peel River just upstream from Point Separation. For its first dozen years of operation, it attracted only Gwich'in, as it was in their territory. The Inuvialuit remained aloof, despite the fact that Gwich'in intermediaries offered them only about one-third the going rate for their furs.[25] One reason given was Indian reports of being poisoned by "fire water" obtained at the post.

A more compelling reason was probably fear of violence. In the spring of 1850, a small group of Inuvialuit were killed at Point Separation, apparently on their way to trade, either with the Gwich'in or directly at the fort. After they had put aside their bows and arrows, they were attacked by Gwich'in with guns, and only two escaped. Adding to the seriousness of the situation, four servants of the Hudson's Bay Company were present. Three had tried to restrain the Gwich'in, but the fourth man had participated in the massacre, and may even have led it. As a visitor at the time remarked:

> The ill consequences of this very melancholy affair will, it is to be feared, be extensive and irredemable, and it must be a source of deep regret to consider how much good might have been accomplished had a different line of conduct been pursued.
>
> The opportunity long and eagerly sought for to conciliate the Esquimaux, and to place them on a friendly footing with the Whites and the Loucheux [Gwich'in] … was most recklessly thrown away. With a display of confidence never before met with in them, these Esquimaux had voluntarily yielded up their arms, and trustingly placed themselves in close proximity to

their hereditary enemies, regarding, I have little doubt, the presence of the Whites as an assurance against treachery. Probably very little persuasion would have prevailed on them to proceed to the Fort [Peel's River Post], where a few presents and judicious treatment would have gone very far to establish a friendly intercourse for the future.[26]

The assessment was needlessly pessimistic. Within two years, direct trade had been established and Inuvialuit were visiting Peel's River Post in ever increasing numbers. By 1854, the annual Inuvialuit trade was worth an estimated £100; four years later 10 times as much.[27]

One early and beneficial effect of trade was a lessening of hostilities with the Gwich'in. The last killing took place in 1856, although mutual fear and suspicion continued well into the 20th century. That same year, the chief factor at Fort Simpson wrote the trader at Peel's River Post encouraging the Inuvialuit trade and suggesting how it could be better managed. But his final remark — "You cannot be too cautious in your dealings with the Esquimaux"[28] — speaks to a continued fear and mistrust of the Inuvialuit despite encouraging developments.

Most of this new-found trade consisted of muskrat and fox pelts, exchanged for items such as metal fish hooks, glass beads, metal pots, iron knives, hatchets and tobacco. Firearms were widely traded to Indian groups but expressly forbidden to Inuvialuit, who were considered too dangerous to be trusted with them. Since guns gave the Gwich'in a considerable advantage in war, the Inuvialuit protested against this unfair treatment, complaining — in the words of HBC trader Peers — that "we furnish the Loucheux [Gwich'in] with firearms & ammunition on purpose to kill them."[29]

Throughout the 1850s, it was mostly western Inuvialuit who were trading at Peel's River Post, particularly the "Mackenzie River Esquimaux" (Kuukpangmiut and Kitigaaryungmiut). The people farther east continued to rely on indirect trade with the Hare, apparently because of a generally hostile relationship with the Mackenzie River people. As Richardson reported, they "do not go as far as the mouth of the Mackenzie, and dread their turbulent countrymen in that quarter."[30] In 1855, Robert Campbell of Fort Good Hope reported sending a party of Indians to open direct trade with the "Esquimaux of Liverpool Bay," and the following year he exchanged gifts with the Avvarmiut of Cape Bathurst. Roderick MacFarlane, a clerk at Fort Good Hope, had high expectations of the results, writing "... there is

Gwich'in warrior, 1851
The Gwich'in live immediately south of the Inuvialuit, and are their closest neighbours. An often hostile relationship between the two people was exacerbated by the establishment of a trading post in Gwich'in territory in 1840.

JOHN RICHARDSON

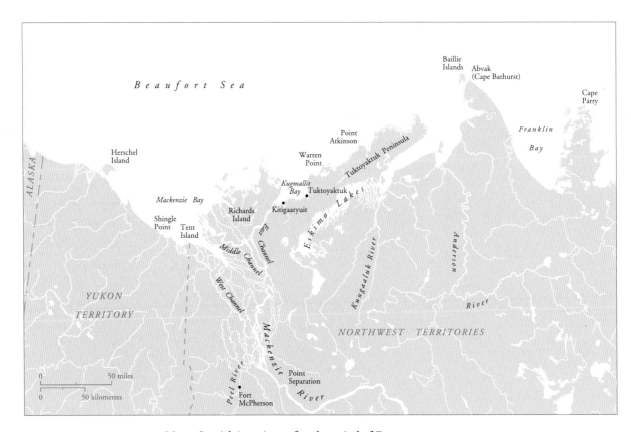

MAP 3 **Inuvialuit territory after the arrival of Europeans**

reason to believe that when [the fur trade's] benefits are felt by these people, and they become in a manner dependent on the Whites for their wants, from their well known industrious habits they would exert themselves in a far greater degree than the Indians and there is also reason to believe that this trade would at no distant date embrace the whole Eastern Esquimaux indirectly through their Countrymen of Liverpool Bay."[31]

MacFarlane was charged with the exploration of the Anderson River, in preparation for establishing a new post to serve the eastern Inuvialuit. In 1857 he canoed down the river with Indian guides — including Iroquois canoemen — from Fort Good Hope, meeting the Inuvialuit just south of the tree line. "The Esquimaux of Anderson River are certainly fine specimens of the race," he wrote, "tall and well formed, active in their movements, lively in their conversation, good-humored, with smiling open countenances."[32] A small present of tobacco ("a commodity of which they seem inordinately fond") secured their friendly cooperation, and MacFarlane was able to continue his voyage almost to the mouth of the river.

Here the situation deteriorated rapidly. The party was threatened with violence by a large and bellicose party of "Western Esquimaux" from the "vicinity of the Mackenzie River," despite the best efforts of their hosts to protect them. These westerners were armed not only with bows and arrows, but with firearms; seven guns "held up to intimate to us that they were as well armed as ourselves." His Hare Indian guides bolted in fear, leaving MacFarlane and his Iroquois paddlers to walk out, abandoning their canoes and everything else they could not carry on their backs. MacFarlane surmised that the westerners had travelled east via the Eskimo Lakes with the express purpose of pillaging his party.

This was not a very auspicious beginning. But after a second, more fruitful journey two years later, MacFarlane and the Hudson's Bay Company did succeed in establishing Fort Anderson on the middle Anderson River in 1861.[33] It was the first Hudson's Bay Company post aimed exclusively at the Inuit trade — previous far northern posts had been oriented more towards the Dene — and for a brief period it flourished.

As clerk in charge, Roderick MacFarlane did more than earn money for his employers. He also played host to the missionary Emile Petitot, an important if not always sympathetic observer of Inuvialuit life. The friendship between the two men was remarkable, considering the usual antipathy between the mainly Scottish, Protestant employees of the Hudson's Bay Company and French Catholic missionaries such as Petitot. In March of 1865, MacFarlane paid a local leader, Noulloumallok-Innonarana, to protect Petitot and convey him to the mouth of the Anderson River, where Petitot hoped to preach. He was disappointed, forced to abandon his trip short of his goal and then pillaged on his way back to the fort.[34]

MacFarlane was also keenly interested in both natural history and in the people he was living with, and spent much of his time at Fort Anderson amassing major zoological and ethnographic collections on behalf of the Smithsonian Institution of the United States.[35] His wonderful collection of traditional Inuvialuit tools and clothing is the largest in existence, and one of the earliest Inuit collections from anywhere in Canada.

In 1866 Fort Anderson was closed because of declining revenues and the difficult overland supply route from Fort

Inuvialuit couple, about 1870

This proud couple, the man in snowshoes, are standing in front of a high-walled sled.

EMILE PETITOT

Inuvialuit dance, Peel's River Post, about 1870

The summer trading season involved considerable ethnic tension between Inuvialuit, Gwich'in and whites. The rumour spread that the Inuvialuit planned to attack the post in revenge for disease epidemics, and even drum dances such as this one, before the gates of the trading post, were often an outward display of bravado.

EMILE PETITOT

Good Hope. The orders to abandon it were issued in secret, Chief Factor Hardisty noting that because of Inuvialuit anger, "care should be taken that the Esquimaux receive no intimation of our designs before they leave for the Sea Coast."[36]

Reasons for this anger are not hard to find. The previous year the Anderson River area had suffered an infectious disease epidemic, identified as measles. According to Petitot, "… because of the measles, all the Eskimos, fleeing the shores of Anderson River, sought refuge on the shores of Liverpool Bay and Franklin Bay … There were 28 deaths from the measles on the Anderson River … and no one can say how many died around the shores of the Arctic Sea."[37] The Hudson's Bay Company reported that "the Esquimaux were exasperated against the Whites, on account of the number of their people who had died of the Measles, which they imagined was caused by the 'bad medicine' of the Whites."[38]

The closing of Fort Anderson seems to have caused some real economic disruption to people grown accustomed to the Hudson's Bay Company and all it had to offer. Instead of reverting to small-scale trade with the Hare, even eastern Inuvialuit now began making the annual trek to Peel's River Post. In 1866, the year Fort Anderson closed, Petitot counted 250 "Anderson Esquimaux" at Peel's River.[39]

Group identity began to blur as the attractions of European trade lured Inuvialuit beyond their community territories. And with increased contact, the Inuvialuit were hit repeatedly by disease epidemics. In 1867–68 they were "decimated" by "typhus or some nervous fever." During the winter of 1869–70, the "Mackenzie River and Anderson bands" were reported wintering together, "camped on the ice hunting seals" and suffering from disease. The following year they were victims of a minor smallpox epidemic.[40] According to Petitot, in the late 1860s there was a rumour that the Inuvialuit intended to seize and pillage Peel's River Post, "on the specious pretext that the whites had brought diseases hitherto unknown among them."[41] But the pretext was not specious; the diseases were of European origin and they were killing Inuvialuit in large numbers. "We are all dying," an Inuvialuit man told Petitot in the 1870s, "we are getting snuffed out day by day."[42]

It was during this period that the Inuvialuit were introduced to Christianity, although they may not have realized it at the time. The first to visit was the Catholic missionary Peter Henry Grollier, who preached to Inuvialuit at Peel's River Post in 1860. He was followed by Emile Petitot, also a Roman Catholic, who made several determined attempts to proselytize, beginning with his Anderson River trip of 1865 and followed by several journeys into the Mackenzie Delta. An Anglican missionary, William Bompas, also visited the Inuvialuit in 1870, but more briefly, "as a spy searching the land." Both Petitot and Bompas were recognized as having spiritual power, and were awarded with the curious title *Tchikreynarm iyaye*, "Son of the sun." Petitot was explicitly blamed for spreading disease and was bullied and robbed on several occasions. None of these early missionaries appear to have had any impact on Inuvialuit religious beliefs.[43]

A final voyage of exploration during this period was that of the English Earl of Lonsdale in 1888.[44] The adventures of this rather ludicrous character tell us more about the culture and mores of Victorian England than they do about the Inuvialuit, but are not without interest. Lonsdale was in official disfavour in England due to a scandalous involvement with an actress, and sought to redeem himself through sport and travel in the far north of Canada. Having read various explorers' narratives, he was especially struck by the "treacherous" and "savage" Inuvialuit, who seemed to impress him as men worthy of his mettle. MacFarlane's account of his trip down the Anderson River in 1857 particularly inspired him. "I should not retreat like Mr MacFarlane, I hope," he wrote in his diary. "They can eat me before that."

Lonsdale contrived to meet these "savages," travelling downriver from Peel's River Post by boat. In his diary and various letters home, he claimed to have discovered a secret route from the Mackenzie into the Eskimo Lakes, a body of water whose existence was then hotly debated by European geographers. He then travelled east to the mouth of the Anderson River, the very scene of MacFarlane's "disgrace." Here he discovered a large Inuvialuit village and was, with his companions, ushered into the "council house" or *qatdjgi*, where his manhood and bravery were severely tested. "They then came at me like tigers plunging at me with knives stoping [sic] within an inch or so of my face & body. I saw this was only nonsense & only sat still laughing at them, which I learned after they thought very odd & brave." Friendship thus established, Lonsdale witnessed a beluga hunt, and was presented with a kayak by a

Inuvialuit dance, Peel's River Post, about 1895
By 1895 the crowds had thinned as disease took it toll. Elders identify the prominent dancer in the foreground as Ovayuak, an important chief at Kitigaaryuit and, later, Tuktoyaktuk.

NATIONAL ARCHIVES OF CANADA, C7519

man named Kagly, a rising political leader. He then returned to Peel's River Post around the outer coast of the Tuktoyaktuk Peninsula.

Much of Lonsdale's account is sheer fabrication,[45] if only because there is no direct water route connecting the Mackenzie River and the Eskimo Lakes. Yet he clearly met Inuvialuit somewhere. His description of the beluga hunt makes that clear, as do the kayak and other gifts and purchases he brought back (whether we can believe any of the accounts of his own bravery seems debatable). Lonsdale may have been the first European to visit Kitigaaryuit, the largest of the Inuvialuit villages, and easily accessible from the East Channel of the Mackenzie. In the 1890s, an important *umialik* at Kitigaaryuit was a man named Kakilik or Kax'alik, who may have been Lonsdale's friend Kagly. Despite the effects of a generation of infectious disease, the Inuvialuit were still able to impress and intimidate the casual visitor.

A CENTURY OF CONTACT, 1789–1889

Perhaps the most striking impression of the first few generations of direct contact is the high level of violence — real or threatened — between Inuvialuit and both the European newcomers and their traditional Dene enemies. Depictions of aggressive and threatening behaviour abound in diaries, letters and published journals, from the earliest secondhand reports by Alexander Mackenzie to the self-serving boasts of the Earl of Lonsdale. As Lonsdale's case illustrates, the depiction of the Inuvialuit as an aggressive and dangerous people owes at least something to European desires to appear as heroes in their own accounts. And it was not absolutely invariable. Some visitors met only friendliness. The Pullen expedition, for instance, visited the Cape Bathurst people under conditions of the utmost cordiality,[46] and years later were still well remembered. "Oh, he was good and kind, that Captain Pullen," remarked one of Petitot's Inuvialuit hosts, who had been a child at the time.[47] Petitot's description of the Inuvialuit as "robbers, the scum of the sea, real evil thugs"[48] is unfair and offensive, but was widely shared. In this, the European experience with Inuvialuit stands in stark contrast to their usual perception of the Inuit as a friendly and non-belligerent people.

In fact, European fears were largely illusory. The only encounter between Europeans and Inuvialuit to end in bloodshed was the treacherous murder of four Inuvialuit in 1850, a massacre perpetuated by Gwich'in, aided or even led by a European (see page 63). The Inuvialuit might pilfer, pillage and

Inuvialuit couple and
fur trader, Fort McPherson
(Peel's River Post),
about 1900

MCCORD MUSEUM, NOTMAN

PHOTOGRAPHIC ARCHIVES,

MP-0000.314.1

intimidate, but they never once violently attacked or injured a European. Even their wars with the Gwich'in did not result in many deaths. Probably the most violent decade was the 1840s, when the Gwich'in were attempting to defend their fur trade monopoly at Peel's River Post and the Inuvialuit were still without firearms. An account of known deaths lists only twenty people killed on both sides during that decade.[49]

One source of European anxiety was the widely believed account of the Livingstone massacre. The story, told by fur trader William Wenzel,[50] describes what would have been the first direct contact between Europeans and Inuvialuit, in 1799. In that year, a party of five Europeans and three Dene led by a North West Company trader named Duncan Livingstone was said to have met Inuvialuit somewhere in the upper Mackenzie Delta. Despite the peaceful intentions of the Europeans, all were killed, although some of the Dene escaped to tell the tale. New evidence suggests that it was in fact the

ALIKNAK

Dene guides who perpetrated the massacre, and that it occurred upriver from the Delta.[51] But the original story was widely believed, and is referred to in Hudson's Bay Company memos fifty years later, urging "the utmost precaution" against the "numerous and fierce" Inuvialuit.[52]

And what did the Inuvialuit have to say about Europeans? Unfortunately they did not write the accounts, so we will never know. In modern presentations, any memory of past conflict seems to have been lost. "The strangers seemed peaceful … We welcomed them openly, fed them, and then entertained them with our games and dances," is how the first encounter with Europeans is described in one modern account.[53]

As we have seen, the real situation was a great deal more complex. Europeans were not always perceived as peaceful, and their intrusion into Inuvialuit territory without permission or consultation was obviously resented. Like many people — most notably the Europeans themselves — the Inuvialuit had a general attitude of superiority towards others, be they Itqilit (Indians) or Kabloonacht (whites), and were clearly angered by the all-too-obvious preference shown by the Europeans to their traditional Dene rivals. And soon they could add infectious diseases to their list of complaints. It was clear that Europeans had brought the diseases, and in the Inuvialuit worldview this could only be explained as malicious sorcery. The great stores of wealth carried by the Europeans must also have been an almost irresistible temptation to pillage and rob. In fact, the truculence displayed by the 19th-century Inuvialuit reflects their fundamental independence from the outside world. Masters in their own house, they were clearly not that worried about what Europeans thought of them.

This does not mean that the Inuvialuit were not keenly aware of the value of European trade. Individual Europeans might have various other goals and purposes for visiting, from the salvation of souls to an interest in natural history, but the relationship between the two peoples was fundamentally a trading relationship. The Inuvialuit eagerly adopted and adapted a host of useful new items into their daily lives. It was their control over the fur trade that gave Europeans whatever standing they had in Inuvialuit eyes.

The items the Inuvialuit valued most were tobacco and metal, particularly iron or steel. Traditional Inuvialuit technology was based on antler, ivory, bone and wood. Iron- or steel-edged tools made it much easier to work these hard organic materials and filled a real need. Iron had actually been available for centuries, but in such small quantities that before the arrival of

Vengeance by Peter Aliknak
Banksland, 1972
In the words of Nuligak, "In the olden days the Inuit slew those who killed their kinsmen. One vengeance followed another like links in a chain."
HOLMAN, STONE CUT, 46 × 61 CM (18 × 24 INCHES), HI 1972-28

direct European trade, most tools were edged with stone or soft native copper. Metal vessels were also in high demand, both as a source of metal and to replace traditional stone and ceramic cooking pots and lamps, which were heavy and fragile.

The large collection of Inuvialuit tools assembled by Roderick MacFarlane in the early 1860s shows how quickly and thoroughly steel and iron were adopted. The arrows and harpoon heads all have steel blades, as do the adzes, skin scrapers and various kinds of knives: crooked or whittling knives, skinning knives, *ulus* (the traditional crescentic knife used by women), snow knives and large daggers with curving hilts. Drills all have iron bits, needles are made of steel and many of the fish hooks are iron rather than bone. All the tools are beautifully made, and in fact were themselves manufactured using steel-edged tools. Almost none is a simple trade item, used as purchased. Adze and knife blades have been re-hafted in traditional Inuvialuit-style handles, drill sets still employ the traditional bow-drill technology, and — beyond the blades themselves — arrow and harpoon heads were still locally made. This was not the wholesale adoption of a foreign technology, but the skillful incorporation of a new and very useful raw material into an already highly developed tool kit.

Inuvialuit craftsmanship quickly extended to the newly available metal itself. The Hudson's Bay Company sometimes provided custom-made articles for the Inuvialuit trade, from their blacksmith's shop at Fort Simpson. But the Inuvialuit quickly learned how to alter metal to suit themselves. They learned how to remove the temper from iron to make it soft enough to cut up, and then how to reapply it with heat and cold water. Clear evidence of metallurgy has been found in Inuvialuit archaeological sites dating from the 1860s.[54]

Perhaps their greatest achievement was in casting some of the softer metals. As we have seen, the traditional Inuvialuit pipe was adopted from Alaska, and ultimately Asia. The wide bowls of such pipes were commonly cast using two metals: copper or brass (probably derived from trade vessels) and lead (from shot), with the one inlaid into the other. Some of the most elaborate examples have small cast-metal figures supporting the bowl. There is no evidence that the Hudson's Bay Company or any other European enterprise manufactured these pipes, which the Inuvialuit must have made themselves.

In return for metal goods, tobacco, glass beads, firearms (after 1870) and a few other items, the Inuvialuit traded furs, mostly muskrat and red and

74

Inuvialuit man and fur trader, Fort McPherson, about 1900
The fur trade at Fort McPherson was undercut by the arrival of American whalers at Herschel Island, who could provide the Inuvialuit with trade items at a far lower price.
MCCORD MUSEUM, NOTMAN PHOTOGRAPHIC ARCHIVES, MP-0000.314.2

(*Facing page*)
Steel-bladed Inuvialuit dagger and *ulu* (woman's crescentic knife)
The Inuvialuit skillfully incorporated steel, iron and other metals into their traditional tool kit, making it one of the most beautiful and practical in the world.
SMITHSONIAN INSTITUTION, COLLECTED BY R. MACFARLANE, 1861–65

white fox skins. Before the fur trade, most Inuvialuit had spent a good portion of the winter in relative ease, living off food stored from earlier in the year. Wintertime trapping may thus have had little impact on the Inuvialuit seasonal round. The fact that it did not compete with an important hunting season meant that it could be adopted easily and with little risk.

One of the most exciting aspects of the new trapping economy was the annual trip upriver to the trading posts at Peel's River and Fort Anderson. The time just after break-up in the early summer was the main trading season, and hundreds attended the various dances and feasts held just outside the forts. Also present were crowds of Gwich'in and Hareskin Dene, and of course the traders and their servants, making this perhaps the social highlight of the year. There were many opportunities to feast and celebrate, and the inevitable inter-ethnic tensions seem to have added spice to the occasion. Watching the Inuvialuit dance at one such gathering at Peel's River around 1870, the Gwich'in "could hardly conceal their scorn" at some of the dance steps, which apparently did not meet Gwich'in standards. A minute later, they turned to our storyteller, Father Petitot, exclaiming, "This will turn out badly. They are going to dance for their dead. Their thoughts will become evil." The post manager and his people closed the gates, the Gwich'in melted away, and the dancing grew to fever pitch. In the end, "nothing tragic happened."[55]

But the Inuvialuit did not have it all their own way. They were not overwhelmed by European culture, nor defeated militarily. But their independence and strength were almost fatally sapped by infectious disease. Like all Native North Americans, the Inuvialuit were essentially free of infectious disease before the arrival of Europeans, and as a consequence had no natural immunities. All over North America, aboriginal populations fell by as much as 95 percent in the first few generations after European contact.[56] The western Arctic was no exception.

It is difficult to know with certainty when the Inuvialuit were first hit with disease. Secondhand testimony from the early 20th century suggests that it may have been as early as the 1840s, when the small community living on Franklin Bay, east of Cape Bathurst, was shattered by disease and starvation. An old woman named Panigyuk, still living at Baillie Island around 1910, had survived these events as a young girl, and was the source of the story.[57] What is uncertain is whether the disease she witnessed was infectious, or simply the result of something like food poisoning. As early as 1825, however, the

Inuvialuit depiction of three white men at Fort Anderson One of the men is probably the fur trader Roderick MacFarlane, another (the man in the black shirt?) the missionary Emile Petitot. Fort Anderson operated between 1861 and 1865.

STEPHEN LORING, SMITHSONIAN INSTITUTION, COLLECTED BY R. MACFARLANE, 1865

Hareskin Indians trading out of Fort Good Hope had been ravaged by "a dreadful sickness … a contagious distemper,"[58] and we know they were in trading contact with eastern Inuvialuit throughout the 1820s, '30s and '40s. They could have been the immediate source of infection.

The Gwich'in were also being decimated by disease from the 1820s on. One historian[59] estimates that their population reached its nadir in the early 1860s, by which time only one Gwich'in was left alive for every six before the epidemics. The general attitude of independence and even hostility exhibited by the Inuvialuit towards both fur traders and Gwich'in seems to have helped postpone their day of reckoning. But it could not be long deferred, and the establishment of direct trade greatly increased the likelihood of disease transmission. It is not until the mid-1860s, however, that we get our first definite indications, in the form of Petitot's measles epidemic. Thereafter, hardly a year went by without some notice of disease or illness. Within ten years, the Inuvialuit could report, "we are all dying."

It is impossible to do more than guess at what the death rates were, perhaps on the order of thirty or forty percent of the total population before 1890. But if the Inuvialuit population was declining rapidly during the early fur trade period, it was to go into free fall with the arrival of the whalers.

The Winds of Change Blow Hard:
The Whaling Era, 1890–1910

David Morrison

The sudden arrival of American whaling ships in August 1889 was to change Inuvialuit life forever. In 1848, American-owned commercial whaling ships based in San Francisco passed through Bering Strait for the first time and began hunting in the rich waters off north Alaska and Siberia. Their prey was the bowhead whale, and vast fortunes were made on the oil and baleen they secured. By the 1860s, the whalers were already an important part of life in Arctic Alaska, particularly at Port Clarence and Point Barrow, where permanent shore stations were established. Their presence was well known to the Inuvialuit, who as early as 1868 told the trader at Peel's River Post of an American ship wintering and trading along the Arctic coast.[1]

Until the 1870s, the fleet was sail-based, with a limited cruising range north and east of Bering Strait. But an increase in the price of baleen to an unprecedented $3.25 a pound helped finance the adoption of auxiliary steam motors. As early as 1873, Captain Owen of the bark *Jireh Perry* was predicting that the Mackenzie River, and even the Northwest Passage, would soon be within the range of the new steam-powered whaling ships.[2]

In 1887 a group of Alaskan Inupiat returned to Point Barrow from a trading trip to the Mackenzie Delta. They told Charlie Brower, resident whaler and fur trader, that they had seen a large number of bowhead whales in the area. The

Inuvialuit crew member "Old Jags" aboard a whaling ship, 1890s
Hundreds of Inuvialuit and Alaskan Inupiat worked on the whaling ships. They lived in close quarters with whaling crews from around the world, and the opportunities for disease transmission were enormous.
ANGLICAN ARCHIVES, STRINGER COLLECTION, 162

following year, Brower outfitted "Little Joe" Tuckfield, one of his boat-steerers, with a whale boat and gear, and instructions to investigate. Tuckfield returned in August of 1889, with news that "made about everybody crazy." He had wintered in the Delta, trading for furs, and even visited the Hudson's Bay Company post at Peel River. He had found a good harbour at Pauline Cove, on Herschel Island near the mouth of the Mackenzie. And best of all, he confirmed the stories of abundant whales, reporting that they were "as thick as bees."[3]

The rush was on, and within a week of Tuckfield's return seven whaling ships — the *Lucretia, Jesse Freeman, Orca, Narwhal, Thrasher, William Lewis* and *Grampus* — were anchored on the east side of Herschel Island. By 1894, 15 whaling ships were wintering there. They brought both prosperity and disaster to the western Arctic. With the arrival of the whalers, everything changed.

The whaling industry quickly established its own seasonal rhythm. Ships sailed from San Francisco in March, heading directly for Unalaska in the Aleutian Islands. There they topped up their coal bunkers and took on water and salt cod before departing for a spring cruise along the shores of the Bering Sea. As they travelled north they stopped at Native villages to trade, particularly for skin clothing. They also signed on crew members, mistresses, hunters and seamstresses. As well as Americans, there were "Masinkers" (Siberian Eskimos), "Nunataarmiut" (Alaskan Inupiat), "Kanakas" (Polynesians from the South Sea islands) and "Portuguese" (as blacks from the Cape Verde Islands were called). The decks were soon a jumble of supplies, equipment, men, women, children and dogs, even a few pigs.[4]

The ships reached Bering Strait in early July, stopped at Port Clarence or Point Barrow to take on more supplies and reached Herschel Island around the middle of August. The whalers discharged their stores and began their hunting cruise, hurrying east to the waters off Cape Bathurst as quickly as possible. Here they met whalers who had over-wintered in the area, and thus had a head start on the season. Over the next three to four weeks, the ships slowly worked their way back west, following the whales, so that by mid-September most were within easy range of Herschel Island in case of an early freeze-up. By late September the migrating whales were well on their way to their North Pacific wintering grounds and the whalers began their own preparations for the coming season. Some ships wintered as far east as Cape Bathurst or even Cape Parry, but most wintered in the harbour Little Joe Tuckfield had discovered at Pauline Cove on Herschel Island.[5]

After a long winter frozen in, the ships were released from the ice again the following July. The hunt continued with renewed enthusiasm, extending over the whole of Amundsen Gulf. Once the ships were filled to capacity they returned to San Francisco, but usually this involved over-wintering a second year. By the 1890s, only a few ships were still equipped with try-works to render blubber. With the short Arctic whaling season and the high price of baleen — now fetching over $5 a pound[6] — most whalers simply took the baleen and cast the rest of the carcass adrift essentially untouched; a terrible waste in an already wasteful industry.

But a highly profitable one. In September of 1892, the steam whaler *Mary Hume* reached San Francisco after a 29-month cruise. She had taken the baleen of 37 whales and her cargo was valued at $400,000, an immense fortune at the time. The following year, the *Narwhal* and the *Balaena* returned with baleen from 67 and 69 whales, worth well over half a million dollars each.[7]

A shantytown of Native houses, shacks, frame huts and storerooms quickly grew up at Herschel Island. During the winter it was home to several hundred people — as many as a thousand during the peak year of 1894–95 — under whatever leadership and discipline the whaling captains could or would impose. Many of the officers and men set up house on shore, generally with Native mistresses, although some of the captains brought their wives and families. The Inuvialuit elder Nuligak recalls his first glimpse: "Herschel! The great big town! I felt very happy at the sight of so many houses."[8]

Wintering Over at Herschel Island by "Johnny the Painter," 1893–94
In this painting, seven whaling ships can be seen frozen into the harbour, as their crews play baseball and soccer on the ice. The on-shore settlement is at top left. The year after this painting was made, there were a thousand men living at Herschel Island.
THE WHALING MUSEUM, NEW BEDFORD, MASSACHUSETTS

A whaling ship frozen into the ice, late 1890s

Although they brought some supplies with them, the whalers depended on fresh local produce, so Gwich'in hunters ("Itqilit" as the whalemen called them) were soon visiting Herschel Island with caribou meat to trade. Alaskan Inupiat ("Nunataarmiuts," or simply "Nunatamas") were also directly employed as caribou hunters. Thousands of caribou were killed each year to support the whaling ships, along with other game such as mountain sheep, geese and seals.

Herschel Island quickly acquired a wild reputation. In the overblown description of one Hudson's Bay Company official, "The arrival of the whaling fleet at Herschel was the signal for a bacchanalian orgy that beggared description. Down the gangplanks surged a motley horde of mixed humanity till the sandspit was overrun with a drunken mob of dark-visaged Kanakas, bearded Russians, ebony-faced Negroes, and the off-scourings of the Barbary Coast. Rum flowed like water. Fighting, drinking, and debauchery became the order of the day."[9] The anthropologist Diamond Jenness called it "a hive of debauchery,"[10] while the Inuvialuit elder Nuligak remembered, "There were drinking bouts almost every day."[11] One of the whaling captains, E. W. Newth of the brig *Jeanette*, was notorious as the "kindergarten captain" because of his sexual involvement with young Native girls. Frequent sexual liaisons between whalers and Native women, often with the bribed consent of husbands or fathers, scandalized many visitors. "The greatest shock I ever experienced," wrote the missionary Charles Whittaker, "was the many white or black children of Eskimo mothers."[12]

THE INUVIALUIT AND THE WHALERS

For the Inuvialuit, the arrival of the whalers and their entourage must have seemed like a foreign invasion, and at first they had little to do with them. Native crews were recruited mainly in Alaska or even Siberia, and the caribou hunters the whalers depended on were primarily "Nunataarmiut" (Alaskan Inupiat) or "Itqilit" (Gwich'in). The whalers called the Inuvialuit "Kogmullicks," a word of Alaskan Inupiat origin meaning "Easterner," or occasionally "Huskies" (a corruption of "Eskimo"). They also considered them poor caribou hunters. As one captain explained, "All the deer-hunting for the ships is done by the Noonatama tribe. The Kogmallicks, who live principally on fish, are not expert deer-hunters. The Itkiliks are good hunters, but live so far inland that we get very little of their game. On the Noonatamas we depend for the great part of what we get fresh to eat."[13] When the missionary Isaac Stringer first visited Herschel Island in 1893, he found that he needed a translator. He had previously visited the Inuvialuit village of Kitigaaryuit on several occasions, and had acquired a slender command of Inuvialuktun. However, the Inuit at Herschel were mostly "Noonatagmiut, speaking a different language from that one he had encountered previously."[14]

According to another captain, the "Kogmallicks" were at first frightened by the noise and smoke of the steam whalers, and fled at their approach. However, once they learned they had nothing to fear they were quite willing to trade venison and fish, and "would come to meet us when they raised the ship."[15] It was trade — especially the fur trade — that cemented the

Whaling station at Herschel Island, 1901
Herschel became a magnet for Inuvialuit settlement, particularly after the abandonment of Kitigaaryuit in 1902. ANGLICAN ARCHIVES, STRINGER COLLECTION, 190

Inuvialuit man checking his fishnets while a whaling ship cruises offshore, early 20th century

The Inuvialuit helped supply whalers with fresh meat and fish. In return, they received an immense variety of manufactured goods, including sleek, seaworthy whale boats, which quickly rendered traditional Inuvialuit boats like this kayak obsolete.

CANADIAN MUSEUM OF

CIVILIZATION, 37133

relationship between the Inuvialuit and the whalers. The whalers arrived with large quantities of manufactured goods: repeating rifles, canvas tents, cotton clothing and even wind-up phonographs and exotic foodstuffs such as coffee and flour. They could import such items much more inexpensively than the Hudson's Bay Company, with its interior supply routes, and were eager to supplement their income by trading for furs. Even after the whalers were forced to pay Canadian customs duties, they could still sell a hundred-pound (45-kilogram) bag of flour for $2, while the Hudson's Bay Company post at Peel's River was asking $30.

The Hudson's Bay Company attempted to fight back. During the winter of 1894–95, John Firth, the factor at Peel's River Post — or Fort McPherson as it was becoming known — threatened to stop forwarding mail to the whalers via the company's string of trading posts on the Mackenzie. The whalers had eagerly awaited the two overland mails that reached them each winter and reluctantly agreed to curtail their fur trading activities. By 1896 Firth was able to report that the fur trade at Herschel had largely ceased. But by then more and more Inuvialuit were joining their Nunataarmiut cousins in the meat trade or working direct for the whalers. Many Inuvialuit temporarily abandoned fur trapping for more lucrative employment.[16]

By the end of the 19th century, Inuvialuit society was awash with the tools and products of Western civilization. One of the most practical and aesthetically pleasing tool kits in the world almost disappeared overnight, but the standard of living was undoubtedly improved by the adoption of a whole host of useful items. Repeating rifles revolutionized hunting. Yields were far higher and caribou and other game became scarcer, while the old communal hunting techniques of the past were abandoned. Another important addition was the whaling boat. Thirty feet long, sail-powered, double-ended and made of cedar planking, these vessels were "light, fast, seaworthy, inexpensive, and maneuverable."[17] Carried in davits on the side of the ship, they were the actual platform from which the whale hunt occurred. At the end of a whaling voyage, captains paying off their Native crew members could often be induced to part with some or all of their boats, which quickly became popular. Skin *umiaqs* had been a sign of wealth for centuries: now only the poor possessed them. With wide-ranging, sea-worthy boats and repeating rifles, Inuvialuit hunters became formidable indeed.

Some idea of the prosperity enjoyed by many can be gleaned from an account written by the naturalist Frank Russell, who visited the western Arctic in 1894. It is not clear whether he is describing Inuvialuit or immigrant Nunataarmiut (both were simply "Eskimos" to him), but his description could probably apply to either:

> As we approached the battures beyond the bay, we were saluted by several rifle shots fired by two Eskimos, whose camp was pitched on the beach, at the mouth of one of the channels. They were living in a new wall tent, which they had obtained from the whalers; several bags of flour, as much as some northern posts receive for a year's allowance, piled under an overturned omiak [*umiaq*], had also come from Herschel Island. A quantity of fresh caribou meat and herring was hanging on a scaffold near by; the woman was kneeling before a wooden vessel of native manufacture … in which she was kneading dough. Such a display of provision and the salute accorded us caused us to land, of course. We were hospitably received by the head of the family, a tall, ferocious looking fellow, whose natural ugliness was enhanced by the presence of a disc labret, as large as a silver dollar, in his lower lip …
>
> They were all dressed in caribou or sealskin garments. Their well-made and serviceable clothing was markedly superior to the tattered and inadequate dress of the Indians. Like many other things invented by the Eskimo, his dress is superior to any which the white man can give him. The woman wore an artega [*atigi*] so broad at the shoulders that she could draw in her arm without using the other hand to assist in the act. The short-skirted artega was at first scarcely distinguishable from the frock worn by the two men, father and son, nor could I have known their sex from their manner; the woman talked with the air of an equal, instead of maintaining silence, or with the slavish behavior of the Indian women in the presence of strangers. Her costume … could but impress one observing such an entire novelty for the first time, as being becoming and sensible. Their clothing was trimmed with the white-haired Asiatic reindeer skin, carcajou [wolverine] and wolf-skin.
>
> The two younger children fried the bread, which had been prepared for us, in a pan of seal oil over an open fire of driftwood. The cakes were of the usual Eskimo shape — oblong, and perforated with three pairs of holes. As soon as

Inuvialuit woman aboard a whaler, 1890s
Many Inuvialuit women served as seamstresses, sewing warm winter clothes and boots for the whalers.
ANGLICAN ARCHIVES, STRINGER COLLECTION, 377

this doughnut-bread was ready, we were invited into the tightly-closed tent where we succeeded in eating *one* meal without being tormented by the ubiquitous mosquitoes. In addition to venison and bread, we were given syrup and coffee, articles quite unknown in the interior; the Eskimos of that coast do not use tea.

As we reembarked, the woman brought some venison from the stage and threw [it] into each canoe; this act of unsolicited generosity but completed the favorable impression which their conduct had made.[18]

Inuvialuit leaders tried to control their people's involvement with the whaling industry. During the 1890s, Kakhilik (likely the same man as Lonsdale's "Kagly") was the most important chief or *umialik* at Kitigaaryuit. He was described as "jealous of his peoples' welfare"[19] and was famous for his temper as he attempted to intercede on their behalf (or his own) with the whalers and missionaries. Another leader maintained the right to boycott trade with particular whaling captains, and demanded a payment when any of "his" people were hired as hunters or crew members.[20]

Nonetheless, the Inuvialuit were sometimes threatened by whaler violence and increasingly came under the discipline of American whaling captains. In 1895 a man named Pysha murdered his little daughter in a drunken frenzy on Herschel Island. He was seized by an indignant crowd of whalemen, handcuffed to an upright log, stripped to the waist and whipped. After receiving a hundred lashes he was ordered to leave the island. Deranged by his punishment, Pysha went on to murder eight Inupiat at Flaxman Island off the northeast Alaskan coast before being himself executed at Point Barrow.[21] Pysha was an Inupiat from Point Hope, Alaska, but his story underlines the apparent power and sovereignty of the whalers. "There being no local police, or other authority, the masters of the ships assumed authority, and in all their dealings with either their crews or the Natives, their word was law, without any court of appeal."[22]

Runaway whalemen could also be a hazard. Discipline aboard the whaling ships was strict, the returns were sometimes poor, and living conditions were arduous by southern standards. Crew members sometimes attempted to desert. In the words of one witness, "Many of the men knew absolutely nothing of the geography or conditions of the country. I have seen such men, who were convinced that a three days' tramp would take them to a railway

Inuvialuit women aboard a whaling ship, 1890s

Sexual liaisons between whalers and Inuvialuit women were common. As one missionary remarked, "The greatest shock I ever experienced was the many white or black children of Eskimo mothers." In keeping with Inuvialuit principles, these children were raised as full members of the community, without stigma.

ANGLICAN ARCHIVES, STRINGER COLLECTION, 381

station, whereas the nearest trading-station was more than two hundred miles, and a post office four hundred miles, with chains of mountains intervening."[23] Poorly dressed, starved and freezing, fugitive whalemen were often desperate and sometimes dangerous. Nuligak remembered a childhood encounter: mm

> One day my little brother and I saw someone coming towards our camp from the west.... we kept an eye on the stranger. He was a white man, with a heavy bundle on his back. About eighty or one hundred yards away, he set down his bundle, sat down, raised his gun and aimed straight at us. He looked dangerous.
>
> Seeing that he meant to shoot us, my stepfather unhesitatingly took a long knife and went towards him. My mother took up her gun, a .45/70. My stepfather advanced straight into range of the stranger's gun. I feared every second to hear a shot. But my stepfather reached him without being killed …
>
> He was one of the sailors from Herschel, who had run away from his ship.[24]

Nuligak's stepfather and the runaway whaler undoubtedly communicated using the trade jargon that appeared with the whalers. Based on "corrupted Eskimo words," it was easily mastered, but of very limited application. "It is a curious thing," remarked one who knew better, "that many white men . . . have mistaken the jargon for the real Eskimo language."[25]

DISEASE EPIDEMICS AND THE NUNATARMIUT SETTLEMENT

More than counterbalancing the economic prosperity brought by the whalers was their other great gift: disease. With the arrival of the whalers, direct, face-to-face interaction with Europeans (or Euro-Americans) became much more frequent, and more intimate, than it had been with the Hudson's Bay Company. Previously the Inuvialuit had rarely been visited in their own territory, and as late as 1890 there were some who had never seen a European. With the whalers, all that changed. They were numerous, they had potential disease links to the four corners of the globe and they were in active, daily contact with the Inuvialuit.

The whalers had already spread havoc in northwest Alaska, where populations fell in some coastal communities by as much as eighty percent.[26] The toll among the Inuvialuit was as high or higher.

Details are sketchy, but it is apparent that during the 1890s the population was collapsing rapidly. Missionary accounts speak frequently of illness and death and of a population that was "greatly reduced."[27] In 1902 there was a major measles epidemic. According to the missionary Charles Whittaker, "the whole population fell ill"[28] and the important villages Kitigaaryuit and Nuvugaq were abandoned. Police reports indicate that by 1905 the Inuvialuit population had fallen to about 250 people, or about ten percent of its level two or three generations earlier. By 1910 the number was further reduced to 150.[29] No culture can sustain such losses. The epidemic of 1902 marks the end of traditional Inuvialuit life. Nuligak remembers:

> That summer the Kitigariuit people fell ill and many of them died. Almost the whole tribe perished, for only a few families survived. During that time, two of the Eskimos spent all their time burying the dead. They were the only ones whom the illness did not touch: Angusinoak and my uncle Kralogark, my mother's brother. Corpses were set on the ground uncoffined, just as they were. Since I could not count at the time I shall not attempt to give the number; but I know that when the people left for Kiklavak they were but a handful compared to the number they had been. It was 1902.
>
> Mother, my little brother Irkralugaluk and I joined those who were leaving. Uncle Kralogark took us with him, for Mother had lost her second

Inuvialuit grave, likely dating to the 1890s
Before they converted to Christianity, the Inuvialuit buried their dead beneath piles of driftwood. The body was often surrounded with tools, weapons, and boat and sled parts. Such graves abound in the western Arctic, mute testimony to the ravages of disease.
DAVID MORRISON, CANADIAN MUSEUM OF CIVILIZATION

husband Avioganak during the epidemic. Once in Kiklavak the Inuit built a large igloo for all. Each and every one gave us food.

Winter came, and one day we saw a huge pack of wolves out at sea on the ice, heading east. There were so many of them that the last ones were still in front of us when the leaders had disappeared on the eastern horizon. It was said that they had feasted on the bodies left on the Kitigariuit land....[30]

As the native-born Inuvialuit were dying, new people were taking their place. According to Mimurana ("Roxy" to the whalers), the first Nunataarmiut entered Inuvialuit territory when he was a boy, sometime in the 1870s, and there were individual Alaskan Inupiat living among the Inuvialuit even earlier. There had probably always been a certain amount of coming and going between Alaska and the Mackenzie area, and the stream of new arrivals continued throughout the first half of the 20th century. But most came with the whalers during the 1890s and the early 1900s.

The name Nunataarmiut means "inland people" or "people of the land," and the majority were indeed Inupiat from interior northwest Alaska, though some were from coastal settlements such as Point Hope and Point Barrow. As primarily inlanders, the Nunataarmiut had previously had little contact with Euro-Americans, and were thus relatively unscathed by the disease epidemics which ravaged coastal Alaska during the 1870s and '80s.

However, they were still fleeing ecological disaster. Beginning in the 1860s, caribou populations in northwestern Alaska began to fail, culminating in a major population collapse between the 1880s and 1920s. The Brooks Range was almost entirely depopulated and people fled to coastal communities in both Alaska and northwestern Canada.[31] Collapsing human populations in both areas must have made emigration doubly attractive, by opening depopulated areas to resettlement. In Canada most of the newcomers settled in and around the Mackenzie Delta, where there was excellent muskrat trapping. They came to be called Uummarmiut, or "people of the green trees and willows," after the lush vegetation there.[32]

To what extent were the whalers responsible for all these ecological disasters? The answer is debatable. Certainly the terrible death rate among the Inuvialuit and many of their Alaskan compatriots was due to infectious diseases brought by the whalers and other Europeans. The destruction of the

Mimurana ("Roxy") and his wife, early 1900s Mimurana was a guide and travelling companion of the explorer Vilhjalmur Stefansson, and the source (via Stefansson) of much of what we know about traditional Inuvialuit life.

caribou is also commonly laid at their door, and understandably so since the whalers introduced both repeating firearms and large-scale commercial meat-hunting in northwest Alaska just before the caribou collapse. Moreover, the situation was soon repeated in the Mackenzie area. Here too caribou populations had decreased dramatically by the early years of the 20th century, after a period of heavy exploitation by and for the American whaling fleet. But the exact kill figures are disputed, and apologists for the whalers cite instead poorly understood long-term natural fluctuations in caribou populations as the more likely culprit.[33] On balance, the impact of the American whaling fleet must be considered at least a very strong contributing factor in the collapse of caribou populations throughout northwestern North America during the late 19th and early 20th centuries.

Understandably, the Nunataarmiut (or Uummarmiut, as they might now be called) were resented when they first arrived in the Mackenzie area. For one thing, they used poison for trapping, which caused needless destruction to wildlife,[34] and were moving uninvited into Inuvialuit territory. Elders like Nuligak found them arrogant and were not happy with the way they over-exploited the Mackenzie Delta, which had previously been left unoccupied.[35] A traditional story relates how the Inuvialuit first noticed Nunataarmiut moving east through the northern Yukon and down to the Mackenzie River. The Inuvialuit were afraid that the Nunataarmiut would discover the excellent hunting offered by the Bluenose caribou herd living farther east. To protect themselves, the Inuvialuit asked a shaman to divert the herd so that it could not be found. Unfortunately, he hid it too successfully, and it was many years before the animals returned to their former haunts.[36]

Soon, however, relations began to improve. Newcomers and indigenous Inuvialuit found they had much in common. They could understand each other's language — although some of the words were different — and shared both a common culture and a common situation. Inter-marriage became frequent and even dialect distinctions began to blur as vocabularies were shared and loan words swapped. By the early 20th century, the Inuvialuit Mimurana reported that "he is so used to Nunatama language now he hardly knows what words are Nunatama (and) has to stop to think."[37] Eventually the newcomers and the Inuvialuit merged into a single people, the modern Inuvialuit of the western Canadian Arctic. Without the arrival of the Nunataarmiut, the Inuvialuit might have disappeared entirely.

THE MISSIONARIES

The Inuvialuit lost more than just their loved ones in the great disease epidemics. They also lost sovereignty over their own lives. As one elder remembers, "In the wake of the explorers our people began to die of many sicknesses which were foreign to us … Our once thriving camps were but empty shells. Many of the elders, leaders, and hunters were gone. In the midst of this sadness and confusion the Tan'ngit [whites] suddenly seemed to be all around. One by one, the fur traders, whalers, missionaries, and government workers had come into our lives pushing and pulling at us."[38] mmmmmmmmmmm

The Inuvialuit were visited by various Christian missionaries during the early fur trade period, but it is doubtful that they had any real effect on belief or practice. It was only when the traditional culture was shattered by disease and foreign intervention that the new religion began to seem attractive. People had seen their traditional leaders and healers helpless in the face of mass death. And while the Inuvialuit died, the whites — now called Tan'ngit (a word introduced by the Nunataarmiut/Uummarmiut) — seemed to thrive. Always there were more of them, and disease and illness seemed to pass them by. Given the cataclysmic events they were living through, it is the Inuvialuit resistance to a foreign belief system which is remarkable.

Kitigaaryuit, 1909
By the time this photograph was taken, Kitigaaryuit had been abandoned for several years, although a few families still camped there in summer to hunt beluga. A late summer snowfall blankets the ground.
NATIONAL ARCHIVES OF CANADA, C23943

In 1890, the Oblate order of the Roman Catholic Church set up a mission house at Fort McPherson under the guidance of Father Constant Giroux. In 1892 he was joined by a companion, Father Camille Lefebvre, known as the "red priest" because of the colour of his hair. Lefebvre became responsible for missionary work among the Inuvialuit and that year travelled to Kitigaaryuit.[39]

The same summer, the Anglican missionary Isaac Stringer also visited Kitigaaryuit. He was greeted by Toowachik, "a prominent Eskimo," and invited to pitch a tent in his "camp" or neighbourhood. On learning that Father Lefebvre was already camped nearby, Stringer chose to live elsewhere in the village. A pattern of enmity was already long established between the two religions, and neither Lefebvre nor Stringer was able to rise above it. According to Stringer, his Catholic rival was in the habit of giving gifts to those who would listen to him. Stringer responded, "telling them of the greater present I was going to give them — the Gospel."

Stringer's interpreter and guide on this trip was an Inuvialuit man from Fort McPherson named Arviuna, also known as George Greenland. Interestingly, he was the same "Arviouna" whom Petitot had met and described at length twenty years earlier.[40] As an adolescent, Arviuna had run away from home and lived with Hudson's Bay Company traders at Fort Good Hope, where he learned English. He helped teach Inuvialuktun to Petitot and later married a Gwich'in woman and settled at Fort McPherson. According to Petitot, "he spoke English and Loucheux [Gwich'in] well enough to interpret between both these languages and Eskimo." Men like Arviuna helped bridge the cultural and linguistic gaps that divided Inuvialuit from Gwich'in and Native from white. He was a harbinger of the multi-ethnic nature of the modern Delta community.

In 1893 Stringer undertook two trips to visit the whalers at Herschel Island, in a commendable and partially successful attempt to control the liquor trade and bring a stop to other abuses. To his surprise he was well received by the whaling captains, who apparently liked him personally and helped support his cause. "I did not *see* [his italics] much liquor or drinking," he later wrote to his wife Sadie, "but I cant [sic] have my ears open without knowing that there is a good deal given to the Eskimos."

Both Stringer and Lefebvre continued to visit Kitigaaryuit on a fairly regular basis over the next few years. In 1893 Stringer met "Kokhlik" (also

Arviuna as a young man, 1870s
Arviuna taught Inuvialuktun to missionary Emile Petitot and served as a guide and translator for Isaac Stringer.
EMILE PETITOT

(*Facing page*)
Anglican missionaries Isaac and Sadie Stringer in Inuvialuit clothing, Herschel Island, 1890s
Isaac Stringer is well remembered by the Inuvialuit, although he did not make a single conversion.
MASON 1910

"Kax'alik," "Kakhilik"), the most powerful *umialik* at Kitigaaryuit, who seems to have acted as something of a sponsor, urging the missionary to camp next to his own tent in the middle of the village. He was allowed to preach in the *qatdjgi,* without an interpreter this time, having made some progress in the language.

In 1894 Stringer finally vanquished his Catholic foe, or rather, that foe vanquished himself. The event happened at Fort McPherson, during the summer trading season. As the Anglicans tell the story,[41] Lefebvre had called on the Inuvialuit in their tents and told them that those who wished to be saved were to come to his house when he rang a bell. Unwilling to be intimidated, the Inuvialuit refused. The *umialik* (Kokhlik?) and his wife climbed the hill to see Lefebvre, but were rudely received by the angry priest. "Taking paper in his hands, he tore it to shreds and flung it into the fire saying that if they were going to be Protestants they would burn like that in hell." Lefebvre was told not to visit the Inuvialuit again, and a few years later the Catholic mission at Fort McPherson closed.

In 1895 Stringer was joined by another Anglican missionary, Charles Whittaker. Together the two men established a permanent mission at Herschel Island and continued to visit Kitigaaryuit and other settlements regularly. A day school was organized at Herschel, attracting an average attendance of about 30 people over the winter months, while a similar number attended Sunday services. But despite the undoubted talents and sincerity of both men, when Stringer left for the South in 1901 they had not effected a single conversion. One of his last diary entries is a cry of near despair: "I feel that the Huskies are no nearer to accepting our religion than they ever were … I feel completely discouraged. Where is the fault? In what have I failed?"[42]

Despite this sense of failure, Stringer seems to have made a good impression. The Inuvialuit praised him for learning to speak their language and trying to protect them from the whalers. Peter Thrasher heard stories about Stringer from his father and grandmother. "You know that time when they first started to come they had no priest. You know that time they started drinking they try and kill each other, fight, drunk. Their wives they lost them to those white people, those people, their daughters they fooled around. When that preacher came just like that all the bad people they stopped. Bishop Stringer, yeah!"[43]

The first Inuvialuit were converted in 1907, and most of the community was baptized that winter or during the following few years.[44] While Stringer's

The Inuvialuit study their catechism, Kitigaaryuit, 1890s
An up-turned *umiaq* provides windbreak or shelter. Despite the rapt attention of the congregation, it would be another ten years before any Inuvialuit were baptized.
MASON 1910; THE PHOTO MAY BE BY STRINGER

Kublualuk the Shaman

Ishmael Alunik (as told to Eddie D. Kolausok)

Kublualuk *means "a big thumb" in Inuvialuktun. Kublualuk was an Inuvialuit hunter. He was also a strong shaman who gained many powers. One of the powers he was known for was the ability to fly. Kublualuk lived along the coast and stayed in Kitigaaryiut during summer months and the winter festive season. Kublualuk had a wife and he lived off the land like all Inuvialuit. He was a good* angatkuq *or shaman and he used his powers in a good way.*

KUBLUALUK RECEIVES HIS POWERS

Long ago during a time of great hunger, Kublualuk was hunting. He travelled inland towards the mountains south of Herschel Island. This was a bad year for game and everywhere Inuvialuit were hungry. Kublualuk thought that the hunting might be better in the mountains. He walked into the mountains for several days but did not see anything. He was getting very tired and discouraged. Kublualuk decided that it would be time to turn back soon but first he would rest. He lay down to rest and felt very sad because he knew his people were very hungry. Despite his hunger and sadness, Kublualuk soon fell asleep with the hope that things would soon change for the better.

Kublualuk slept peacefully in the mountains. He dreamed of better days and of happy times when food was plentiful. He also dreamed about hard times where people were hungry and starving. While he was sleeping, the wind began to grow and the clouds went away and the moon filled the mountains with brightness as it shone off the snow. Suddenly Kublualuk was jolted awake by a strong wind and the loud ruffling of feathers. Startled, he saw a giant falcon looming over him. Kublualuk shuddered with fear as the giant falcon flapped its wings and clasped its sharp talons over Kublualuk, making him feel trapped and helpless. The giant falcon's eyes seemed to pierce Kublualuk's eyes, scaring him even more and holding him in a trance-like state.

Kublualuk the shaman with his wife and children, Herschel Island
Kublualuk, the last great Inuvialuit shaman, was said to have the ability to transform himself into a falcon. He is remembered with pride by modern Inuvialuit.
YUKON ARCHIVES, FINNIE COLLECTION, 81/21, #206

Sensing that Kublualuk was in great fear, the giant falcon began to speak in a strong but gentle voice. He told Kublualuk, "Do not be afraid, I am here to give you strength and good power." Kublualuk relaxed and listened keenly. The falcon said, "I will show you how to transform into a falcon, for you will need this power to help you and your people in hard times." The giant falcon reached up over its head and made the motion of putting on a jacket. Kublualuk watched and got up to do the same thing. "When you wish to transform for good purposes, think about what you will become and put this falcon jacket on like this," said the giant falcon. Kublualuk reached high over his head and made the motions of pulling on a falcon jacket. He used all his will to think of the falcon as he made the motions. He was soon amazed to find that he had turned into a falcon.

The giant falcon then told him, "You now have a strong power but you will have to use it for the good of your people. Do not use it in a bad way or you will be dealt with in the way you use the power. Remember this well, Kublualuk, and always think of the good of the people before you think of yourself and you will be taken care of."

Kublualuk was amazed that he was now a falcon and he screeched and nodded his head, saying, "Yes, I will remember this always." The giant falcon then said, "I must continue on my journey into the good dark light that you will come to know as you grow older." With a thundering snap of his beak and a thrust of his wings the giant falcon lifted off into the air. As Kublualuk watched the giant falcon take off, the wind roared stronger than any west wind on the coast of the Arctic Ocean that Kublualuk had ever witnessed. Soon the giant falcon vanished into a grey mist that blew off into the mountains and up into the high clouds, quickly disappearing out of sight.

Kublualuk was excited and scared at the same time. He flapped his wings and quickly rose high into the air. He soared to heights he had never dreamed of and saw great distances in every direction. He was happy. He knew that this new power was to be used only for situations like the hard times he and his people were experiencing at that moment. As he soared towards home he came across a flock of ptarmigan and he quickly took seven of the birds. He then transformed back into a human and walked the last few kilometres home with his catch.

Kublualuk arrived at his home to see his hungry wife smiling at the sight of the fresh ptarmigan. They ate the ptarmigan and gave thanks for the food they had that day. They also made sure to save some of the ptarmigan for the other people who were hungry. Kublualuk did not tell his wife or anyone about his newly gained power. He was still very afraid of the new gift he had received. From that day on, Kublualuk knew he would need to pay attention to the words of the giant falcon and use his power in a good way. That is how Kublualuk received his power to turn into a falcon and fly.

KUBLUALUK MEETS THE POLICE

. . . .

One time at Herschel Island when the North-West Mounted Police first came into Inuvialuit traditional territory, Kublualuk had an encounter with the police. It was in the latter part of October and people were continuing to hunt as they had at this time of year since their ancestors could remember. Kublualuk was walking along the beach on Herschel Island and he came across a nice cross fox [a colour phase of the red fox]. Kublualuk took aim and shot it. Kublualuk was very happy, as he knew the fox would bring him a good trade for goods.

Instead of being happy for long, Kublualuk was soon confused by how he was treated by the police, who were newcomers to the area. This was at the time when the government first introduced hunting laws, where you could not kill or trap at certain times of the year. The law was already in place up the Mackenzie River area but it was the first time the law was being enforced on Inuvialuit traditional territory. The North-West Mounted Police arrested Kublualuk and put him in jail because he shot a fox before the coloured fox fur season opened.

So Kublualuk was put into a jail cell on Herschel Island. Kublualuk smiled at his people when he was led into the jail. He stayed in jail late into the night. When the fire went out and the chimney cooled off, Kublualuk turned into a feather and used the updraft of the chimney to get out of the jail. Kublualuk then went to his sod house. In the morning the police were surprised that Kublualuk was gone, but there was no evidence of a break-out. They went to Kublualuk's sod house, where they found him and told him, "You escaped from jail, we are going to have to put you in again."

Kublualuk was again put in jail. The next morning the police went to wake up Kublualuk but he was gone again. They went back to his house and arrested him for the third time. Again Kublualuk was able to get out of the jail without anyone seeing him and without any evidence of a break-out.

The Inuvialuit living in the area told the police that Kublualuk was a strong shaman. The police were puzzled, but instead of trying to arrest Kublualuk for a fourth time, they hired him as a guide.

They must have realized that he did not use any physical force, nor was there any harm in how Kublualuk left the jail. Maybe the police respected Kublualuk or feared him, but one thing is certain — he was hired on in a capacity of goodness as he worked alongside the police, even though he did not understand English. If there was no interpreter, they used sign language to communicate. The police never had any trouble with Kublualuk again, and they seemed to understand that laws made in the South had to be dealt with in a different manner in the North, as the traditional people of the North already had an understanding of conservation practices that were balanced with the need to survive in the harsh Arctic environment.

KUBLUALUK VISITS HIS NIECE

. . . .

One time Kublualuk was at Herschel Island and he decided that he would visit his niece who was in the Delta about 150 kilometres [90 miles] away. He told his friends that he was going to go and visit her. Kublualuk then quickly vanished from Herschel Island.

It took him only fractions of a second to get to his niece's house. Kublualuk showed up as a falcon. He flew above his niece's sod house and fluttered over the gut window. His niece came out to see what was happening. Kublualuk did not want to frighten her so he flew off back to his home at Herschel Island.

When Kublualuk returned to Herschel Island, he told his wife that his niece was okay and that she was sewing and putting new soles on a pair of mukluks [boots]. His wife was happy with this report.

In the springtime the hunters and trappers came to Herschel Island to trade their furs for goods. Kublualuk's niece came with her husband to sell furs. Kublualuk said, "I seen you sewing soles on your mukluks through your window. The time when you were sewing your mukluks you came out to see what was going on and you saw me as a falcon." His niece was amazed because she knew exactly what he was talking about. She knew that Kublualuk was using his power for good things and she felt very good. Ever since that time, when people see a falcon they say "Kublualuk!" because of this story.

successor Charles Whittaker credited the long-standing labours of the Anglican mission, it was, ironically, Alaskan Inupiat who converted the Inuvialuit. Kotzebue Sound was one of the first toe-holds of Christianity in northwestern Alaska, where between 1896 and 1902 a Christian community was founded by Uyaraq ("Rock"), an Alaskan Inupiat, and two Quaker missionaries. From here the new religion spread rapidly. Most Alaskan Inupiat were converted by other Inupiat, and given their important connections with the Nunataarmiut community in northwestern Canada, it was only a matter of time before Christianity spread there too. Nuligak recalled the Nunataarmiut holding outdoor prayer services at Baillie Island, "to everyone's astonishment." The sermon was delivered by a man named Okritlaik, who dressed in a long, white gown, like that of a bishop.[45]

It was the Anglican Church, however, which baptized the Inuvialuit. Nuligak recalled that the baptismal ceremony was fairly meaningless to some of the participants:

> A minister, Mr. Whittaker, arrived. He poured water on a great number of people. I got in line and did as the others did. During the ceremony the minister said to an Eskimo, Oyangin, "I give you the name of Haydn." Oyangin answered, "What a queer name you are giving me." He did not want to be called that way. Furthermore a number of them did not even know what this ceremony was all about — even the adults did not bother to ask for explanations, and they knew nothing of the meaning of the prayers.[46]

Needless to say, early Inuvialuit Christianity retained many elements of traditional belief, as Stefansson records: "There are also in every community Eskimo who are in the habit of visiting heaven and conferring there with Christ Himself, with Saint Peter and others, quite in the manner in which they used to visit the moon while still heathen, and have discussions with the man in the moon."[47] There was also a strong emphasis upon taboos, including a strict keeping of the Sabbath that would have impressed the staunchest Presbyterian. According to Nuligak, an early Inuvialuit preacher named Tanomerk referred to the commandments of God as *Pinailat,* or evil spirits: "in the listeners' minds these Pinailat were like taboos which, when broken, spelled doom for the offender."[48]

Although Stefansson called the new religion "Eskimo-ized Christianity" and laughed at some of its incongruities, it was warmly embraced by Charles

Whittaker and the Anglican mission: "The acceptance of Christianity has dispelled their fears of malignant nature and given them such a confidence in the overruling beneficence of the greater powers, that their minds have been set free to expand in many directions. Stefansson declares that the old beliefs persist under or behind the newer. One observing their daily life, hearing their conversation, seeing their methods, their houses, their furnishing and, above all, their animated faces and sparkling eyes, has no hesitation in saying that life is far richer and more worth while to them than ever before."[49] One wonders how he would have felt had they converted to Roman Catholicism.

Not only were many traditional beliefs "Christianized," some survived more or less intact outside of the Christian fold. One of the last great shamans was Kublualuk. In the early days of the 20th century, at a time when the Inuvialuit were converting to Christianity, Kublualuk decided instead to become a shaman or *angatkuq* (for more on Kublualuk, see pages 98–102).

Royal North-West Mounted Police officers, Herschel Island, about 1904
The two men are Sergeant Fitzgerald and Constable Sutherland. Fitzgerald later won immortality with the "The Lost Dawson Patrol," where he lost his life.
CANADA'S VISUAL HISTORY, 50-25

THE POLICE

The presence of the American whaling fleet operating unsupervised in Canadian waters, and of a permanent American settlement on Herschel Island, was a source of great embarrassment to the Canadian government. Law and order was imperilled, Canadian sovereignty was in jeopardy, and the Hudson's Bay Company was complaining of unfair competition in the fur trade. Belatedly, and with the impression of reluctance, the Dominion government finally responded, and in 1903 Sergeant Fitzgerald and four constables were sent north to Fort McPherson to establish the first North-West Mounted Police detachment north of the Arctic Circle (the North-West Mounted Police became the Royal North-West Mounted Police the following year, and the Royal Canadian Mounted Police in 1920). In August of 1903, Fitzgerald and Constable Forbes Sutherland landed at Herschel Island, "the first Mounted Policemen to tread it, make official contact with the Eskimos and sight the North-West Passage."[50]

The western Arctic was still an exotic place for visitors from the South. In a letter to his mother, Constable Sutherland describes a dance or "houla-houla" (as it was called by the whalers) he witnessed en route to Herschel Island that first summer:

At Shingle Point, out thirty miles from the mouth of the Mackenzie, we struck a Huskie village where they entertained us with a "Houla-Houla," their native dance. It is something like a "Pow-Wow" dance of the Indians, but the spectacular part is in the way they use their knives. Each man has a fine steel knife of his own make from six inches to two feet long. Flourishing this is an important feature of the dance. Then when the "Houla-Houla" drum beats in a certain way, one man grasps his neighbour by the left hand with his left hand. They lift each other's arms and make motions as though they were driving their knives into the arm-pits of their partners. They do it so quickly that it takes some time to see where the blade goes, but they twist it off some way. They dance around a fire to start with, but end up dancing all around the camp, brandishing their knives, houla-houlaing, shrieking & yelling. One of them kept dancing around me for some time brandishing his knife, of course, I had to smile & look as though I liked it, until finally he came a little closer, slashed off one of my brass buttons & danced away laughing.[51]

The reader is reminded of the Earl of Lonsdale's reception fifteen years earlier.

Fitzgerald must have quickly realized the difficulties of enforcing the laws of Canada in so remote a place. The police were few and the whalers many,

Herschel Island, 1909
The central building is the Royal North-West Mounted Police station. It housed a barracks as well as the jail from which the shaman Kublualuk escaped.
NATIONAL ARCHIVES OF CANADA, PA211734

and he was a long way from civilization. At first he had almost no real power, writing to his superiors: "They [the American whalers] think that I have the same power as the officers on their own Revenue cutters. If they once found out that I could only make a report, I am afraid plenty of liquor would come ashore. As it is they are very careful while there are Police on the island."[52]

Clearly the Arctic coast could not be policed from Fort McPherson. In 1904 an independent detachment was established at Herschel Island under Sergeant Fitzgerald. In 1905 he was granted full powers to enforce "all the laws of Canada" and "to deal summarily with most cases of crime."[53]

Sergeant Fitzgerald's first task was to control the illicit liquor trade, and several Inuvialuit were arrested for public drunkenness. According to Constable Sutherland, again writing to his mother, "So far we have had no serious trouble. A Husky fired a shot at the sergeant, but he was drunk and we got him in irons … Our prisoners are all very docile and obedient. We gave them fourteen days apiece, and they will have enough wood sawed up to last all winter if they keep on at the rate they are going. We made a guard-room out of an old wood shack, and lock them in there every night and make them work all day. They are much better than the average white prisoners outside, and we don't have to watch or nag them at all."[54] It was from this guard-room that Kublualuk would later escape, helped by his shamanic powers.

The whalers who were actually supplying the alcohol were almost all American citizens and had to be approached more cautiously. They could only be charged if caught ashore with alcohol in their possession, a situation that evidently frustrated the police. Constable Sutherland writes of being "kept fairly busy, going into the country chasing up sleds from the ships, which eluded us here and got away with liquor to trade the Natives for deer meat and furs inland."[55] The captain of the *Beluga,* however, showed his support by clapping his steward in irons for giving alcohol to a Native woman. Arrests continued, and within a year "the worst was over" and the whalers were made aware of Canadian jurisdiction and forced to pay Canadian import duties.[56] In fact, many whaling captains seem to have found their crews difficult to manage and welcomed the arrival of the police.

Law and order had been asserted, but in many ways it was too late. By 1905 the whaling industry was dying and the cultural and environmental damage had been done. The land and sea had been despoiled, a culture shattered, and now the Inuvialuit were subject to police arrest and Canadian law.

THE END OF THE WHALING ERA

By 1895 the best days of the whaling industry were already over. Whales were becoming progressively scarcer and several bad ice years in the late 1890s resulted in poor yields and the loss of several ships. The industry tried moving to Cape Bathurst to take advantage of previously unexploited waters farther east. A harbour was found at Baillie Island, but it was windswept and poorly protected, making Pauline Cove seem luxurious by comparison. Captain Bodfish of the *Beluga* took the last good catch of the fishery off Cape Bathurst in 1899.[57] As profits suffered, the quality of the crews declined to the point where they were described in the American press as "demons of debauchery" and by their own captains as "an inferior grade — some of them being, emphatically, hard cases."[58]

The shore station at Baillie Island became — briefly — a miniature Herschel Island. The whalers traded alcohol for furs, meat and sex and attempted to teach the local Inuvialuit how to hunt whales "American-style." But to no avail. There were just not enough whales left to catch. The fur trade became an important hedge against failure, and often the only source of profit in a bad year. Captain Bodfish records trading for 1,400 fox skins and four bear skins on one occasion at Horton River.[59] As of 1907, the total value of furs exchanged between whalers and the Inuvialuit has been estimated at $1.4 million.[60]

By the early 20th century it was clear to all that unless whaling ceased quickly, the bowhead would soon be extinct. The invention of cheap artificial substitutes for baleen — including spring steel, celluloid and "featherbone" (an amalgam made from processed goose quills) — helped make that possible. The year 1908 saw the last real attempts at systematic whaling in western Arctic waters. In that year the entire fleet took only 24 whales, and when they reached San Francisco they found that the price of baleen had collapsed. The leading operators laid up their remaining vessels. In 1909 only three ships went north, almost solely to trade furs. By 1910 there were no buyers for baleen whatsoever and the industry was effectively dead.[61]

THE PIVOT OF INUVIALUIT HISTORY

Between 1890 and 1910, the Inuvialuit suffered one of the most dramatic cultural dislocations of any people in recorded history. The greatest change was

in the size and nature of the population itself. The native-born Inuvialuit community plummeted from perhaps 1,500 people in 1890 (already down by about forty percent from 1850) to 150 people just 20 years later. At the same time, the survivors were swamped by Inupiat (Nunataarmiut) newcomers from Arctic Alaska. Some came on a temporary basis — in 1894, for instance, most of the inhabitants of Point Barrow, Alaska, and nearly a hundred people from Point Hope were living on Herschel Island, working for the whalers — but many stayed and founded families. By the early 1920s, the "Inuit" population of the western Arctic numbered just four to five hundred people, fewer than half of whom were of local origin.[62]

A number of whalemen also stayed and started families, especially the so-called "beachcombers" or "squawmen" who married local women and took up trapping and fur trading as the whale industry died. By the first decade of the 20th century, a new Inuvialuit people was being born, with both local roots and genetic ties to the four corners of the globe. Many modern Inuvialuit have ancestors who a hundred years ago came not only from Arctic Alaska and the Mackenzie area but from Siberia, Polynesia, the Cape Verde Islands, the United States and Europe. They are all now Inuvialuit.

Society was changed fundamentally. Old territorial divisions disappeared, ancient villages were abandoned and Christianity was adopted. The old subsistence economy was disappearing, replaced by a cash economy based on fur trapping, sealing and trading. Schooners and whale boats were widely available and many Inuvialuit were poised to become prosperous entrepreneurs. They had suffered greatly, but they had also learned much. The whaling era is the pivot around which Inuvialuit history turns.

5

Trappers, Traders and Herders, 1906–

David Morrison and Eddie D. Kolausok

The demise of the whaling industry left the Inuvialuit with both opportunities and threats. Could they maintain their economic prosperity? Could they begin once again to take charge of their own lives? And could they rebuild their culture, shattered by disease and foreign intrusion?

From the Inuvialuit point of view, the whaling era did not come to an abrupt end in 1908. Many whalers had long been active in the fur trade. When the market for baleen disappeared some stayed on, particularly those who had married Inuvialuit women and fathered local families. Much of the early 20th-century fur trade continued to be schooner-based and many of the old whaling ships, such as the *Rosie H*, the *Belvedere* and the *Polar Bear*, continued in operation as floating trading posts, plying the waters of the Beaufort Sea from community to community.

Nor did Herschel Island immediately die as a population and trading centre. In 1915 the Hudson's Bay Company established a trading post there, its first on the Arctic coast.[1] When the Hudson's Bay Company fur trader Phillip Godsell visited the island in 1921, he described a bustling scene that had changed little in some ways over the last twenty years:

The place was crowded with Mounted Police, missionaries, also traders and trappers of many nationalities from Negroes and Hawaiians to Portuguese.

Iglukitallok ("Kitallok's camp"), Mackenzie Delta, about 1915
The early 20th century saw a dramatic rise in fur prices and soaring prosperity, as the Inuvialuit became dedicated and highly skilled fur trappers. They still depended on fish and game for most of their diet, but had access to flour, tea and a wealth of manufactured goods.
CANADIAN MUSEUM OF CIVILIZATION, 43215

Drawn up along the shore were about sixty motor schooners belonging to the Nunatagmiut Eskimos. That they had become quite sophisticated in their ways was evidenced by the strains of "Red Hot Mama," "Dardanella" and "How Are Ya Gonna Keep 'Em Down on the Farm" which were wafted on the Polar breeze from the gramophones within the cabins.[2]

The 60 motor schooners belonging to "Nunatagmiut Eskimos" (as Godsell called all Inuvialuit) are a clue that for many people, prosperity remained high or even achieved new heights in the years after the whaling boom. The schooners were two-masted and 12 to 15 metres (40–50 feet) long with powerful gas engines. They replaced the earlier sail-driven whale boats after 1912 and cost about $6,000 each, a considerable fortune ninety years ago.[3] According to one observer, the average standard of living for Inuvialuit during the early 20th century was higher than that of many working-class southern Canadians.[4] At a time when the fortunes of Native Canadians generally were at an all-time low, the ability of the Inuvialuit to prosper and achieve some kind of control over their own economic destinies is remarkable.

It was the fur trade that supported this prosperity. The Inuvialuit had been involved in trading furs since 1850, but before the whaling years, it had not dominated their lives. The whalers had taught them to value and depend upon a whole range of trade items which the 19th-century Hudson's Bay Company could not supply: gramophones, cotton clothing, imported food, sewing machines, frame houses with glass windows, even typewriters. To pay for these things, the Inuvialuit became adept and highly focused fur trappers. The shift to an economy that depended more and more on trapping was also encouraged by a sharp rise in the price of furs. Between 1915 and 1919, the price of white fox in the western Arctic rose from $2.50 to $50 a pelt, marten from $2.50 to $55, mink from $1 to $20 and muskrat from 40¢ to $1.50.[5]

With this kind of economic inducement, some Inuvialuit were even able to step into economic roles previously occupied only by whites. They were not just hunters and trappers; some were now traders and entrepreneurs as well. Beginning in 1910 and picking up momentum after 1920, a string of trading posts was opened in the Mackenzie Delta and along the western Arctic coast. About fifty posts were opened before 1945, by the Hudson's Bay Company, the Canalaska Trading Company and other small companies and independent traders. Most lasted no more than a decade. At least eight were owned and operated by Inuvialuit.[6] Inuvialuit schooner captains were also active in trading.

Dog teams, Yukon Arctic coast, about 1915

The Inuvialuit had always depended on dog teams for winter travel. But with the new prosperity of the 20th century, the size and quality of teams was much improved. For a subsistence hunter, dogs are expensive animals to keep.

THE RISE OF AKLAVIK AND THE DELTA MUSKRAT TRAPPERS

In 1912 a small Hudson's Bay Company post was opened at Pokiak Point, opposite the present town of Aklavik in the western Mackenzie Delta. It was followed by a Northern Traders Ltd. post the following year, and in 1918 H. Liebes and Company established a post at the present site of Aklavik. Within a few years the other posts had re-located and the important settlement of Aklavik began its bustling existence. By 1945 another 18 independent posts had opened (and often closed) there.[7]

From its earliest days, Aklavik — "place of the grizzly bear" — was a multi-ethnic town, home to Inuvialuit (mostly Uummarmiut) as well as white, Metis and a few Gwich'in. During the first half of the 20th century, all depended on the fur trade and particularly on the excellent muskrat trapping in the Mackenzie Delta. As Herschel Island fell into its inevitable decline — the RCMP re-located to Aklavik in 1922 and the last trading post closed in 1940 — Aklavik rose to the forefront as the transportation, commercial and administrative capital of the western Arctic. It soon boasted stores, schools, a hospital, hotels and even an Anglican cathedral.[8]

Aklavik was well positioned. It sits within the low-lying, meandering maze of the Mackenzie Delta, one of the richest fur areas in Canada. In earlier times, the Delta had been largely unoccupied. Home to few large animals but a huge population of muskrat and mink, it was a poor place for hunters but a rich one for trappers. Its human population rose dramatically during the first decades of the 20th century. By 1931, 411 people lived in the Aklavik area, 140 of them Inuvialuit.[9] Hundreds of thousands of muskrats were taken — as many as 250,000 in some years[10] — and Aklavik was soon known as the Muskrat Fur Capital of the World. By 1924 the steamer *Distributor* was making two annual supply trips. By the 1930s, Aklavik was one of the most important fur-trade centres in Canada, both in the number of people involved and in the value of furs traded.

Active trappers, of course, did not live in Aklavik itself but were scattered across the landscape "on the land." All had to fish in order to feed their dog teams, and during the summer most Inuvialuit travelled to the Beaufort coast to hunt seals and beluga whales. They relied on motor schooners for the beluga hunt and to get people to the whaling camps at Shingle Point and elsewhere. Schooner owners were addressed as "Captain" and enjoyed some of the prestige

Hunting muskrats in the Delta, early 1960s

DEREK SMITH

(*Facing page*)

Spring break-up at Aklavik, 1922

NWT ARCHIVES, N-1979-004-0242

Pokiak and family, Aklavik, 1922

"Old man" Pokiak was one of the founders of Aklavik. In the early 1900s, Aklavik quickly became the fur trade capital of the western Arctic, eclipsing Herschel Island as the commercial and administrative capital of the region.

NWT ARCHIVES, N-1979-004-0261

of the old *umialit*, organizing the hunt and sharing out the spoils. Cabin sites or camps often had evocative names such as Kawmijyuq, "bright place." Cabins were made of logs but in a modified Euro-Canadian style, with horizontal log walls, hinged doors, glassed windows and a wood-burning stove. Doors were left unlocked so that travellers could always make tea or find shelter for the night. Near the cabin stood a smokehouse and a four-pole shelter cache, entered by means of a ladder and used to store food and other perishables beyond the reach of wolves, wolverines and sled dogs. People travelled into Aklavik on a seasonal basis, to visit, trade, buy supplies and attend church.[11]

In an effort to regulate the trapping industry, government officials began to map out trapping areas. In 1949 a law was passed requiring trappers to register individual traplines through the purchase of an annual trapping licence. Mandatory registration was ended in 1957, but the program did minimize conflict and help local people deal with an influx of non-local, non-aboriginal trappers.[12]

What was Aklavik like during the heyday of the fur trade? Fur trader Dudley Copland described the town as it appeared in 1935:

THE INUVIALUIT MOVE EAST:
BANKS ISLAND AND HOLMAN

Before the arrival of Europeans, the eastern limit of Inuvialuit territory was Cape Bathurst or Franklin Bay; about 400 kilometres (240 miles) of uninhabited coast separated them from the Copper Inuit living on Victoria Island and around Coronation Gulf. Early in the 20th century, lured in part by the opportunities of the fur trade, the Inuvialuit began to move east into this uninhabited territory and beyond. Two important individuals in this process were Charlie Klengenberg and Natkusiak, or Billy Banksland.

Charlie Klengenberg was a Danish whaler turned fur trader. He was married to Qimniq (Gremnia), an Inupiat woman,[16] and together they had eight children and founded a fur trade dynasty. In 1905 Klengenberg was given charge of the trading schooner *Olga* and ordered to take her from Baillie Island to Herschel Island. Instead (he later claimed) he was caught in a storm and blown east and could not make landfall until he reached the west coast of Victoria Island, where he over-wintered. At that time, Victoria Island and the western part of the central Canadian Arctic were almost entirely unknown to the outside world. The area had not been visited by a European since the 1850s, and even appeared on Dominion of Canada maps of the day as "uninhabited."

Setting a fish net, Kugluktuk–Victoria Island region, about 1915
The Stefansson-Anderson Arctic Expedition (1910–12) and the Canadian Arctic Expedition (1913–18) brought Inuvialuit trappers and hunters into the central Arctic, where they later played an important role in founding towns such as Kugluktuk and Holman.
CANADIAN MUSEUM OF CIVILIZATION, 38613a

On board the *Olga* were several Inuvialuit families including two men, Kromamak and Tadjuk, and their wives. They set up traplines around the ship. While checking them one day they met three people, members of the Kangiryuarmiut branch of the Copper Inuit, who were in fact the local inhabitants. According to the story told by Kromanak and Tadjuk the following year, "While they were talking, Kromanak, who felt like smoking, filled his pipe with tobacco, took out a match and lit his pipe — and the three visitors cleared out as fast as they could [frightened by such magical power] … As they fled, Kromanak and Tadjuk had a good time firing shots close to them to make them go faster!" When the "Krangmalit" or "Easterners" — as the Inuvialuit called their hosts — asked them later, "Where in the world did they come from, to act as though they were dangerous men?" Kromanak and Tadjuk did not answer, but instead replied that they had come from Abvak, or Cape Bathurst. At this the easterners declared that they must be related, as their ancestors had come from the same area.[17]

Klengenberg and his crew eventually came to a satisfactory trading relationship and bargained the ship's manifest for fox furs. After a year away, they went home to Herschel Island, where Klengenberg was promptly arrested for the theft of his ship and for murder in the suspicious deaths of four of his crew. He was eventually acquitted, although many, including Stefansson and Nuligak, considered him guilty.

The door to the East had been opened, and Klengenberg was one of the first to take advantage of it. In 1916 he established the first permanent trading post in the central Arctic, at the mouth of the Coppermine River, the origin of the present-day hamlet of Kugluktuk (Coppermine). His many children, all of them socially Inuit (or Inuvialuit), continued his legacy. His daughter Etna and son-in-law Ikey Bolt (another Inupiat/Inuvialuit), son Patsy and daughter Lena were particularly active in developing the fur trade among the Copper Inuit, founding trading posts and stores in various locations on western Victoria Island and around Coronation Gulf. The Klengenberg family is now one of the largest and most prominent in the central Arctic, and is also represented in several Inuvialuit communities.[18]

The explorer Vilhjalmur Stefansson was at Herschel Island when Klengenberg returned from Victoria Island during the summer of 1906. He was intrigued by what Klengenberg and his crew had to say about the Inuit they had met, and in particular by the report that many had light-coloured hair and blue eyes and looked like Europeans. He proceeded to make plans to

Charlie Klengenberg and his family, about 1915 Charlie Klengenberg (*far right*) and his wife Qimniq (*holding baby*) founded a fur trade dynasty in the central Arctic. A former whaler turned fur trader, Charlie was considered by many to be a murderer.
CANADIAN MUSEUM OF CIVILIZATION, 36912

visit them, and during his second expedition to the Arctic (1908–12) travelled overland from the western Arctic to Victoria Island accompanied by Natkusiak, "the best of all Eskimo hunters that I have known."[19]

Stefansson's constant guide and travelling companion, Natkusiak was another Alaskan-born Inuvialuit. Ironically, the Copper Inuit took him at first for a white man, perhaps because he was travelling with Stefansson and was armed and equipped in the same fashion. The racial misidentification went both ways: Stefansson was delighted with his "Blond Eskimo," as he called the Kangiryuarmiut, and loudly proclaimed them to be — in all probability — descended from survivors of the "lost" medieval Norse colonies in Greenland. In fact, the Kangiryuarmiut have the same colour hair as other Inuit, and the occasional blue eyes were the result of structural damage due to repeated bouts of snow blindness. Stefansson may have simply been looking for publicity when he made his entirely erroneous claim.[20]

If so, his efforts had the desired effect, as he quickly found financial backing for his last, and by far his most ambitious, adventure, the Canadian Arctic Expedition of 1913–18.[21] It had two parts: a Southern Party, charged with geological and anthropological work in the Coronation Gulf region, and a Northern Party, led by Stefansson, which set out to discover new lands in the

Natkusiak ("Billy Banksland") on the *North Star,* August 1915
Natkusiak (*left*) was the constant guide and travelling companion of the explorer Stefansson, who said Natkusiak was the most skillful hunter and traveller he had ever met.

ACROSS TIME AND TUNDRA

unexplored regions north of Banks Island. Natkusiak, who accompanied Stefansson once more, became so well acquainted with Banks Island over the course of the expedition that he was soon being called by a new nickname, Billy Banksland. As payment for his services, he was given one of the expedition schooners, the *North Star,* and with several Inuvialuit companions he stayed on after the expedition ended. By the time they left Banks Island in 1921, they had trapped about a thousand white foxes. With his profits in hand, Natkusiak returned west, living at Baillie Island with his wife Topsy Ikiuna, whose family had also worked for Stefansson.[22]

Other Inuvialuit soon began to exploit the rich fur resources of Banks Island. Before the 20th century, this large island, unlike nearby Victoria Island, had been essentially unoccupied. In 1921, a hopeful Canadian government declared it a game preserve open only to Inuit (or Inuvialuit) hunters and trappers. In 1928, three Inuvialuit-owned schooners arrived carrying the families of Lennie Inglangasak, David Pektukana (Pirkuqana) and Adam Inoalayak. They spent the first winter at the old base camp of the Canadian Arctic Expedition at Sachs Harbour (named for Stefansson's schooner *The Mary Sachs*). It was a bad trapping year on the mainland, but the Banks Island families did fairly well, and from that time on, the seasonal community on Banks Island began to grow. Each summer they would journey to the western Arctic mainland, first to Herschel Island and later to Aklavik, to sell their fox furs and buy supplies. In autumn they would return to Banks Island for the winter's trapping, spreading out around the island in a number of winter outcamps. Different families made the trip each year and there was considerable movement back and forth between Banks Island and communities such as Aklavik and Tuktoyaktuk.

Some of the Bankslanders also began trading into Walker Bay on Victoria Island, where there were both Hudson's Bay Company and Canalaska Company trading posts. Some began over-wintering in this area, trapping foxes. It is from this group — which included Alex Stefansson (son of Vilhjalmur by his common-law Inuvialuit wife Panigavluk), Fred Wolki, Andy Klengenberg, David Pektukana and Natkusiak himself — that the community of Holman eventually grew.

During the 1930s, the local Copper Inuit (Kangiryuarmiut) were still basically subsistence hunters, little interested in the fur trade. From their

Etna Klengenberg, about 1915
Th eldest daughter of Charlie and Qimniq Klengenberg, Etna (*right*) and her husband Ikey Bolt became key figures in the central Arctic fur trade.
CANADIAN MUSEUM OF CIVILIZATION, 51333

perspective, the Inuvialuit — Uallingmiut ("Westerners"), as they called them — were wealthy people who, though they were fellow Inuit, possessed items normally associated only with white traders. As one Copper Inuit elder reported some fifty years later, "I remember those Westerners. Those people used to come here to trap and trade. Some of them were pretty wealthy. They were able to buy lumber to build wood houses. They were mostly trappers, while the people around here were still mostly hunting and only doing a little bit of trapping."[23]

Of course, not all of the Bankslanders moved to the Holman area. Most continued to winter on Banks Island, where they grew affluent on the white fox trade. The schooner fleet continued to grow during the 1930s and '40s. By 1936, 41 trappers or fully forty percent of all Inuvialuit trappers in the western Arctic had trapped on the island for at least one season. Two of the best trappers, Fred Carpenter and Jim Wolki, got together and bought a 17-metre (57-foot) schooner they called the *North Star*. Named for Natkusiak's boat, which had since been lost, it was the largest and finest schooner ever brought into the western Arctic. For 26 years it was the "flagship" of the Banksland fleet. It cost $35,000 at the time, or about $300,000 in modern funds. In 1935–36, another trapper was able to afford a year-long holiday with his family in San Francisco and Vancouver.

PAULATUK AND THE EASTERN MAINLAND COAST

Located in Darnley Bay on the mainland coast of Amundsen Gulf, Paulatuk is the third community of the eastern Inuvialuit diaspora. The hunting and trapping potential of this area was first explored, at least in modern times, by Natkusiak. Between 1908 and 1912, Stefansson and his expedition, including Natkusiak, were headquartered at Langdon Bay, only a few kilometres to the east.

But it was another decade before Inuvialuit families began settling there. Beginning in the early 1920s, families such as the Rubens, Thrashers, Greens and Kolausoks all settled in the area around Cape Parry and Darnley Bay. In 1927, the Hudson's Bay Company opened a post at Letty Harbour, named for the schooner *Letty*, owned by Qupatquq (Kopatkok) Johnny Green and his wife Ulurraq, both from Alaska. The following year a Roman Catholic mission was set up and another post opened at Pearce Point, where a small group of white trappers had been eking out an existence since about 1920.[24]

Fred, Agnes and Andy Carpenter aboard the schooner *North Star*, about 1950
Fred Carpenter opened the first trading post at Sachs Harbour, and was a very successful trapper. His schooner the *North Star* was the largest ever built for the western Arctic.
NWT ARCHIVES, N-1990-004-0392

Unfortunately, trapping success was short-lived. Some people moved on; others began to do more subsistence hunting than trapping. In about 1935, Billy Thrasher (from Baillie Island) and Father Biname explored the area around modern-day Paulatuk to see if it offered any advantages over Letty Harbour, where Father Biname was priest. It did; they found both better hunting and trapping and an easily accessible source of coal on the nearby Hornaday River (Paulatuk, or Paulatuuq, means "place of soot"). In 1936 the Catholic mission moved to Paulatuk, where it operated its own trading post and store, and by 1937 Letty Harbour had been abandoned. Billy Thrasher served for years as pilot on *Our Lady of Lourdes,* the Roman Catholic supply ship. The coal was traded locally and used for fuel.

As they did elsewhere, people continued to live in various outpost camps around the Cape Parry peninsula, hunting and trapping. The mission store at Paulatuk was rarely if ever profitable. It finally closed in 1954, causing some hardship, although the Hudson's Bay Company re-opened its post at Letty Harbour the same year. Many people moved to Cape Parry for work on DEW Line construction, but they missed Paulatuk. Eventually they sent a petition to the Canadian government asking for help in moving people back there. The Paulatuk Co-op Association was organized, and a post at Paulatuk re-opened in 1967. People began moving back into the settlement, houses were built and the community as it is today came into existence.

THE END OF TRAPPING AS A WAY OF LIFE

In the 1940s the people of the western Arctic were still largely reliant on the fur trade. Fur prices were high during World War II, reaching their all-time peak in constant dollars in 1945–46. But outside forces were conspiring to bring about the end of trapping as a way of life within a generation. The two most important factors were not unrelated: an unstable and generally declining market for furs and the increasing attraction of town life and wage employment.

Fur prices collapsed in 1948–49, causing widespread economic hardship.[25] Fortunately, the government had established family allowances a few years earlier, and most people were able to survive in the short term on a mixture of trapping and social assistance. But the trapping industry never really recovered in most areas of the western Arctic. The construction of DEW Line sites during the mid-1950s brought a timely and very welcome source of wage

TRAPPERS, TRADERS AND HERDERS, 1906– 129

employment, as did the construction of Inuvik a few years later (see chapter 8). Slowly at first, and then with increasing speed, people gave up trapping — and life on the land altogether — for town life and wage labour. The fact that social assistance was tied to school attendance was another powerful impetus for people to move off the land, as many families wanted to live with their children.

In the Aklavik region, the number of active or full-time trappers began to decline as the town grew. Over the course of the 1950s, the number of people engaged in muskrat trapping in the Delta fell from 369 to 236, a figure that includes even part-time trappers. By 1961 the total population of the Aklavik region was 711, of whom 328 — almost half — were classed as Inuvialuit ("Eskimos"). Of these, 222 — or 68 percent — lived permanently in town, compared with no more than a handful a generation earlier. And the Inuvialuit were the only ethnic group still living on the land; none of the 383 "Indians" (Gwich'in), "Multi-breed" (mixed, or Metis) or whites in the region lived outside the town. By 1963–64, only five Aklavik area trappers were earning over $2,000 a year and most were making less than $500.

In the Tuktoyaktuk area, the trapping life also collapsed in the 1950s. The rise of Tuk as the only permanent settlement on the western Arctic coast meant — as elsewhere — that too many people lived in one place for the efficient harvesting of furs. Alone among western coastal settlements, Tuk survived because of the wage employment available there. By the late 1950s, only 11 percent of Inuvialuit income in Tuktoyaktuk was derived from trapping, while wage labour supplied 60 percent.

The building of Inuvik in the late 1950s and early '60s accelerated the process of "micro-urbanization." By 1961 the population of Inuvik had already reached 1,248, including 309 Inuvialuit, 210 of whom were employed, 120 of them permanently, at salaries of $300 to $450 a month. Trapping just could not compete with wages like that.

Only on Banks Island did trapping recover from the "bust" of the late 1940s. By 1948 most Banksland trappers, like trappers elsewhere, were seriously in debt to mainland traders. Without credit and in the grip of a region-wide flu epidemic, none of the Bankslanders was able to return to Banks Island in the autumn of 1948, and for several years they were grounded on the mainland.[26]

Most settled around Aklavik and Tuktoyaktuk, where their situation was not a happy one. The majority tried to take up trapping, but though they fared adequately by local standards they could only make a fraction of their past incomes. They were also widely resented, both because of their former prosperity and because they were entering an already declining trapping market. They had no capital to make repairs, so their schooners were falling into ruin; by 1950 probably only four or five were seaworthy enough to make the return voyage to Banks Island.

Bankslanders were unwelcome on the mainland, and it was in everyone's interest to help them return home. The Canadian government had a particular interest in the matter. During the Cold War after World War II, the American military began to take an interest in the unoccupied islands of the Canadian Arctic. The resettlement of Banks Island could help defend Canadian sovereignty there. The government therefore urged the Hudson's Bay Company to open a post — which it refused to do — or at least to advance the necessary credit to allow the Bankslanders to return home. Nine trappers were prepared to try again, supported by their own resources and by the Hudson's Bay Company, with a small loan guarantee by the Canadian government. In September 1951, two schooners returned to the island. Prices were slowly recovering and foxes were abundant that winter. Loans were repaid, and by 1954–55, fully 20 trappers were once again flourishing on Banks Island.

Fred Carpenter had long been a leader of the Bankslander community. The cabin he built at Sachs Harbour in the 1930s is the oldest building still standing on the island and, as late as 1953, very nearly the only building. In 1958 Carpenter opened the island's first trading post, again at Sachs Harbour, and life was changed forever. Outpost camps at Sea Otter, Lennie Harbour and De Salis Bay were abandoned and by 1961 everyone lived at Sachs Harbour. Frame houses were built, and Catholic and Anglican missions were opened in 1962. No longer tied to the mainland for trading, people began to live at Sachs Harbour all year round, and schooner traffic came to a rapid end. The *Fox* made her last voyage in 1960 and the venerable *North Star* in 1961.

On Banks Island, as nowhere else in the western Arctic, trapping continued to thrive for another 15 years. The fox population on the island was (and probably still is) the highest in the Canadian Arctic. The community of Sachs was small enough — 143 people in 1974 — that town activities did not compete with trapping as a way of life. And the introduction and rapid adoption of snowmobiles after about 1968 greatly extended a trapper's range and mobility. During the 1970s, many Banks Island fox trappers ran 800 to 1,000 traps on lines up to 500 kilometres (300 miles) long. Typically, checking such a trapline took two weeks on the trail, with six or seven trips a season. The task of skinning and preparing the hides, which fell to the trapper's wife, was equally daunting. In the opinion of one expert, the Bankslanders were the best fox trappers in the world.[27]

It took the development of a new social consciousness to finish off the fur trade on Banks Island. The anti-fur lobby was (and is) a social and political movement dedicated to fostering the humane treatment of animals and the advancement of animal rights. Their first victim was the sealing industry. With effective television advertisements and direct action, the anti-fur lobby quickly made its presence known throughout Canada, Europe and the world. Newspaper headlines and television news stories showed seal pups being clubbed by seal hunters off the east coast of Canada. Anti-sealing moratoriums were organized and protests staged, and within a few years the seal hunt was essentially over. Many Inuit communities in the eastern Arctic suffered serious consequences, since the sale of seal hides had been an important source of income.

Attention then turned to the trade in fine furs. Television commercials produced by anti-fur groups and seen by millions of viewers around the world showed graphic images of animals suffering at the hands of trappers. Other commercials showed well-dressed women in fur coats smeared with blood to symbolize the cruelty of the fur trade. Displays of furs were vandalized and people wearing furs were attacked on the streets.

It could not have come at a worse time. Fur prices were high in the early 1970s,[28] the Banks Island fur trade was buoyant, and there were hopes of a more general recovery in the trapping industry. The Canadian government responded to the threat by creating the Federal-Provincial Committee on Humane Trapping (FPCHT) in 1973. The FPCHT undertook the first scientific research on the suffering and stress experienced by animals in traps and demonstrated a commitment by government to address issues raised by anti-fur lobby groups and animal welfare organizations. Soon other initiatives such as trapper training and public education campaigns were launched to counter the anti-fur lobby movement.

Like other aboriginal groups across Canada, the Inuvialuit found themselves defending the trapping life in the public media. According to the National Film Board documentary *Pelts*, "The anti-fur movement has challenged all segments of the fur industry. In the North Native people fear that a collapse of the fur trade would finally destroy their way of life."[29] Their

Inuvialuit Reindeer Herders

Buster Kailek with reindeer
in fancy harness, 1961

NWT ARCHIVES, N-1993-002-0629

. . . .

In the 1920s, the Canadian government approached the Inuvialuit, and particularly Mangilaluk, the chief at Tuktoyaktuk. The government was interested in negotiating a treaty. Instead, Mangilaluk suggested they should provide something of direct use, like reindeer for the people to eat.

Reindeer and caribou are members of the same species, *Rangifer tarandus*. Reindeer, however, are native to Eurasia and have been domesticated for centuries; caribou are only found in North America and are invariably wild. By the end of the whaling era, caribou were almost extinct in the western Arctic, due to over-hunting and other factors. Mangilaluk hoped that imported reindeer might take their place, supplying both food and the hides that people still preferred for winter clothing. The government agreed, hoping too that reindeer herding might provide more reliable employment than trapping, given the ever fluctuating price of furs.

In 1929 the Canadian government signed a contract with Lomen Reindeer Company of Alaska to deliver approximately 3,500 reindeer to the Mackenzie Delta. The company hired Andrew Bahr, a respected Saami herder (the Saami are sometimes called Lapps or Laplanders), to lead the herd, along with other Saami and Alaskan Inupiat herders. The herd left Alaska in December of 1929, on what was supposed to be a two-year journey. Instead, it took five years. But eventually, on March 6, 1935, 2,370 reindeer were delivered to a prepared corral and reindeer station built near Kitigaaryuit on Richards Island. The government paid $65 a head. They also established the huge Mackenzie Reindeer Grazing Reserve, covering 17,094 square kilometres (6,838 square miles) between the Anderson and Mackenzie rivers. This angered many Inuvialuit, who now needed a permit to hunt or trap on traditional lands.

From the beginning the government decided to follow a "close herding" technique, which meant that the reindeer were not allowed to wander freely. Herders stayed with the animals at all times, to keep the herd together and protect it from wolves and other dangers. Local Inuvialuit and even Inuit from the central Arctic were hired as herders. Some of the Saami and Alaskan Inupiat also stayed on, eventually marrying into the Inuvialuit community. Some of the herders include Jimmy Komeak, Joseph Avik, Donald Pingo, Otto Binder, David Roland, Charlie Rufus, Mikkel Pulk (Saami), Peter Kaglik and Joe Illasiak. In all, dozens of men were employed over the next few decades. Each received a small cash salary ($25 a month in the 1930s) and a generous meat ration. As one herder, Ned Kayotuk, remembered, "we never bought meat: we had rations all the time. Just clothing we bought …"

The herds produced both meat and hides. In the 20 years from 1935 to 1954, 9,083 animals were slaughtered. About twenty percent of the meat was donated to the Anglican and Roman Catholic missions, for use in their schools and hospitals and for general welfare. Another third went to the herders themselves, leaving 4,129 carcasses and about 3,500 hides to be sold. By the 1950s the meat was being marketed through the Hudson's Bay Company, who paid about 35¢ a pound; the retail price was between 52¢ and 62¢ a pound, more than most local people could afford to pay.

Some men liked the herding life, but for most it was a gruelling existence. The herders travelled mostly on skis and were exposed to all kinds of brutal weather with little or no shelter, particularly in the winter. Especially when fur prices were high, it was difficult to attract and keep good employees.

In 1938 the government loaned 950 reindeer to Rufus Kalialuk and his son Charlie Rufus. By 1942 their herd had increased to about 2,500 animals and they were able to repay the loan. In 1940 a second Native herd was started with a loan of 825 reindeer. But disaster struck in 1944, when the Rufus schooner *Calla* sank off Cape Dalhousie in one of the worst storms of the year. Eleven people were drowned, including all of the herd managers and some children. Many of the animals were lost after the accident. Although other Inuvialuit-owned herds were established during the late 1940s and early 1950s, none prospered. In total, just over 7,000 reindeer were loaned for Native herds, but fewer than half were returned.

During the 1950s it became progressively harder to hire herders as other, far more lucrative forms of wage employment came on the horizon. Fewer and fewer people were willing to put up with the hardship and isolation of the herding life at a time when many were moving off the land and into towns like Aklavik, Tuktoyaktuk and eventually Inuvik. As Native-owned herds began failing, the government was left with the dilemma of what to do with such an expensive but unprofitable resource. The rapid increase in the local caribou population drove down the value of reindeer as a source of meat. In 1974 the herd was finally sold to Silas Kangegana, an Inuvialuk, who sold it a few years later to William Nasogaluak of Tuktoyaktuk. At the time of writing, in 2003, the Binder family of Inuvik was in the process of buying the herd.

Under modern Inuvialuit management, the western Arctic reindeer herd is a financially viable concern. It numbers several thousand animals and is managed using the most modern techniques and equipment. The herders do most of their work by helicopter and keep in constant contact by radio and cell phone. The use to which the animals are put, however, may seem bizarre. They are rarely slaughtered, nor are they much valued for their meat or hides. Instead, the main source of revenue is their antlers. In East Asia, many people believe (quite erroneously) that ground antler in velvet — when it is still growing and full of blood vessels — is a valuable male aphrodisiac. Every summer at "round-up" time the herders gather the reindeer together and saw off their antlers. Tens of thousands of dollars' worth of reindeer antler are sold each year to East Asian markets, where it helps prop up (if only in the imagination) the declining virility of the old and impaired.[30]

efforts were rewarded when the environmental group Greenpeace made the significant decision to end their anti-fur activities, largely because of the effect it was having on Native people. But public opinion against the fur trade continued to mount and prices plummeted. By the 1980s, only a bare handful of Inuvialuit were still engaged in full-time fur trapping.[31]

And still the battle raged. The European Union announced that it would seek a total ban on all animal pelts caught by leg-hold traps by the end of 1996. Rosemary Kuptana, an Inuvialuit leader, was president of the Inuit Tapirisat of Canada when the European Union's decision was under discussion. As she testified to the European Parliament:

> Trapping is integral to the economic and social life of all hunting people such as ourselves. Our culture is sustained by our ties to the land, and provides an opportunity to pass along traditions and skills to our young people. The cash earned by the sale of pelts allows us to live an independent, dignified life, according to our traditions … Without this important part of our mixed cash economy, we would not be able to afford the tools necessary to hunt for food: snowmobiles, guns and ammunition … implementation of this regulation at this time, will contribute to the further destruction of our way of life.[32]

Again aboriginal lobbying efforts resulted in a reprieve of sorts, when the European Parliament decided to delay the implementation of their ban until January 1, 1997. But it was too late. There was almost no market for furs and the last full-time Inuvialuit trappers had been out of work for a decade.

The Inuvialuit still trap, but on a part-time basis and more as a hobby or traditional activity than because it pays. With changing public attitudes and government support, the industry may recover some day. But it will never again be the sole economic support for so many people. With the death of trapping, a way of life came to an end, and an important link between the Inuvialuit and their land was snapped.

Inside a snow house, De Salis Bay outcamp, Banks Island, 1958

A soapstone lamp provides light and heat. During the 1950s, Banks Island still lacked a trading post or store, a Christian mission, government offices, or any permanent white residents. Schooner travel provided almost the only link with the outside world.

NWT ARCHIVES, N-1993-002-0190

6

Nuyaviak's Story: Life around Tuktoyaktuk Long Ago

Ishmael Alunik (as told to Eddie D. Kolausok)

A long time ago life around Tuktoyaktuk was much different than it is today. I want to tell stories about some of the activities and some of the people who passed on stories to me about what it was like in the old days around Tuktoyaktuk. The following is a mix of stories from around Tuk long ago. I hope you enjoy them and get an understanding of what it was like back then.

Felix Nuyaviak's father-in-law's Inuvialuk name was Mangilaluk. In his time, Mangilaluk was Head Man or Leader at Kitigaaryuit and later at Tuk. Mangilaluk was a well-liked man. Every Inuvialuit trusted and liked him very much as he was a wise and strong man. He led his people very well by teaching them how to live peacefully with each other and how to hunt sea mammals such as beluga whales and seals. Mangilaluk was a good man and a strong leader.

Mangilaluk showed his strength in different ways. Once, a long time ago in Tuktoyaktuk during freeze-up, four Inuvialuit were trying to pull a whale boat that was almost 30 feet long. The four men put skids at the bottom of the boat but they kept getting stuck. So Mangilaluk asked the men if he could try. He put the rope around his shoulders and without stopping, pulled the boat about 30 feet up the beach just like it was a 12-foot canoe. The whale boat was very heavy. Mangilaluk helped the men and showed that he had physical strength.

Drummers including Felix Nuyaviak, about 1950
Felix Nuyaviak (*left*) was one of the most respected of all Inuvialuit elders, and the son-in-law of the famous *umialik* Mangilaluk.
NWT ARCHIVES, N-1979-062-0064

Log house at Tuktoyaktuk, 1950

Two generations ago, most houses at Tuktoyaktuk were still locally made from milled lumber and driftwood logs. As Ishmael Alunik remembers, it was a small, friendly town, with close ties to the past.

Oliver Kikiktak, an Inuvialuk, also spoke of Magilaluk's strength. He said that one time three Inuit men were trying to pull the tail part of a beluga whale that was about four feet long. The piece of whale must have weighed about 400 pounds. Mangilaluk lifted it and put it on his shoulders just like it was nothing. Stories like this were often told about Mangilaluk and increased his reputation as a strong man.

Mangilaluk was a good leader. He was the first to build a log house at Tuktoyaktuk. He chose that spot because it had a good harbour and it was a good spot for fishing. There were lots of herring and whitefish around Tuk Harbour. Once Magilaluk built his log house, others soon began building log houses at Tuktoyaktuk. I did not get to know him because when I first went to Tuktoyaktuk in 1941, Mangilaluk had just died.

I first went to Tuktoyaktuk around Christmas of 1941. There were not even 15 houses then. The only other buildings were the church and the Hudson's Bay trading post. There was no government facilities or anything like that. The people lived by making their own homes and looking after themselves.

Christmas was an exciting time in Tuk. Many other Inuvialuit trappers and their families came to Tuk from Baillie Island and other places along the coast to trade their furs. There were hardly any white people around Tuk at that time. Only the Hudson's Bay staff. When everyone got together for Christmas, people attended church services, then there was a drum dance and big feast. People really liked sharing stories, dancing, sharing food and enjoying the company of each other. After the Christmas season everyone would travel back out onto the land to hunt and trap. That was what it was like in Tuk in 1941.

In the latter part of the 1940s, there was a very strong storm with flooding around Tuk. Some people say the Bay building drifted across the Tuk Harbour. That's about the time Charlie Rufus — Killie was his Inuvialuk name — was shipwrecked. Killie's whole crew drowned in that shipwreck [his family perished also].

Today Tuktoyaktuk has many houses that are not made of logs. Eddie Gruben has a large, modern log house and is a big businessman. Tuktoyaktuk today has hundreds of people living there but when I first went there, there was no school, no nurse, no RCMP. Now Tuktoyaktuk has everything, roads, an airport, police station, nursing station, a community centre called Kitti Hall, a large school, and a general store. There are lots of Ski-doos and speedboats. Some Inuit still own dog teams.

Now I'll tell a story about whaling before the Europeans came, as told by Mangilaluk's son-in-law Felix Nuyaviak. Long ago, Inuvialuit were well trained by their elders. The beluga whales would arrive in the Tuktoyaktuk and Kitigaaryuit waters around late June or early July. This is the best time to hunt them. There weren't any strong winds for a couple of months around this time. The leader would help teach the hunters about the weather, including the tides in the area in which they hunted. They were taught that often in the early morning the tide would rise very quickly. This was a sign that it was going to storm soon. They were also taught that if clouds came from the northwest fast, it meant there was going to be a strong wind and the waters would get rough quickly. If the tide came up after the sun had risen high in the sky, like around midnight or early in the morning, usually the tide came up slowly, then it would get calm later in the day. These were a few things Inuvialuit elders and the leader would teach their people. The people needed to know about the weather in order to hunt whales and travel safely on the coast.

Hunting beluga whales was important for the people. The leader would tell the men to wait in the shallow water away from the main channel that goes out to sea. The men would wait until the whales went by. The whales would enter the shallow waters to feed on herring and other fish. The whale calves would also travel into the shallow waters with the adult whales. Once the whales entered their feeding area in the shallow waters, it was time to hunt. The leader told the men to go around very quietly and follow the whales by entering the feeding area from the deep side of the channel. If the whales are in deep water they can escape easily, so the men in kayaks would trap the whales in the shallow water.

The beluga hunters would then bang their paddles on their kayaks and make a lot of noise. They would herd the whales into shallow water until they got stuck and could not turn around. The chief hunter would then tell the hunters when it was time to harvest the whales. They would use a long-handled knife similar to a spear to poke the whales. They would poke the whale between the ribs right into their lungs and heart. That is how they killed whales back then.

Men repairing fishing equipment, near Tuktoyaktuk, 1927
Tuk is only modern Inuvialuit town which was occupied during the 19th century (and earlier). The excellent fishing in Tuktoyaktuk Harbour has long been an important resource.
NATIONAL ARCHIVES OF CANADA,
PA101960

After a whale was harvested, Nuyaviak said the Inuvialuit would then turn the whale belly-up and poke a small hole under the throat and in the belly area. They would also use a short stick to make a hole between the *maktak* and meat and carve with a hard-pointed stick a few feet under the skin. They would put a tube in this area. They would then blow air into it. This would keep the whale from sinking and it would make it easier to tow the whale back to camp.

Nuyaviak said when he was a small boy he saw one kayak pull five whales. He would see a lot of kayaks if the weather was good and there would be a good catch. Nuyaviak said sometimes they killed close to a hundred whales in one season before the white man came. Back then there were a lot of Inuvialuit.

Felix Nuyaviak told his son Norman (Shepherd) where they used to take the whales in the shallow water. Shepherd said his dad told him the water wasn't even a foot and a half deep in that area. *Kapokvik* in Inuvialuktun means "place where Inuvialuit poke whales." In those days the whale hunt was done in a day or two if the weather was good and there wasn't any wind. After the Inuvialuit hunters got enough whales, they were ready for seven or eight months of winter — until spring anyway.

The people worked hard during this hunting time. The women used to use bearded seal and other seal skins for storing meat and making whale oil.

The skin from the head and beside the neck on a seal had to be cleaned really well. The women would leave the flipper arm on or tie them off. They always took most of the blubber off. After the skin was cleaned, the women would blow air into it until the skin had become balloon-shaped. They would often fill the balloons with *maktak* and blubber strips.

The blubber in the sealskin storage containers would turn to oil over time. This oil would be very tasty to eat with whale meat and other food. In the smaller bags they would put the whale flipper and flipper joint muscle parts. They would add in strips of blubber to preserve it. It's really delicious when eaten raw. These sealskin bags full of food were stored in a cool place in permafrost. They would also put herring, whitefish and other dry-fish in bags and place them in cool storage places so the food would not spoil. They would cover it with whale skin or seal skin.

The women would also make a bag out of a whale stomach by taking the inner lining out and tying both ends by the bowel side. They would then blow air into it and it would become a good-size bag. Some of the bags were more than two feet in length. They used to use these bags for storing berries. Yellow berries are plentiful all along the western Arctic hills. There are all kinds of berries for the picking. The berries used to be put in bags made from whale or caribou stomachs. The bags helped to store and keep food for a long time. The Inuit really enjoyed berries as a dessert in the winter.

Our ancestors worked hard in the summer hunting and fishing, for they knew that in winter food was harder to come by. During the summer months fishing and sealing was an ongoing activity. Sinew nets made from thin strips of caribou skin and coated with seal oil were used to catch fish. All of the materials and tools used to harvest and store the foods were made from natural resources. This meant that the materials and tools like fishnets had to be taken care of good. If a net was left in the water over a day, the net would have to be pulled out and dried before it could be used again. People were strong in the old days and they never let anything go to waste.

I thank Shepherd and other elders for sharing their stories about what life was like around Tuktoyaktuk and the Beaufort Sea coast long ago. It was a tough life but it was also a good life. All Inuvialuit had to work hard to survive and shared with each other to ensure everyone was taken care of.

Unidentified Inuvialuit elder scans the Arctic Sea for beluga whales, early 1960s

The brass telescope is likely a legacy of the whaling era that ended sixty years earlier.
DEREK SMITH

7

A Trapper's Life in the 20th Century

Ishmael Alunik (as told to Eddie D. Kolausok)

GROWING UP ON THE LAND

. . . .

I was born on February 19, 1923, in Old Crow, Yukon. There was no doctor or nurse to help deliver babies in that time — just midwives. From as early as I can remember things were tough. Even when I was born they thought I was dead, but I came back after half hour. Those days were tough but everybody worked hard to help with all the family needs and everybody, even the children, had chores to do. Families and people living in camps worked together and looked after each other in the old days. That was the way it was then.

I remember when I was around four years old, our whole family walked over the mountains from Crow Flats back to our camp on the other side of the mountains. It was hard walking. My parents packed my younger brother and sister. My grandmother packed me over rough areas but because she was old she would let me walk. I held her hand but after a few days I walked on my own. It was tough walking and my grandmother always encouraged me even though it was really tough going. When we walked to our log cabin at Head Point on the Yukon coast, it took about two weeks. We had about 15 pack dogs that packed our supplies. We made this trip from the coast to Old

Dog travel in the
Richardson Mountains,
circa 1950s
ISHMAEL ALUNIK

Crow Flats and back many times. We travelled to Old Crow Flats to trap muskrat, then we travel back to our camp on the coast for the summer.

The men would use dogs for packing sometimes when they had to go on long trips. Dogs were really dangerous. My uncle was killed by a trapper's dog team. Us small children, we had to listen to our parents and grandparents and stay away from the dogs. That was how it was when I was young, travel by walking mostly in spring and summer and by dog team in the winter.

Our clothes were made out of caribou skins. We all had caribou pants, caribou parkas and caribou mitts. Our *kamiks* (boots) had sealskin bottoms that were waterproof, with fur from the front legs of caribou for the top part. Our clothes were really warm. We used every part of the animals that were harvested for all our clothing, tools and supplies. Our dog packs were made out of seal skins and they were waterproof. Dog harnesses, floor mattresses, rope and other things we needed came from the animal hides from animals we harvested.

One time when my parents walked to Old Crow Flats for ratting season, they left me behind to stay with my grandparents, Charlie and Rebecca Koruguk. It was really hard on me to be away from my parents but I really like staying with my grandparents. They told me stories about legends and things that happened long ago. They talked to me in our language all the time. We snared ptarmigan, ground squirrels and rabbits. I used to watch my grandparents and I learned how to do many things from them. When my parents came back after ratting season I was really happy.

When we lived on the coast at Head Point in the summer, I remember we lived in a log house that was made of drift logs gathered from the coastline. Sod was used to seal the cracks and help insulate the house. We lived off the land. We caught lots of fish. Char, herring and fresh-water salmon. We put quite a bit of herring and char away in the ice house for wintertime. Lots of herring was caught for us and to feed our dogs. My mother and grandmother made smoked fish and dry-fish. My grandmother mixed cranberries with fish livers and it was like a delicacy. They also put dry-fish in sealskin bags and mix it with *oksook* (whale oil), but we mainly used seal oil because not much whales around Head Point.

We hunted geese, ptarmigan and even small shorebirds and seagulls. Young seagulls were good to eat in the fall time when they were fat. We put seagulls away in the ice house for when it was tough times — when we couldn't get caribou or fish. In the springtime we ate seagull eggs.

When berries start to get ripe we pick *ukpicks* (cloud berries), blueberries and cranberries. We put lots of berries away in sealskin bags in the ice house for wintertime. We even gather roots up along the rivers that flow out of the mountains, and some rhubarb. The roots and rhubarb was put in sealskin bags with *oksook*. We mostly eat it with *quiqsak* (frozen meat or fish). It is very healthy food.

In the fall time we start fishing with fishnets. We catch lots of whitefish in inland lakes during caribou hunting time. The caribou are really fat this time of year and we get enough, if they are plentiful, to last us for long time. When the ptarmigan start moving around we would start snaring them. I would go with my grandmother to snare them. Sometimes pretty near every snare get a ptarmigan. It helped for winter food. Our parents continued to hunt seals, polar bear, grizzly bear, caribou and mountain sheep throughout the seasons. I remember that my dad hunted polar bears around Head Point and they tasted different from the polar bears around the Delta.

First time I seen dance was in 1928 or 1929 in Herschel Island. I thought it was strange because I was young and people really dance and really make noise — especially at New Year's. They used to go outside after dance and bang, bang, bang, shoot their guns. In July on big days before hunting whales, after Christmas and New Year's, big dances at big gatherings.

This was what I remember as a child. It was hard work but everyone helped out and everyone had a purpose. Even though it was tough we were all happy to be living off the land.

MISSION SCHOOL

. . . .

In 1928 an Anglican Mission School opened up at Shingle Point. I went to school at that mission school for four years straight. Our parents come to visit at Easter and Christmas time and in the summer. The rest of the time they live on the land and make a living travelling, trapping, hunting and fishing in all the good places they always travel to. Boys live in big log house that used to be old Hudson Bay office. Girls live in another house that used to be old Hudson Bay staff house. We go to school in mission schoolhouse. Mr. Shepherd had his own house. Thomas Umauk was the Anglican deacon and he had his own house.

Everyone had chores to do all year round. Big boys helped by getting wood, ice blocks in winter from inland lakes and water in summer from same place. They do little hunting too. We all learn lots of cultural stuff from Thomas Umauk. Us little kids used to help him check net in summer. That time net was set with no boat, just use long poles to push net out to set it. Catch lots of herring. We help gather wood from the beach all summer and pile it in big piles like a teepee shape. We did this so snow can't cover it in wintertime. All summer we worked.

At Shingle Point we were free to speak our language. Thomas Umauk taught us how to read in Inuvialuktun, it was easy. Thomas mostly taught in church time. He read the service in Inuvialuktun and once in a while he preached. There was a Hudson Bay store at Shingle Point and people lived around there because of the mission and the store. All the children had chores to do like getting wood and ice for the mission. We were young and there was strict discipline, but we were tough even though we really miss our parents lots.

In 1935 the mission closed and later a big storm flooded the Hudson Bay store and did so much damage they shut it down. People had to go to Aklavik then to buy groceries and all that so they started moving into the Delta.

In 1930s, Delta people been getting schooners with engines. Ten-horse Johnson was the fastest kicker. We had a small 25-foot schooner with one-cylinder engine. We travelled in the summer with this. We put it up with block and tackle on shore of coast for winter. Had to winterize the engine and drain everything.

So in 1936 I went to mission school in Aklavik with the other kids from around Shingle Point. There were Gwich'in kids there and lots of kids from all over the Delta because their parents put them in school for the winter while they were out trapping. At Shingle Point we were free to talk our own language, but in Aklavik it changed and we were only allowed to speak English. In Roman Catholic mission school they said Native language was pagan language not Christian, so they couldn't talk their language there too. Our principal was Gibson. He was an Anglican minister and on Sundays we got taught about religion. Gibson forbid people from talking their own language and it got worse for others later I heard. The ministers learned Inuvialuktun from prayer books, but they wanted us to learn English so much that they never talked Inuvialuktun to us.

Thomas Umauk, about 1952
The first Inuvialuk to be baptised, Thomas Umauk went on to become an Anglican clergyman. He built the first church in Tuktoyaktuk, and is remembered as a defender of Inuvialuit culture.

All the kids had chores to do and we ate lots of fish and food from the land. School was lonely and the young kids sometimes cried and get really lonely for their parents. Kids get sick with measles in school too. Measles was first disease I experienced. Some people died from it. In 1930s we were in school and in isolation we survived. The school went up to grade seven so everybody had to go home after grade seven.

FIRST TIME I SEE WELFARE

. . . .

Around 1938, it was really tough and I saw poor people getting some welfare. I remember a family got 25 pounds of flour, one sugar, baking powder, little salt, little bit of lard. Just enough to eat. They always gave a case of canned tomatoes and three pounds of oats. Them days they only gave welfare to widows or families in need. Before this the church helped people if they had enough to spare. Really hard-up people they would give them little groceries. Government had a list of food the poor people could get from the store. This was called relief and it was the first welfare.

Jane Klengenberg and friends with a snowman, All Saints School, Aklavik, 1937

LEARNING TO HUNT AND TRAP
ON MY OWN AT 14

. . . .

After I came out of Anglican residential school in Aklavik I stayed with my grandparents. I was about 14 years old. My parents were in the Yukon trapping rats. I learned from my grandfather how to make traditional log traps for mink and weasel. Then I started seeing Delta people using snare tied to a willow — jump snares. I learned how to trap and set snares from my grandfather and my parents when I was young. In Aklavik, in March, we trapped on the lakes we staked — there was no registered traplines and no restrictions back then. When you go trapping you get everything ready the night before you travel. Early the next morning, you have to wake up and work hard checking your line during the day.

GROWING UP FAST

. . . .

When I was 17, I started working after my father died. I waited for steamboat to come to work. We get fifty cents an hour for working hauling freight. Few more years it become dollar an hour. Peffer used to haul freight with big horse that pulled a log sled. Horse pulled about one thousand pounds like nothing. We get two free meals, breakfast and dinner when we work hauling freight. First time we eat like a hotel food. The rest of the time when no work we hunt, fish and trap. I used to sell fish to Peffers once in a while for seventy five cents each. Not too much work that time.

MY FIRST CARIBOU

. . . .

In 1939 I started to learn how to hunt big game. I used my grandfather's 25-20. It was pretty much like a .222 rifle. I used a 30-30 carbine to kill my first caribou.

The night before my first caribou hunt I prepared everything for the hunt. I woke up early in the morning, had breakfast, hitched up my dogs and started travelling to the mountains. It took me about two hours to reach the mountains. I hunted and stalked caribou for another two hours. It was the middle of the day when I see a bunch of caribou. I got downwind because I learned you got to get away from where they could smell you. I shot a dry cow [a female caribou that is not lactating] that was really fat. I had to skin and clean it in 40-below weather. It was normal. It took about half an hour to skin and load onto my sled. It took about two to three hours to get back home with the load and about one hour to put the meat away and tie up the dogs.

Parents always be really proud when you kill your first big animal. They say things like, "This is a day you will never forget, for it's a day you killed your first big game." According to Inuvialuit, when you kill your first caribou you have to give some to your grandparents. They were about 200 miles away. We sent them the fat. It was about one inch thick. If my grandparents were at the same place as us, my parents would have given them the whole caribou, but grandparents were too far so we could only send the fat. It was the way of our tradition, right from elders' stories, they say you must give to your elders.

GRIZZLY BEAR HUNTING

My grandfather taught me how to hunt bear. Grizzly bear is a dangerous animal. Children did not go on dangerous hunts for bear. You have to be experienced to hunt it. My grandmother always said my grandfather came from a bear family because he eat big bowl of yellow berries and he snore like a bear. He was told that since he come from a bear family he is not to kill a bear with a bald head because he would get a curse on him. He didn't listen and he killed one like that, the kind with no hair on its head. When he killed it he got paralyzed on the right side as soon as the bear hit the ground. He lived the rest of his life using only his left arm just like a bear mostly uses its left arm.

The first thing my grandfather told me is if you see a bear don't be thinking in your mind that you will catch it right away. First bear I saw I said to myself, I am going to catch you right away. I made big mistake saying going to catch you quick because you are slow. Bear could see me and he get suspicious and start down the mountain fast. So I started running real fast but he disappear over some hills. It was a big grizzly bear — over 12-foot

A trapper's cabin at
Kuugaaluk River, 1985

DAVID MORRISON, CANADIAN
MUSEUM OF CIVILIZATION

skin. I lost sight of him for long time. When I saw him again he was walking slow so I walk slow too. I put my pride down and then I caught him. I learned from my mistake not to think proud. Grandfather taught me first thing you do when you kill a bear is bust the eyes. Because next time you hunt bear he will never see you. When I kill him, I do what my grandfather teach me. Grandfather, Abraham Tigilik, was right again.

The next bear I shoot I used a .303 British rifle. He was at our caribou cache. He dig it up and eat all the fat on our fresh-killed and cached caribou. It was covered up good with skins and rocks to keep the ravens away but the bear must have smell it and he dig it up. I get close and wait for him. He stand up and I shot three times and he never dropped. He turned around and ran away. He was a real fat bear. It was late in the evening and getting dark. We were taught not to hunt dangerous animal like bear in the night but I wounded him. So I told my partner I'm going to get him because I wounded him in the leg. I never got him. I learned a lesson. Never think in your own mind you're going to get bear fast. The next day I saw him going over the mountain. I try to find him but he must have not been too wounded. That was most dangerous hunt I made. It made me think hard again about what Grandfather taught me, "Don't even think you are going to get that bear that easy."

Second bear I got with one shot. He was about two years old. It just dropped dead when I shot. When I skin it I notice that the bullet hole was through the high part of the leg — so it must of died of heart attack. I was glad my grandfather teach me to respect bear and be patient in hunt.

ACTIVITIES IN WINTERTIME

. . . .

We always prepare for the next day the night before. We get up early. The father of the house get up and make fire. It might be 30 to 60 below out. The house had to be warmed up. We used woodstove that burned driftwood. We gathered the driftwood from the beach. If we were in the mountains we had to look for willows for fire. Once the house is warm we had breakfast. We had slapjacks or what we call pancakes today. We also ate oats with powdered milk. A bowl would be good and you don't get hungry for quite a while. We drink tea, ice water or snow water. Our parents talk about where we will go and about the hunt. We know how to kill and we know how to skin. We know how to take the guts out so it don't spill all over inside. Them days we had to take all sinew out. If no caribou, sinew not easy to get and we need sinew to sew clothes and for other things.

I learned how to handle three to four dogs. They were pretty well trained and they behaved good. After we eat and talk about what is going to happen on the hunt we go outside and load up our sled. We hook up our dogs. Make sure everything tied down good. I had three big dogs. They could pull three big caribou. When dog get four or five years old they are well behaved. Once everything ready in morning we take off with dog team.

One time I shot caribou and wounded it and needed to save shells. I let the dogs go and they get the caribou and hold it down until I get there. Then I kill the caribou with a knife. Dogs work hard. I share some liver with them.

I made a mistake once coming down the mountain with a load of caribou. I went up one way and I tried to come back a different way. I ended up getting stuck in a narrow place with big rocks. I had to work really hard that day and I remember what my parents say: "When

Spring travel in the Aklavik area, early 1960s
During spring break-up, travel could require both a dog team and a canoe. On snow and ice the canoe can be loaded on the sled; when crossing open water the situation is reversed.
DEREK SMITH

you travel into the mountains, look back to remember where you come from and use that route to go home." We learn everything about the land and animals, weather and everything from our parents because we have to know how to survive off the land. It was tough but it was a good time because everyone worked together and cared about each other.

NAVIGATING ON THE TUNDRA

The Inuvialuit had to be able to find their way around in the winter, when there are few landmarks. We used many different ways to navigate. Stars, the moon and snowdrifts were used as reference points like a compass.

We watched snowdrifts carefully in the winter to help us tell the direction we were going. There are many different types of snowdrifts. In very strong winds with gusts of up to 100 or 150 miles per hour, snowdrifts become hard-packed. I travelled in winds of 70 miles an hour with gusts of up to 120 miles per hour in Yukon Territory and Alaska myself. Once I was travelling by dog team and twilight faded on me and it got extremely dark. I couldn't even see the stars. It was blowing real hard. I had to hang onto the sleigh real hard on this trip. The wind was gusting to over 100 miles per hour. I could hardly see my dogs. I had to watch the snowdrifts to keep my direction straight for home. In our area, our people had observed that the winds blow from the east or the west the majority of the time. Any person would be observant of this and could quickly get a rough bearing by looking at the direction of the snowdrifts. During that trip I had to pay close attention to the snowdrifts. But I must admit that we Inuit also had lots of respect for our dogs in weather like this, to help guide us home.

Hard snowdrifts are found along the shore of the sea. A traveller or hunter can use these drifts to tell the direction also. Again the prevailing winds are from the west or east in the area I lived and most of the big snowdrifts pointed in these directions.

In the winter during night-time when the skies are cloudy there is no moonlight. In conditions like this it is easy to get lost. But if the moon and stars can be seen, a traveller can read them like a compass. Inuit were taught by their fathers as youngsters how to watch the snowdrifts and the moon and stars for travelling. Their fathers would make their sons learn if the wind is blowing from the north, west, south and east. Sometimes they would watch the drifting snow becoming snowdrifts if the wind lasted more than two days. Wood or ice markers were also used out on the land where there were no prominent land markers to help provide reference points for travelling.

We also make observations to foretell the weather. I was taught to keep a good watch on the ocean in the summertime when we lived on the coast. When the water came up really high all of a sudden with no wind, we could tell that a big northwest wind was on its way. Usually the wind followed the change in water level by eight to ten hours. We had to understand these signs as our lives depended on a good understanding of the weather in our environment.

FAMILY LIFE AND THE DEW LINES:
THINGS CHANGING FAST

. . . .

I married my wife Ruth in 1944 in Aklavik. I was 21 years old. There was no Anglican minister in town so Principal Gibson married us. We had three children, Angus, Mary-Allen and Dennis.

One time there was a big flu at Aklavik. I got it but I got through it. It was not as bad as the one that killed off Kitigaaryuit people. I was getting over flu but still feeling weak. Father France came along and he had big Thermos full of liquor. He said drink it down, you will get better. I did and next morning I felt better. It was rum … but I do not advise people to take that. The flu killed off a fair few people.

When the DEW Lines started I was hired as a labourer at Shingle Point. They called that site Bar B. We started as labourers and we were not allowed to drink. There was no training for us. This was first time we started using small fuel stove with five-gallon tank in our tent. Labourers had tents. All white people lived in a caboose, Natives in tent with fuel stove. It was cold. This was first time people start working out of town. Hans Hansen was foreman. He knew how to handle any problems. He do all the talking for us.

One time they had a four-propeller cargo plane landing on ice. First time I saw loaders, cats coming out back of plane. We had to mark off the airstrip on the ice and chisel a hole in ice to see how deep it was for the plane to land. First landing it cracked the ice. That was in 1952, a little before Christmas.

When foreman find out I had experience on coast he let me be guide.

Trucks were out on coast working. When we were working on module construction it became big wind. The snow was blowing and it was hard to see. I worked as guide especially during storms. We get paid less than three dollars an hour. This was double what Northern Affairs paid. It was first big money people start making from work around Delta but not enough to buy trucks and things like that.

Later on in the 1950s the workers at DEW Line started inviting us into their bars. Government find out they were supplying alcohol. At that time Natives were not allowed to drink. Liquor store in Aklavik open around 1956. It was only for whites. That's why certain people became white status … later on I learned that this was not worth it. Only Inuit could get licence to drink that time. Indians were not allowed to drink. If Inuit get licence to drink you could get a ration of two bottles and one case of beer or something like that. Some places they invite husband and wife to drink at DEW Lines or in Aklavik. Before the liquor store came around, people used to drink American beer and whisky at the DEW Lines. DEW Lines give parties once in a while but never sold alcohol. Most Inuit were good trappers and they learned to drink from DEW Lines. Later when oil companies and Navy moved here, everything changed. Since liquor store came things changed. Women, mostly smart ones, run the family when their husbands drink too much or play poker too much. I'm proud of those women. I never heard of anybody kill themselves before liquor store started. Then we start hearing about suicide, mostly older sons who were getting mixed up. That was what I saw at DEW Lines and around Aklavik and Inuvik when drinking start to get bad that time.

THE EARLY YEARS OF INUVIK

. . . .

When government start to look for new site to move Aklavik to, I work for Northern Affairs. I worked for people who tested ground. In some places were just ice. Some places ice with gravel and mud. We looked for gravel and found good gravel around Blueberry Hill. In 1955 lots of people start getting work building Inuvik. I cut brush for Northern Affairs, who ran the town that time. I worked clearing roads and helping surveyors. In 1955 I went to Wabamun Lake, Alberta, to train to be a crusher operator. We still trapped once in a while, especially in winter because not much jobs in Inuvik in winter.

Peffer was building Mackenzie Hotel about 1957. One job I had this time was working with electricians as a lineman. We drill holes, put crosspieces on logs, then put wires up. Then I got a job working on a rock crusher at the airport with Aklavik Contractors. I slipped on a conveyor belt and got a broken arm. I stayed in a hospital in Edmonton for seven months. When I came back I couldn't do any heavy work so I started working as custodian at schools. The schools were 512s [buildings 512 square feet in size] at that time. When Samuel Hearne school opened up, I started working there as head caretaker. I left that job to go back trapping for four years. First time people get electricity it was something. It seemed strange. It was too easy.

ALCOHOL

In early years of Inuvik I got caught up in drinking and I did not know how to handle it. Some white people say drink some more, drink some more and we didn't know how to handle it. We find out later that they just like to play around with us. It was difficult for us. Some white people used it because they could get a woman. So people learned from this to use alcohol to get women … because they are drinking they think they are man enough to ask. People start drinking mostly to satisfy themselves. Then they really get hooked on it … next thing you wake up in jail cell and find your companion there. Lots of complaints, trouble and jail. People experience first fines. Fifty dollars first offence. Hundred dollars second offence and it goes up after that. Everything start getting hard. You could see it among the children … not good clothes or food. It made me remember what Bishop Fleming said at a church service once when I was about 17 years old. He told us that drinking was serious and that it could take control of your life and your family and children could suffer lots. He was the only Anglican minister I ever heard talk about drinking. Later I was thankful for his words. Alcohol was really hard on the people and the liquor store didn't care. The government own the liquor store at that time.

In the 1960s I work in Inuvik but I also trapped and hunted to help make extra money. One time in the 1960s, two springs in a row we get about 2,000 shot rats and we get seventy cents a rat. Semmler bought them.

Around 1970 I stopped drinking because I did not like seeing the problems. It was not good for family and not good for children because once you learned to drink it became a habit. Once you stop, your children start trusting you again. Once you stop, you learn better. We tried to teach our children softly with love and care.

END OF THE OLD WAYS

Around 1970 sometime was last time I used dog team. Skidoos started coming, I was one of first ones to get Skidoo. Before that Bruno and Alex Stefansson had Skidoos that were different. They had track like caterpillar. Then I start working at Samuel Hearne High School for about four or five years. After that I worked as Inuvialuktun radio announcer for CBC for 17 years. I retired in 1989.

After I retire I still trap and get out on the land. I really enjoy the fresh air and good land we have. Sometimes I worry about our children because they have seen so much and their parents too. Things change too fast. Our language is almost lost and I worry that soon it will be gone. It was around 1970s when people really start to mix with each other that our language really started to get lost. My children know and understand Inuvialuktun but their children don't. If you told them to go out and get *loche* [ling cod or burgot], they would not understand.

From the late 1970s they start teaching students Inuvialuktun but they just learned a few words. They never learned how to talk. Before this I still remember mission school in Aklavik, where we were not allowed to speak our language. Us Native people were treated different from the white man that we helped on our own land. We shared with them. We taught them how to survive on the land and hunt and trap. But we were not good enough to go into their hotel in Aklavik or get the same benefits as they got when they first moved to Inuvik. We only learned about voting in 1950s because they said we could vote then. Then when alcohol came it really change things, especially for behaviour and language. Long ago I never hear or see children misbehave. It all came from how people were treated and with alcohol it only made things worse. Some people really got hurt and we lost lots of young people too early in life because of the changes and treatment our people got.

Today we are starting to speak out and try to relearn our history and culture. We have a land claim and we are getting self-government. This is a good chance for our children to get control of their lives and for us to make the decisions that are best for us.

It has been a long time now since I remember walking over the mountains as a child with my family. Today I can fly in a jet to down South in one day. Even though things were tough in the old days, people had pride and there was healthy family relations. Our land was healthy and our people were healthy. I pray that the children can learn something from our past and make sure they work hard and be healthy and strong and stay away from alcohol and drugs. I hope they learn respect and above all learn that they are special and that they can live happy lives if they choose and really try hard. Many of us elders had to do the same thing in our lives. Soon I will be walking in the mountains with my ancestors again. I hope this story about my life as a trapper, and later a wage trapper, helps the youth and other people understand some of the things our Inuvialuit people experienced. We need to encourage one another and treat one another with respect. Just like our ancestors did. Thank you.

8

Boom, Bust and Balance:
Life Since 1950

Eddie D. Kolausok

As late as the early 1950s, most Inuvialuit were still living on the land. Hunting, fishing and trapping were their main economic activities. Life on the land was tough, and they had to be healthy, strong and capable to survive. People lived in tent frames or log cabins in small family communities scattered across the land. They hauled their own water and wood, taught their children about life on the land and still practised many traditional cultural activities. With few health services available, diseases such as tuberculosis and influenza continued to ravage the population. People who contracted these diseases either died or had to spend long periods of time in mission hospitals or be flown to southern hospitals for treatment. Inuvialuit territory was dotted with trading posts, some destined to disappear, others to become modern communities. People travelled to Aklavik, Holman and Tuktoyaktuk to trade furs, purchase supplies and, increasingly, to visit their children who were going to school there.

Canadian government policy was originally one of non-interference in the daily lives of aboriginal Northerners like the Inuvialuit. "The federal government," explains historian William Morrison, "had based its policy with respect to the Indians and, even more, the Inuit of the Yukon and Northwest Territories on the position that the less their indigenous way of

Old boat stuck in snow near Aklavik, early 1970s
MARIE KEENAN

161

life was interfered with, the better. According to the official views, it was impossible — and undesirable in any case — to integrate them into the wider Canadian society; therefore they should be left alone to pursue their traditional occupations on the land."[1]

THE NEW WELFARE STATE

Government policy began to change after World War II. With the new tensions of the Cold War, the Canadian government focused more attention on the North for reasons of sovereignty and national security. It took a little longer for the government to concern itself with the health and welfare of northern aboriginal people. This was partly because of considerations such as cost and distance, and partly because there was still little government infrastructure or services in most northern communities. The Inuvialuit received the right to vote in federal elections in 1950, but they still had little real voice in the government that administered their territory. Federal policy was usually developed with little or no consultation, although it had an increasingly corrosive effect on the Inuvialuit and their traditional way of life.

Other people, however, took note of their situation. Farley Mowat's widely read books *People of the Deer* (1952) and *The Desperate People* (1959) raised awareness among southern Canadians of the miserable conditions faced by Inuit in many parts of the Arctic. Newspaper accounts of starvation and death at Garry Lake in 1958 added pressure on the government; they caused "a scandal and impelled the government to focus more attention on social programs in the North."[2] While the Inuvialuit situation was far less desperate, there were still many health and welfare issues in the Western Arctic, particularly as trapping incomes fell. Many of these were exacerbated — or at least made more visible — by the increasing concentration of the Inuvialuit population in new "micro-urban" towns such as Inuvik.

The first government social program to touch Inuvialuit communities was the Mother's Allowance. The 1944 *Family Allowances Act* introduced the "Family Allowance" or "baby bonus," which provided mothers with a tax-free monthly benefit of five to eight dollars for each child under the age of 16. All Canadian women received the bonus, but aboriginal women in the Yukon and Northwest Territories were treated differently. Initially, instead of receiving the allowance in cash like other women, these mothers got payments in kind, in the form of clothing, groceries and other supplies. "The philosophy behind this policy was pure paternalism," writes William Morrison; "in the government's view the mothers of First Nations people were not sufficiently educated or mature to make the proper choices in spending the money."[3] It continued an earlier practice, in which the government — through the church or trading post stores — provided goods in kind to widows, the chronically ill and others unable to take care of themselves.

The Mother's Allowance had a profound effect on Inuvialuit culture. If a mother wanted to receive it, her children had to attend school. For most Inuvialuit, a good traditional education in how to live off the land was more important than formal instruction in reading, writing and arithmetic. But the collapse of fur prices in the late 1940s made the Mother's Allowance too valuable to refuse. The desire to be with their children, and the need to support them while at school, pushed many Inuvialuit off the land and into villages like Aklavik, Tuktoyaktuk and Holman.

The Mother's Allowance had the same effect all over the North. Writing about the Dene around Fort Norman, Father Bern Will Brown notes:

Although this tribe was still to some degree dependent upon their traditional hunting and trapping for a livelihood, their mobility had been curtailed the previous year when the government put up the first of many day schools. Previously their children had been educated in the mission-run boarding schools in Fort Providence and Aklavik. The problem with a day school was that the mothers would have to stay home to take care of the children instead of accompanying their husbands on their trap lines. Then the men did not go out as far or as long, with the resulting loss of the fur harvest. When the people predicted this outcome the Department of Education told them not to worry because they would be given rations to compensate. Thus began the era of crippling welfare in the Northwest Territories.[4]

Government policy helped speed the population movement from small camps and settlements into the larger towns. The federal government established a day school in Aklavik in 1951. Four years later it took control of all public day schools in the Northwest Territories; before then schools had been administered by the Anglican or Roman Catholic churches, with limited government funding. "The Ottawa bureaucracy had decided that all Native children must attend school," explained Leonard "Laco" Hunt, a government administrator in Aklavik during the 1950s. "To make this

possible, it was necessary to provide facilities in every village, settlement and hamlet, whether the local residents wanted them or not."[5]

The once independent and semi-nomadic Inuvialuit found the adjustment to settlement life challenging. Life was becoming more and more controlled by a government thousands of miles away in Ottawa. In the words of Vince Steen of Tuktoyaktuk:

> After the white trappers and the fur traders, we have all the settlements, all the government people coming in and making settlements all over, and telling the people what to do, what is best for them. Live here. Live there. That place is no good for you. Right here is your school. So they did — they all moved into settlements, and for the 1950s and 1960s they damn near starved. Most of them were on rations because they were not going out into the country any more. Their kids had to go to school.[6]

Justice Thomas R. Berger paints a similar picture:

Barbara and Leslie Carpenter, 1959
NWT ARCHIVES, N-1993-002-0599

(*Facing page*)
Lena and Susie Tiktalik and Florence Carpenter, Sachs Harbour, 1959
The women are in front of Susie's tent, protected by a wall of snow blocks.
NWT ARCHIVES, N-1993-002-0348

> Federal policy in the North since the late 1950s has proceeded on the assumption that the traditional way of life was dying, and that Native people had no alternative but the adoption of the white man's way. The short-run solution to the northern crisis was the provision of heath and welfare measures. The long-run solution was the education of Native people to enable them to enter the wage economy. The Native people who were still living in the bush and on the barrens had to live in the settlements if they were to receive the benefits of the new dispensation, and if their children were to attend school. Doubtless, the promise of greater comfort and ease made the move to settlements seem more attractive; but evidence given at the Inquiry reveals that many people do not remember the move as entirely voluntary. Many were given to understand that they would not receive family allowances if their children were not attending school. At the same time, the children in school were being taught a curriculum that bore no relation to their parents' way of life or to the traditions of their people.[7]

Another government initiative that had a dramatic effect on life in the North was the construction of the Distant Early Warning or DEW Line, a product of the Cold War between the United States and the Soviet Union that followed World War II. The military observed that the shortest air route between the two superpowers was over the North Pole, making America vulnerable to attack from the north. The solution was to build the DEW Line — a string of radar sites stretching from Greenland across the Canadian Arctic to western Alaska — to give "distant, early warning" of a Soviet military strike.[8]

With the haste of Cold War paranoia and the financial backing of the United States, the construction of the DEW Line began in 1955, at a cost of $500,000. There was no consultation with the Inuvialuit about the building of giant radar sites in their traditional territory. "It was a surprise to the people, you know," recalls elder Ishmael Alunik. "They're supposed to get information from Yukon and our government just said there was jobs down there at Early Warnings."[9]

The DEW Line brought the first large-scale wage employment and modern training opportunities to the Inuvialuit. Men began to work as heavy-equipment operators and labourers loading and unloading freight from aircraft. Jimmy Jacobson, a respected elder from Tuktoyaktuk, remembers:

> When they first started, I even used to travel in dog team. Dogs used to be inside the plane every day! Finally they learned how to go in the plane. No problem! Marking out the air strip where it was going to be. Marking where the modules were going to be built. I used to haul 800-pound engine with my dog team. Finally when I found out my dogs get paid, I bring more dogs so I could get more money! That time it was a dollar a dog and they feed them, eh! It was good because those days a dollar was like ten dollars now … Anybody who wanted to could work and you could put in as much hours. Could even sleep two, three hours, unloading planes day and night with fuel. They come by 45-gallon barrels. So, you just put in your time sheet. Was making big money that time because DC-3 were coming day and night and you had to be up … There was about three hundred to each camp. Because there must have been about hundred tents, two man to a tent, and then they got a kitchen. When the whistle blows, start running for the dining room! … Took about two, three years [to build].[10]

It was an exciting time, when traditional forms of transportation such as the dog team came face to face with the modern aircraft and heavy equipment involved in DEW Line construction.

Inuvialuit workers proved to be excellent employees. They learned fast, performed well in the Arctic environment and knew the land intimately. Some maintain that they were paid less than their southern counterparts for similar work, but they enjoyed the work, wages and learning new skills. Some took advantage of training opportunities in Leduc, Alberta, to become skilled heavy-equipment operators.

Of the 41 DEW Line sites in Canada, one of the largest was at Cape Parry, on Inuvialuit land. Smaller sites were also built at Shingle Point, Tuktoyaktuk, Pearce Point and eight other locations within Inuvialuit territory. Large sites like Cape Parry employed upwards of forty full-time workers once construction was completed. Smaller sites had from five to twenty-five staff members. A small number of Inuvialuit families settled around Cape Parry and Tuktoyaktuk to take advantage of job opportunities, but there was no real settlement at other sites.

DEW Line construction helped to open up the North by creating a military system that needed supplies and services. Airports and radio and weather monitoring stations were built, helping to develop the northern infrastructure. The Inuvialuit community that benefited most was Tuktoyaktuk, which soon had an airport with regular mail, freight and passenger service. Marine services were also developed, with the Northern Transportation Company setting up a base in Tuktoyaktuk to supply 25 DEW Line sites along the Arctic coast. These new services provided additional jobs to the Inuvialuit.

"During the past 10 years the economy of the Tuktoyaktuk region has changed from one based on hunting, fishing, and trapping to one of wage employment," notes a 1966 report. "The establishment of a transportation centre, government services, and the building maintenance of the Distant Early Warning Line system have resulted in wage employment providing 66 percent of the population's cash income."[11] The historian A. M. Ervin observed a similar situation in the Mackenzie Delta: "Ten years ago the large majority of Native people in the Delta were 'bush-oriented,' and active fur trappers. But since the DEW Line construction era, the majority have become dependent on wage-labour." He goes on to state, "The DEW Line was finished in the late 1950s, but the building of Inuvik had begun, and there was a continuation of construction work."[12]

**DEW Line site at
Tuktoyaktuk, 1995**
This is one of the 12 sites
built on Inuvialuit land in
the late 1950s.
EDDIE D. KOLAUSOK

Aklavik airstrip, 1970

The oil boom of the 1970s saw
the rapid development of
modern transportation systems in the western Arctic.
Today, most travel between
communities is by air.

NWT ARCHIVES, N-1979-051-0440S

In 1953 the government decided to replace Aklavik, the administrative centre for the western Arctic, with a new town. Aklavik was subject to seasonal flooding and considered unsuitable for further expansion, and the government had ambitious plans.[13]

The new town was to provide expanded government services to the people of the North, including improved access to educational, health and welfare facilities. It was to be "a model Arctic town, proof that living facilities of southern Canada were viable in the Arctic."[14] It was called Inuvik, an Inuvialuit word meaning "the place where people live." Southern engineers and federal bureaucrats selected the site and planned the new town after little or no consultation with local people. However, an Aklavik Relocation Advisory Committee was founded in 1954, and the local newspaper, *The Aklavik Journal,* monitored events closely.

The site chosen for the new town was on the east branch of the Mackenzie River about 100 kilometres (60 miles) south of the Beaufort Sea. It was originally known as East-3, or E-3 for short. Construction began in 1955, and a garage, shop and government dock were erected the following year. Work soon started on the airport. Two stores and two missions were relocated from Aklavik and a temporary school began operating. In May of 1956, *The Aklavik Journal* was able to advise its readers: "Home-owners in Aklavik who wish to move will be paid what their house would cost to build at E-3, less depreciation, plus 15% for disturbance. A gov. assessor will be in to do this job this summer. Lots at the new townsite will cost nothing and present lot owners in Aklavik will get first choice ... Individuals may build their own homes provided they can pass the building standards."[15]

Many Inuvialuit, Gwich'in, Metis and other Northerners began to work at the new townsite in various construction jobs. Mostly untrained, they entered the labour market at the low end of the wage scale. Tommy Ross was an Inuvialuit man who travelled from Aklavik seeking employment. "When I first came here I got a job cutting the brush at the beach," he remembers. "We lived in tents. We didn't get paid much — about a dollar an hour. That was a lot then. You could buy cigarettes for 75 cents a package in those days."[16]

In 1957, a new Conservative government came to power in Canada. Prime Minister John Diefenbaker initiated a "Northern Vision" that would accelerate development. Alvin Hamilton, Diefenbaker's Minister of North-

Inuvik from the air, 1990
Inuvik is located along the eastern edge of the Mackenzie Delta, just south of the tree line. The administrative and business capital of the western Arctic, it has almost all the amenities of a southern Canadian city.

DAVID MORRISON, CANADIAN MUSEUM OF CIVILIZATION

(*Below*)
Building the airport at Tuktoyaktuk, 1956

NWT ARCHIVES, N-1979-062-0078

Semmler's Store

· · · · · · · · · · ·

One of the first stores in Inuvik was built by Slim and Agnes Semmler. Slim and Agnes had operated a mink ranch and lived off the land by trapping, hunting and trading. When Inuvik was under construction, Slim and Agnes moved from their bush camp to the banks of the new townsite, where they set up a small store in a tent. They sold dry goods and other supplies and bought furs from local hunters and trappers. It was tedious work: "Instead of sweeping dust from the floor like most people would, we shovelled out the mud!" Agnes remembered. She and Slim later opened a store on the main street of Inuvik. Elders and local people would gather there to purchase goods, sell furs, buy and sell northern foods such as fish, rabbit, caribou and maktak, or simply to have fun telling stories or sharing news. Slim and Agnes helped many local people by providing credit for grocery or other supplies. They were greatly respected for their generosity.

Some funny stories are told about Semmler's Store. One concerns a colourful character named Sweeney Loreen. Sweeney was a hunter and trapper of Inuvialuit descent. One day during the spring muskrat-hunting season he arrived at Semmler's Store in a terrible hurry. He had a gunnysack full of muskrats and wanted Slim, who was busy with other customers, to buy his rats immediately. Sweeney was in a rush to get new supplies and head out of town — or so he said. Slim understood trappers, so instead of checking the gunnysack he just looked in the top and asked Sweeney how many rats he had. Sweeney said a hundred, so Slim took his word and paid for a hundred rats. Sweeney grabbed the money and moved on. Later Slim emptied the sack of rats and was surprised to find that it was full of old clothes, with just a few rats on the top!

Semmler's Store served the local people for close to thirty years, but was eventually closed in the early 1980s because Slim was getting old. The store is still fondly remembered by the people of the Delta.

ern Affairs and Natural Resources, explained that his party's "great historic mission" was "the development of Canada and the building of a nation in the northern half of this continent truly patterned on our way of life."[17] This commitment to the goals and lifestyles of southern Canada ("*our* way of life") continued to inform government policy for decades.

As the new administrative centre of the western Arctic, Inuvik soon offered more services and facilities than any other town in Canada of its size (a few thousand people), including an airport, a hospital, an army base and a radio station. Its two residential hostels brought in hundreds of aboriginal children from all across the North to attend the new federal day school.

On July 21, 1961, Prime Minister Diefenbaker attended the official dedication ceremony. He unveiled a monument with three arches curving upwards, joined by a metal ball. The arches represent the Inuit, Dene and non-aboriginal peoples of Inuvik, living in harmony. A plaque on the base of the monument states: "This was the first community North of the Arctic Circle built to provide the normal facilities of a Canadian town. It was designed not only as a base for development and administration but as a centre to bring education, medical care and new opportunity to the people of the Western Arctic."

Diefenbaker unveils the Inuvik monument, 1961
At the dedication of Inuvik, the Prime Minister unveiled a monument symbolizing the peaceful co-existence of its Inuivaluit, Gwich'in and non-Aboriginal citizens. However, Native Northerners were still subject to discrimination in employment and access to housing and other services, and were rarely consulted in decision-making.
NWT ARCHIVES, N-1993-002-0480

These new opportunities brought great change to the Inuvialuit and other aboriginal peoples who decided to make Inuvik their home. TV and Hollywood movies began to replace traditional storytelling. Dog teams gave way to snowmobiles. Oil and gas exploration brought new jobs. These were changing times, and Inuvik was a government centre with opportunities and challenges. There is no doubt that new opportunities helped to raise the material standard of living enjoyed by most Inuvialuit. However, the negative social and cultural effects were also great.

NEW RELATIONSHIPS IN A NEW TOWN

During the early years of Inuvik, the Inuvialuit were often treated like second-class citizens in their own land. Their voice was rarely heard when government decisions were considered, and policy still emphasized their "protection" and assimilation, not their empowerment. But with the civil rights movement in the United States and the Quiet Revolution in Quebec, the movement to eliminate poverty, prejudice and unfair treatment was gaining momentum. Things were beginning to change.

Inuvik was the first place where the Inuvialuit came face to face with large numbers of southern Canadians, who came north to work in government or industry. "In the eyes of the Northerners," wrote one observer, "the 'Southerners' fall into various categories. At worst, the Northerners view the Southerners as opportunists and selfish intruders who are a threat to the well-being of the North, coming there to exploit, to exercise power over local people, and to create little or nothing of positive value in or for the area. At best, the Northerners see the Southerners as rather impersonal and disinterested persons, apparently not willing, or giving much indication of trying, to interact with or understand the Native peoples."[18]

Segregation was a fact of life, as the same observer explains: "There seems to be little intermingling or conversation between members of the two groups. Southern transients (except for construction workers) drink almost exclusively in the quiet atmosphere of the Mackenzie Hotel's cocktail lounge, while the groups of Native peoples drink in the one beer parlour, or 'zoo,' as it was called ... This theme of separateness is apparent also at the Hudson's Bay Store, at baseball games and sports events, and such public events as Inuvik Sports Day."[19]

Southerners took control of much of the economic and social life of Inuvik. They had good jobs, received subsidized housing and telephone service and in some cases subsidized food. In contrast, as Ervin points out, "the vast majority of Natives live in the unserviced end of town, where housing is crowded and living costs are higher ... Also, since the Native people are unskilled for the most part, large numbers of transients have been introduced into the area to fill administration and skilled construction jobs. A Native person, having at most quasi-vocational training (not fully useful in the bush or in the town), rarely achieves a position other than one of unskilled labour."[20] To many Inuvialuit, Inuvik seemed like a town built by and for Southerners.

The segregation was obvious in both design and practice. Most Southerners lived in the East End, which had modern conveniences such as roads, sidewalks and houses with hot and cold running water and electricity. It also featured a utilidor system, an insulated structure that housed and heated the above-ground water and sewer lines. In the permafrost environment of Inuvik, this was the only way to provide running water and flush toilets.

The West End, where most aboriginal people lived, was very different. Here there was no utilidor, so people had to haul their own water and dispose of waste in green plastic "honey bags," picked up once a week by the municipality. Houses were tent frames, shacks and "512s," government buildings so named because they only contained 512 square feet of living space. "We could characterize the shift from Aklavik to Inuvik as the shift from egalitarianism to discrimination, from attitudes of acceptance to attitudes of prejudice against Native people," explained one resident. "If in Aklavik the honey bucket was the great equalizer, in Inuvik, particularly during the early years, the utilidor was the great discriminator."[21]

THE CHALLENGES OF ALCOHOL

Prior to the 1960s, the Inuvialuit were allowed to drink if they bought a liquor permit or "licence to drink" from a government administrator. A person could then buy two bottles of hard liquor and a case of beer each week from the Aklavik liquor store (Indians, however, were still not legally allowed to drink). Later, a new liquor store was opened in Inuvik, along with several bars. Faced with a great deal of social stress and easier access to alcohol, some Inuvialuit and other Northerners began to abuse alcohol. This had many negative results, including suicide, crime, family break-up, violence, loss of employment, exploitation of women and a widespread loss of self-esteem.

These problems both reflected and worsened the serious social and cultural breakdown that the Inuvialuit were already experiencing, and to some extent continue to experience. Southern encroachment was destroying the Inuvialuit way of life, causing massive suffering and hardship for those caught in the transition. In the words of Yellowknife physician Ross Wheeler, "The common theme running through all these social problems is alcohol. This single drug, more than any other factor, has been, is, and will be at the root of most of the social problems in the Territories … While treatment programs are necessary, they do not affect the basic problem causing alcoholism. Only the restoration of self-respect and a meaningful place in a society to which a person can relate, only basic dignity as a human being will reduce the problem of alcoholism."[22]

The landmark Drybones Case exposed the different treatment given to Inuit and Indians by the Canadian government in the North in the 1960s. The Crown charged Joseph Drybones in Yellowknife of being intoxicated off reserve. Justice Morrow acquitted Drybones, noting "in the Northwest

Territories the authorities, in enforcing liquor legislation, if the Indian Act provisions are acceptable, must of necessity treat Indians not only differently from white Canadians but also from other groups of aborigines, namely Eskimos … I feel I must differ from them, and hold that the intoxication sections of the Indian Act 'abrogate, abridge or infringe' the Canadian Bill of Rights." Morrow's decision was appealed to the highest court of Canada and on November 20, 1969, "the Supreme Court of Canada held that the use of the racial classification of 'Indian' violated the equality provisions of the Canadian Bill of Rights." This ruling ended discrimination, but at the same time opened the door to even greater "equality" in access to alcohol.

In the 1970s, the territorial government began to fund drug and alcohol programs. But the devastating social problems associated with alcohol continue to haunt northern communities. In the words of elder Ishmael Alunik, "Seventy percent of people in the graveyard is caused by liquor and drugs."[23] More and more Inuvialuit and other Northerners who have suffered from alcohol abuse are taking the challenge into their own hands and becoming healthy successful people living without alcohol. These people are role models for youth and those who continue to battle the insidious problem of alcohol abuse.

THE 1970S OIL BOOM

The first oil well in the Northwest Territories was drilled at Norman Wells in 1920. In 1958, Imperial Oil started seismic work in the Mackenzie Delta. Ten years later a major oil strike was made at Prudhoe Bay, Alaska, and the stage was set for one of the most important events in Inuvialuit history.

The Canadian government responded almost immediately to the Prudhoe Bay strike by establishing the Task Force on Northern Oil Development.[24] The fear was that the Americans would develop their Arctic oil resources without regard to Canadian sovereignty and without benefiting Canada. The task force was set up to gather information on the petroleum situation in the North, including transportation routes to southern markets.

In 1970 Imperial Oil made a significant oil find at its Atkinson H-25 well, in Inuvialuit traditional territory. Dreaming of another Prudhoe Bay, the industry stepped up its exploration. The Canadian government proposed guidelines for the construction and operation of oil and gas pipelines in the North a few months later. The same year Jean Chrétien, then Minister of Indian Affairs and

Northern Development, announced a government plan to complete a high-way to the Arctic by 1974, in time to aid in pipeline construction. With the energy crisis of the mid-1970s spurring production, the boom was on.

Inuvik was the first community to experience the boom. Southern welders, mechanics, electricians and other tradespeople moved into town, trailer parks sprang up and an industrial area appeared. Imperial Oil and Shell Oil established base camps. Airstrips, marine services and winter roads were built to transport seismic and drilling rig crews. Inuvik was a bustling boomtown where accommodation was hard to find and jobs plentiful.

Inuvialuit got jobs as equipment operators, cooks, camp attendants, roughnecks, derrick hands, bear monitors, expediters and truck drivers. People who were used to driving dog teams could now afford to buy snow-mobiles. Air travel, by helicopter or plane to and from oil rigs and base camps, suddenly became common.

The social impact of the 1970s oil boom was enormous. It brought work, money and many southern transients. Inuvik's bars were often rocked with scenes of drunken conflict. Young people dropped out of school to take high-paying — but temporary — jobs in the oil industry. Violent assault, break and enter, theft and suicide all increased. Drugs and sexually transmitted diseases appeared. Even trappers living far from town would sometimes come face to face with oil workers moving heavy equipment across their traplines.

Oil platform in the
Mackenzie Delta
ROBERT SEMENIUK

By the mid-1970s, oil companies were drilling in the Beaufort Sea. But the bubble was about to burst. In 1977 the Berger Commission (see pages 180–81) recommended a 10-year moratorium on pipeline development. The world energy crisis was ending, and with markets facing an oil glut, the northern oil boom went bust. Even the opening of the Dempster Highway linking Inuvik with southern Canada failed to revive it. The first companies began to pull out of Inuvik in 1979. The oil boom ended with the decade.

THE COMMITTEE FOR ORIGINAL PEOPLE'S ENTITLEMENT (COPE)

Like other aboriginal peoples in Canada, the Inuvialuit have long experienced a pattern of exploitation, coercion and neglect at the hands of government and industry. When oil was discovered on their land in 1970, many began to wonder about the implications this discovery would have for their future. During a meeting held in Inuvik on January 28, 1970, 19 people decided to form the Committee for Original People's Entitlement (COPE) to represent their interests.[25] The Committee and its supporters were well aware of the ambitious plans the government and the oil and gas companies had for the western Arctic. They also knew that most of the benefits were flowing into southern pockets, leaving aboriginal Northerners with little but long-term social problems. With these concerns in mind, COPE identified its main objectives: to provide a united voice for all original peoples of the N.W.T. and to work for the establishment and realization of the original peoples' rights.

By 1973, COPE had accomplished many things. It organized the first conference of Arctic Native People in Coppermine (now Kugluktuk), helped people in Arctic Red River (Tsiigehtchic) get compensation for damage to their fish nets, helped start the Northern Games (see pages 208–9), produced weekly CBC Radio broadcasts in Native languages, helped preserve the history and heritage of Native people by interviewing and taping elders, helped refurbish and support the Native community hall in Inuvik, supported Native business ventures and promoted and lobbied for adequate housing for low-income families. Above all, COPE became the voice of indigenous people seeking their rights and entitlement to the land they had occupied for time immemorial. This did not sit well with government or the Southerners who controlled most of the power, the jobs and the companies profiting from development.

From the beginning, COPE stood up for its members' rights. In 1970 the hunters and trappers of Banks Island became increasingly worried about oil companies doing seismic work on their land. They sought assistance from the government, but the bureaucrats sided with the oil companies. COPE assisted the people and threatened a court challenge to stop the work. In 1971 the government capitulated and created the Territorial Land Use Regulations to manage land access in the N.W.T. This important and progressive piece of legislation was a victory for all the people of the North, giving local authorities a strong voice in land development for the first time.

But the path was not a smooth one. In 1969 the federal government under Prime Minister Trudeau issued "A Statement of the Government of Canada on Indian Policy." This White Paper sought to eliminate the Department of Indian Affairs and rapidly integrate Native people into Canadian society, at the same time extinguishing all special rights.[26]

COPE and other aboriginal organizations protested vigorously. With changing public opinion and a new court case — the Calder case — the federal government changed its position in 1973. It began to support the concept of aboriginal title and set up an Office of Native Claims in the Department of Indian Affairs and Northern Development the following year.

COPE joined the Inuit Tapirisat of Canada in 1972 and worked with the Inuit of the eastern Arctic on a collective land claims initiative. A land claim proposal was submitted in 1976, but retracted a few months later because the Inuit of the east wanted more time to study it. COPE was reorganized to represent specifically Inuvialuit interests, and in 1977 proposed a separate, regional land claims process to the federal government. Negotiations began and an Agreement in Principle was signed in Sachs Harbour the following year. After six more years of intensive negotiations, the Inuvialuit Final Agreement (IFA) was approved by Ottawa and ratified by the Inuvialuit in 1984. COPE's work was completed and it was dissolved, making way for the Inuvialuit Regional Corporation to implement the new agreement.

THE INUVIALUIT FINAL AGREEMENT

On June 26, 1984, the Inuvialuit Final Agreement (IFA) was passed with three readings in the Parliament of Canada with all-party agreement in one day — a precedent for land claims. A month later, on July 25, *The Western Arctic*

The Berger Commission

. . . .

O n March 21, 1974, Justice Thomas Berger was appointed Commissioner of the Mackenzie Valley Pipeline Inquiry. His mandate was "to examine the social, economic and environmental impact of a gas pipeline in the Northwest Territories and Yukon, and to recommend the terms and conditions that should be imposed if the pipeline were to be built."[27] Berger travelled to all of the communities in the Western Arctic and set a new standard for consultation with regard to development. Aboriginal people spoke to the commission and expressed their feelings with conviction and compassion. Ishmael Alunik told Berger, "This land is our industry, providing us with shelter, food, income, similar to the industries down South supporting the white people … We do not think of our jobs as a substitute for living off the land. Jobs are another way to help us live. We still want to trap and eat the food from our land."[28] In Tuktoyaktuk, Vince Steen provided the following historical view on how the Inuvialuit had been treated:

> A lot of people seem to wonder why the Eskimos don't take the white man's word at face value any more … Well, from my point of view, it goes way back, right back to when the Eskimos first saw the white man.
>
> Most of them were whalers, and the whaler wasn't very nice to the Eskimo. He just took all the whales he could get and never mind the results. Who is paying for it now? The Eskimo. There is a quota on how many whales he can kill now.
>
> Then next, following the whales, the white traders and the white trappers. The white traders took them for every cent they could get. You know the stories in every history book where they had a pile of fur as high as your gun. Those things were not fair. The Natives lived with it — damn well had to — to get that gun, to make life easier for himself.
>
> After the white trappers and the fur traders, we have all the settlements, all the government people coming in … then came the oil com-

panies. First the seismographic outfits, and like the Eskimo did for the last 50 or 60 years, he sat back and watched them. Couldn't do anything about it anyway, and he watched them plough up their land in the summertime, plough up their traps in the wintertime. What are you going to do about it? A cat [caterpillar tractor] is bigger than your skidoo or your dog team.

... People won't take a white man's word at face value any more because you fooled them too many times. You took everything they had and you gave them nothing. You took all the fur, took all the whales, killed all the polar bear with aircraft and everything, and put a quota on top of that, so we can't have polar bear when we feel like it any more. All that we pay for. Same thing with the seismic outfits ...

Now they want to drill out there. Now they want to build a pipeline and they say they're not going to hurt the country while they do it. They're going to let the Eskimo live his way, but he can't because ... the white man has not only gotten so that he's taken over, taken everything out of the country ... but he's also taken the culture, half of it anyway ...

For the Eskimo to believe now that the white man is not going to do any damage out there ... is just about impossible, because he hasn't proven himself. As far as I'm concerned he hasn't proven himself worthy of being believed any more ...

The Eskimo is asking for a land settlement because he doesn't trust the white man any more to handle the land that he owns, and he figures he's owned for years and years.[29]

The Berger Commission was broadcast on television and radio across Canada and internationally from 1974 to 1977, giving a large audience a better understanding of the interests, concerns and rights of Northerners and aboriginal peoples. In 1977 Justice Berger submitted an extensive report to the federal government. In it he recommended a 10-year moratorium on the building of a pipeline, stating "If it were built now, it would bring limited economic benefits, its social impact would be devastating, and it would frustrate the goals of Native claims. Postponement will allow sufficient time for Native claims to be settled, and for new programs and new institutions to be established."[30] The Berger Commission was greatly respected by aboriginal Northerners because it listened to what they had to say. And it gave the Inuvialuit time to negotiate a land claim agreement so they could position themselves for future development in their traditional territory.

Chief Justice Thomas Berger
During the 1970s, the Berger Commission recommended a moratorium on pipeline construction in the western Arctic, pending the settlement of land claims.
RENE FUMOLEAU, NWT ARCHIVES, N-1995-002-7018

(*Inuvialuit*) *Claims Settlement Act* was proclaimed into legislation, becoming the first comprehensive claim settled in the Northwest Territories.

Page one of the IFA clearly states the goals of the agreement:

(a) to preserve Inuvialuit culture identity and values within a changing northern society;

(b) to enable Inuvialuit to be equal and meaningful participants in the northern and national economy and society; and

(c) to protect and preserve the Arctic wildlife, environment and biological productivity

Kids playing outside, Paulatuk

In negotiating the Inuvialuit Final Agreement, Inuvialuit leaders were motivated by a concern for the future of their children and grandchildren.

EDDIE D. KOLAUSOK

Under the IFA, the Inuvialuit came to a land claim and resources agreement with the Canadian government. They received $45 million in direct compensation (in 1977 funds) and over $17 million to promote social and economic development. They also received title to 236,600 square kilometres (91,000 square miles) of land, including surface and sub-surface rights to 1,820 square kilometres (700 square miles) around each community. Rights to sand and gravel, but not oil and gas, were granted for an additional 78,000 square kilometres (30,000 square miles). Hunting rights were also protected. The Inuvialuit have the exclusive right to hunt bears and muskoxen within the Settlement Region, and also enjoy preferential rights to all other species except migratory birds. Representatives of the six Inuvialuit communities were also guaranteed participation on all advisory boards responsible for the management of land and other resources.[31]

SELF-GOVERNMENT

The Inuvialuit lost the practical power and authority to govern themselves with the arrival of Europeans over a hundred years ago, and did not fully recover these powers with the signing of the Inuvialuit Final Agreement. The IFA is a land claim, establishing rights to the land and its resources under a corporation. Self-government is another matter.

When the IFA was signed in 1984, the Canadian government did not yet have a policy on aboriginal self-government, although the question was explicitly reserved for a future time. In 1993 the Inuvialuit, Gwich'in and Beaufort/Delta municipal governments decided to work together on self-government, and in 1996 began formal self-government negotiations with the governments of Canada and the Northwest Territories.

The Inuvialuit and Gwich'in self-government negotiations are about the vision of those communities to take control of their destinies. They foresee a public government that has a guaranteed number of seats for aboriginal people. They also envision distinct aboriginal governments to serve aboriginal people only.[32]

Signatories to the Inuvialuit Final Agreement

. . . .

The following Inuvialuit signed the agreement:

For the Committee for Original Peoples Entitlement:
Peter Green, President • **Charles Haogak,** Vice-President and Director, Sachs Harbour • **Sam Raddi,** Director, Inuvik • **Billy Day,** Director, Inuvik • **Eddie Gruben,** Director, Tuktoyaktuk • **Bertha Ruben,** Director, Paulatuk • **Annie C. Gordon,** Director, Aklavik • **Elsie Klengenberg,** Director, Holman

Negotiators: **Nellie Cournoyea,** Tuktoyaktuk • **Andy Carpenter,** Sachs Harbour • **Robert Kuptana,** Holman • **Nelson Green,** Paulatuk • **Mark Noksana,** Tuktoyaktuk • **Renie Arey,** Aklavik • **Agnes Semmler,** Inuvik

The agreement was signed on behalf of Canada by:
The Right Honourable Pierre E. Trudeau, Prime Minister of Canada • **The Honourable John C. Munro,** Minister of Indian Affairs and Northern Development • **Simon Reisman,** Chief Negotiator

Dennis Patterson, Minister, Aboriginal Rights and Constitutional Development, signed on behalf of the Government of the Northwest Territories

Chris Pearson, Government Leader of the Yukon, signed on behalf of the Yukon.

In October of 2001 the Gwich'in/Inuvialuit Self-Government Agreement-in-Principle (AIP) was initialled by federal and aboriginal negotiators. On April 16, 2003, negotiators signed the AIP in Inuvik; a final agreement could be reached in a few years. If it is administered properly, Inuvialuit–Gwich'in self-government will be an example to all of Canada of respect, integrity, accountability and the recognition of aboriginal rights. Most of the old colonial order will finally be abolished.

NEW ECONOMIC OPPORTUNITIES

The Inuvialuit corporate structure starts with Inuvialuit individuals. Every eligible man or woman receives one non-transferable unit in the Inuvialuit Trust at the age of 18. As long as he or she lives in the Settlement Region, each beneficiary can vote in community corporation elections and receive benefits from the corporation entities. At the moment, the trust represents about 3,300 Inuvialuit.

Non-profit community corporations were established in the six Inuvialuit communities: Aklavik, Holman, Inuvik, Paulatuk, Sachs Harbour and Tuktoyaktuk. Together they make up the Inuvialuit Regional Corporation (IRC), which is responsible for managing the compensation and benefits received under the IFA.

The Inuvialuit Corporate Group is a combination of the IRC and its four wholly owned subsidiaries, responsible for oil and gas, land, development and investment. The IRC is involved to some degree in almost every significant economic venture in the western Arctic. In 2000, the IRC and the Inuvialuit Corporate Group earned a total profit of $52.5 million after taxes, and held total assets less liabilities of $309.6 million.[33]

The Inuvialuit continue to demonstrate the business skills learned from a hundred years of boom and bust economics. They are determined to become, as the IFA states, "equal and meaningful participants in the northern and national economy and society."[34] With another oil and gas boom on the horizon, Nellie Cournoyea, Chair and Chief Executive Officer of the Inuvialuit Regional Corporation, said this to Inuvialuit beneficiaries:

Many of us who now witness the exploration activities on our traditional lands can honestly say "we have been here before." We have already seen the

hustle and bustle of oil and gas exploration and its impact on our communities and our people. The last time around it had come and gone in less than twenty years. A few of us did well during that hectic time, but most of us just made a few dollars and then went back as best we could to the lives we lived before the boom. It was quite a learning experience.

Now, two decades later, we are better prepared to meet this oncoming development head-on and benefit from it. Our claim has given us the means to ensure we are full participants in the many economic opportunities that have already begun. If a pipeline becomes a reality, these opportunities will continue for decades. IRC and the business members of the Inuvialuit Corporate Group have worked diligently during the past year to provide beneficiaries with employment, training and business opportunities wherever the oil and gas industry is active in the ISR. This will continue to be one of our primary and collective goals for 2001 and beyond ... The future is positive and filled with new opportunities as we move ahead.[35]

THE INUVIALUIT AS BUSINESSPEOPLE

A generation ago, the Inuvialuit still lived on the land, but were already developing their business skills as trappers and traders. Since the move into towns, this entrepreneurial spirit has flourished. For a people who once devoted a great deal of time and ingenuity to travelling from place to place, it is perhaps not surprising that the transportation industry has been an area of particular investment interest. Transportation is still very important in a region where people and resources are scattered widely across a huge landscape.

One of the most successful Inuvialuit to own and operate a transportation company is Eddie Gruben of Tuktoyaktuk. Like most Inuvialuit in the 1930s and '40s, Eddie started out as a hunter and trapper. He worked hard and raised a large family, and was probably the first Inuvialuk to own and operate a snow machine (the precursor to the snowmobile), which he was using on his trapline in the 1950s. While the DEW Line sites and then Inuvik were being constructed, Eddie built up his own company. He started out by purchasing a gravel truck and gradually turned his company — Eddie Gruben Transportation — into one of the largest of its kind in the Arctic. Eddie is a well-known Inuvialuit elder who has helped many people. Through his company, many Inuvialuit have benefited by working and learning new skills.

Other successful Inuvialuit businessmen in Tuktoyaktuk include Jimmy Cockney of Cockney Services; Emmanuel Felix, who operated Felix Enterprises; and William Nasogaluak, who ran Canadian Reindeer Limited (see pages 133–135). In Aklavik, David "Buck" Storr operated D. Storr and Sons Contracting, while in Inuvik, Jimmy Gordon ran Beluga Transportation, a small tug and barge operation, and Frank Hansen operated Hansen Petroleum Products. In Paulatuk, Garrett Ruben founded a company that leased heavy equipment.

Through the Inuvialuit Development Corporation (IDC), the Inuvialuit are involved in other business enterprises such as oil and gas development, charter and regular air service (Canadian North & Aklak Air), environmental services, construction, modular home manufacturing, logistics and real estate.

The Inuvialuit have also embraced the marine transportation business, with excellent results. Through the IDC, Inuvialuit beneficiaries own 50 percent of Northern Transportation Company Limited (NTCL), the largest inland water transportation company in northern Canada. NTCL is the main transporter of bulk petroleum products and dry cargo to communities, defence installations and oil and gas exploration sites in the North.

Tuktoyaktuk is NTCL's Arctic hub. Tugboats start their voyages from Tuk to points as far west as Point Hope, Alaska, and as far east as Taloyoak on the Boothia Peninsula. NTCL provides a wide variety of jobs at the Tuk terminal and other facilities and on their boats. From managers to apprentices and labourers, NTCL is providing quality employment opportunities for Inuvialuit, other Inuit and Northerners, and all Canadians.

From kayaks and *umiaqs* a hundred years ago, to owning and operating vessels like the M.V. *Edgar Kotokak* and the 62-metre (205-foot) MV *Alex Gordon*, the Inuvialuit have come a long way in a short time.

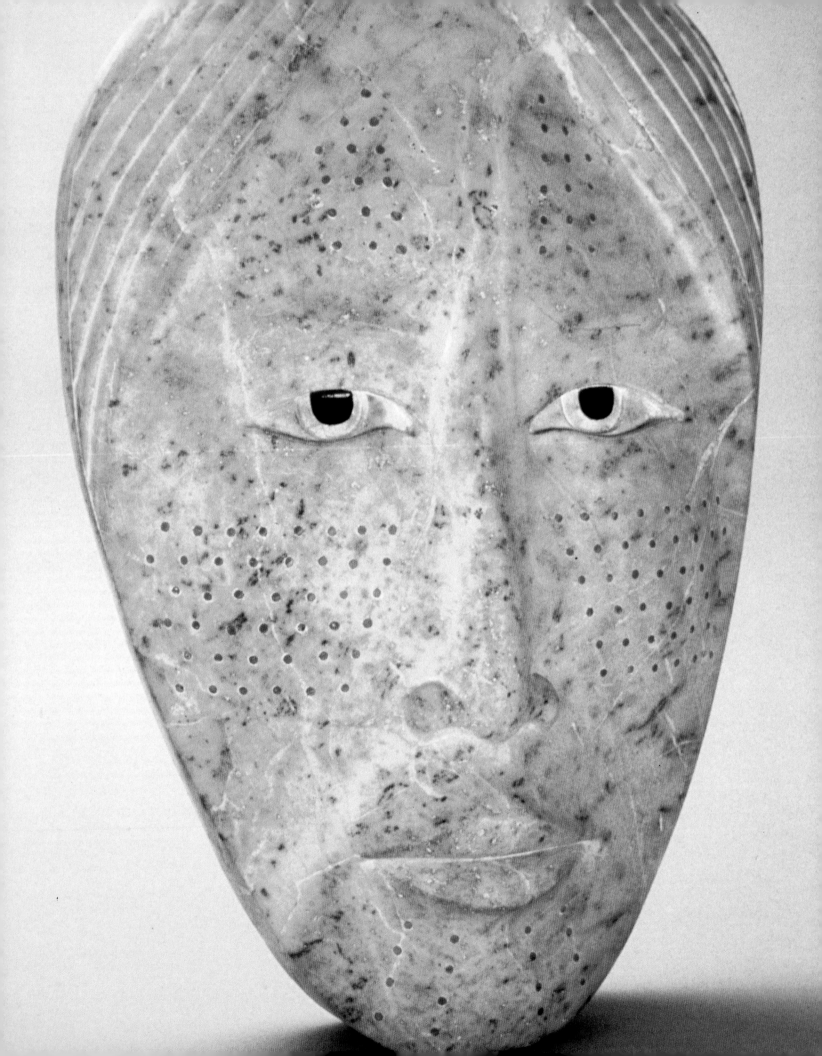

Contemporary Inuvialuit Art

Maria von Finckenstein

In contemporary Inuit sculpture, the trailblazers from the Inuvialuit region have been two brothers, David Ruben and Abraham Anghik. Both started making art after leaving their hometown of Paulatuk. Anghik moved to Fairbanks, Alaska, to study art in 1971, while his brother David has mostly lived in the Toronto area since becoming an artist in the early 1970s.

Their art is characterized by composite, elegant and highly stylized forms and the use of mixed media and a diversity of stones. They use the underlying symbolism of Inuvialuit oral history passed on by their elders in Paulatuk to make bold social and personal statements. Both products of residential schools, which cut them off from their cultural roots at an early age, the brothers have found art-making to be a powerful tool for personal expression. Anghik stated in 1993: "When a sculpture … can elicit emotion in someone, stir up something, then the work has succeeded."[1]

Their three cousins, Bill, Joe and Eli Nasogaluak, were all born and raised in Tuktoyaktuk and, like the Ruben brothers, find inspiration for their art in the stories and legends of their elders. Emphasizing the heroic side of traditional Inuit culture, they tend to celebrate their heritage through their art. There is much movement and drama; "I try to produce work that shows a lot of action and strength," explains Eli.[2] Unlike their colleagues in the eastern Arctic, Bill and Eli have their own dealer and sell their art through a website.

Tattooed Face by Abraham Anghik, 1986

PAULATUK, BRAZILIAN SOAPSTONE, ARIZONA SOAPSTONE, BLACKSTONE AGGREGATE AND RED STONE, 15.3 × 49.4 × 34.5 CM (6 × 19.5 × 13.5 INCHES), GIFT OF BEVERLEY AND IRWIN BERNICK, TORONTO, 1987, CCMC IV-D-2183

Also from Tuktoyaktuk is Stanley Felix, who is proud to be the great-grandson of the famous *umialik* (leader) and shaman Mangilaluk. His work is often based on legends and stories about his venerated great-grandfather.[3]

A video producer as well as a carver, Angus Kaanerk Cockney is also from Tuktoyaktuk but now lives in Yellowknife. In *Reflections: Tuk in Stone*, a 1992 catalogue of his work, he speaks for the new generation of Inuvialuit artists when he says, "It is my ancestry that has inspired me to create in stone the traditional values of my people, combined with the issues of today."[4]

The youngest artist of the group is Floyd Kuptana, a resident of Paulatuk who has been actively carving since 1992. A recent exhibition at a Toronto gallery — on display on a website — shows the influence of his cousin David Ruben. His work is very accomplished technically, using complex inlay and mixed media, and shamans are often the subject. The flair for the dramatic, so evident in the work of the Nasogaluak brothers, is pushed one step further. Intricate figures display distorted, mask-like faces which border on the grotesque. As he says himself, "I really like to carve strange transformation pieces."[5]

Printmaking is another aspect of contemporary Inuvialuit art. The print shop in Holman on Victoria Island, representing artists of both Copper Inuit and Inuvialuit ancestry since 1965, has issued numerous prints based on Agnes Nanogak's drawings. These show the same flair for movement and drama characteristic of Inuvialuit sculpture. Nanogak and her brother Alec Banksland were both born near Tuktoyaktuk, and moved to Holman in 1934. Banksland's drawings are very controlled and meticulously executed, with fine, naturalistic detail. Nanogak's grandson, Rex Goose, is also an accomplished graphic artist. Apart from drawing, he specializes in miniature sculpture, using ivory, antler, whalebone and muskox horn for intricate narrative scenes and delicate animal figures.[6] Other talented Holman artists of Inuvialuit origin include Mary Okheena, Elsie Klengenberg, Louie Nigiyok and Roberta Memogana. Sachs Harbour also has a number of excellent artists of Inuvialuit ancestry.

Altogether, artists from the Inuvialuit region are urbanized and closely connected to the southern art market. They have developed a collective style quite distinct and separate from that of their colleagues in the eastern Arctic.

The Survival of a Culture

Eddie D. Kolausok

A hundred and fifty years ago, the Inuvialuit were a vibrant, flourishing society. Their culture was their own, unmonitored by outsiders. They spoke their own language, practised their own religion and ordered their own lives. This enviable situation began to change with the arrival of Europeans.

First came the fur traders of the Hudson's Bay Company, who brought disease and a growing dependency on foreign trade goods. The arrival of American commercial whalers had more dramatic effects. They established posts or stations on Inuvialuit territory (which the fur traders did not), without permission or consultation. They despoiled the environment and, uninvited, brought in large numbers of outsiders as crew members or hunters. By living directly among the Inuvialuit they increased the transmission of foreign diseases, with truly horrifying results. And then, fortunes made, they sailed away. The presence of the whalers also brought two other groups of newcomers who sought to change and control the Inuvialuit: the Royal North-West Mounted Police (now the RCMP) and Christian missionaries. The first brought the Inuvialuit under the legal control of the Canadian government. The second abolished traditional religious beliefs and, in an attempt to "educate" the Inuvialuit, began the long, slow process of cultural assimilation.

None of these intruders was malicious, and some — particularly the missionaries — were consciously motivated by "high ideals." Most probably

Inuvialuit girl at Tuktoyaktuk with whale vertebra, 1969

NWT ARCHIVES, G-1979-023-1390

thought of themselves as agents of inevitable change and development, exporting a higher civilization to "the uttermost ends of the earth." But in hindsight they were often — by modern standards — arrogant and patronizing. By right of birth or culture, missionaries, traders and police assumed that they knew best and that their needs and wishes should take precedence over those of the people they sought to control and govern. The same failure of imagination and conscience continued to inform Canada's "colonial" policy towards the Inuvialuit, and the North in general, throughout much of the last century. One of the cornerstones of that policy was the residential school system.

CHRISTIAN MISSIONS, RESIDENTIAL SCHOOLS AND CULTURAL LOSS

During the early 20th century, the Canadian government showed little concern for the well-being of aboriginal Northerners such as the Inuvialuit. Social services such as medical treatment and welfare for the destitute were ignored or left to the church. There was little interest in integrating aboriginal peoples into mainstream Canadian society, as was the case in the South. As the historian Kenneth Coates has noted, this decision "rested more on the desire to limit federal spending than on a belief in the value of the Native lifestyle."[1]

The churches — most notably the Anglican missionary Charles Whittaker — vigorously protested what they saw as government neglect and demanded greater support for their program of Christianization and civilization. Civil servants and politicians in Ottawa may not have shared their enthusiasm, but were left with little room to manoeuvre in the face of public opinion. Education emerged as the cornerstone of church plans for Native "improvement." To save money, the government was content to leave education in the hands of the religious missions, which were given some supplementary funding.

The battle for Inuvialuit souls had been won with seeming decisiveness by the Anglican Church in the years before the First World War. But the Roman Catholics regained some ground over the next few decades. Not welcomed by the mainly Protestant Hudson's Bay Company, Catholic missionaries were willing to live closely with the Inuvialuit. Particularly in the Paulatuk/Letty Harbour area, where they operated a non-profit trading post, the Catholic fathers became a significant element in the religious life of the Inuvialuit. But Anglicanism remained the predominant religion in most communities.

The rivalry between the churches in their race for souls introduced a new and divisive factor into Inuvialuit society: religious factionalism. Coates describes the often bitterly competitive relationship:

> Both believed their spiritual interpretations and religious path offered salvation and, equally, that the opposing faith offered only false hope … Both groups hastened to mark out their territory, struggling to baptize and hence lay claim to as many Natives as they could before their rivals arrived. The "rush for souls" hardly endeared the missionaries to the Natives, nor did it provide a useful model of Christian ethics at work. The endless back-stabbing and name-calling substantially hampered the missionaries' efforts.[2]

Residential school students at Aklavik, about 1940
Elders remember that residential school students had to work hard fishing, cutting wood and hauling water. Discipline was strict, and the use of Inuvialuktun and other aboriginal languages was discouraged, and finally forbidden altogether.
NATIONAL ARCHIVES OF CANADA, PA101771

At the same time, many of the missionaries were sincere and dedicated men. F. D. Clarke of All Saints Anglican Church in Aklavik kept a journal which shows the extent of his work among the Inuvialuit.[3] During the summer of 1922, Clarke travelled to Shingle Point on the Yukon Arctic coast, where he helped build a new church, taught students, fished, gathered wood and assisted in church services. The following winter he travelled by dog team throughout Inuvialuit territory, performing marriages and church services. On March 23, 1923, he arrived in Tuktoyaktuk, where he found "a nice group of people, including … Mangilaluk the Chief and his family." He visited other camps at Aklavik, Kitigaaryuit, Baillie Island, Atkinson Point, Horton River and 23 other locations; by his own count he held over 50 services and "encouraged 150 souls." After completing this trip, Clarke noted in his journal, "Our physical self was better than when we started, notwithstanding the fact that the palate was often put to the test with … seal-meat, blubber, polar-bear, white whale, musk-rat, dried fish and meat."

Missions were soon established across the western Arctic, beginning with Aklavik in 1919. Others were built at Shingle Point, Stanton, Baillie Island, Holman, Letty Harbour, Paulatuk and Tuktoyaktuk. Anglican (1919) and Roman Catholic (1927) hospitals were also built in Aklavik. The Inuvialuit population was rebuilding after the traumatic experiences of the whaling era and the missionaries were often viewed as generous, kind and considerate. In turn, they relied on Inuvialuit for food and clothing. They also hunted, trapped and traded for furs in some places. The missionaries learned to speak Inuvialuktun, and during the early years were looked upon as members of the community. Life was hard and the missionaries provided spiritual as well as medical and social assistance to those in need.

The first school in Inuvialuit territory was operated by the Anglican church at Herschel Island in the 1890s. It was run on a part-time, voluntary basis. The first residential school in the Northwest Territories was opened by the Anglicans in 1902 at Hay River, far south of Inuvialuit territory. Some Inuvialuit children were sent there, for up to five years. Some died of disease. Others survived, only to have to re-learn their language and culture when they returned home.

In 1919 an Anglican residential school was built in Aklavik; not to be outdone, the Roman Catholics opened their own school there in 1925. In 1928, a second Anglican Mission School was opened in Shingle Point.

Inuvialuit elder Ishmael Alunik, who attended the Shingle Point Anglican Mission School during the early 1930s (see pages 147–48), pointed out that children attended the school for years at a time, and loneliness for parents and family was common. They worked hard at chores and were expected to assist in fishing, wood gathering and other tasks while attending school. By forbidding the Inuvialuit language, mission schools assisted the assimilation process desired by the Canadian government.

Eddie Kikoak, an Inuvialuit elder who lives in Gjoa Haven in the central Arctic, remembers his time at the Aklavik Roman Catholic Mission School in the 1940s:

Students and teachers from the residential school at Shingle Point, about 1935

NWT ARCHIVES, N-1979-050-0412

ACROSS TIME AND TUNDRA

The R.C. Mission boat called the *St. Immaculata* with a wooden barge arrived in Tuk [Tuktoyaktuk] and would pick us children up. Sometimes it would take all the kids from Tuk.

When we were at the mission we wake up at 5:45 A.M. to wash up. Then we empty all the buckets from the bathroom. We carried these full buckets from the top of the stairs down to the main floor then to the river where we dumped them. Everything was done like in the army: when sisters clapped, you had to be ready. After wash-up and emptying buckets, we went to morning mass. In mass you had to look straight ahead. Sisters used a heavy piece of wood split in half that they clap with. Clapping the wood instructed us to stand up, kneel and sit down in mass. Right after church, just before breakfast, we had to get wood. We carried four-foot-long timbers for the furnace from the wood yard to the cellar. Outside of building was a chute where we put wood in. We slide the wood down into cellar where others stacked it.

After hauling wood, we had breakfast. Before breakfast we pray. It was quiet. There was no talking allowed. Breakfast was porridge with little bit of brown sugar. After you finish porridge you get beans. That was breakfast.

After breakfast, before 8 A.M., we looked after younger children which were about two or three years old. We mend their socks. If their coveralls need mending, we do that. Sisters never did that. They used sewing machines if the holes were too big.

At 9 A.M. we went into the classroom. We were taught religion first. Then we were brainwashed to learn the Ten Commandments as fast as we can. If you could not repeat it right, you got slapped on the hands with a ruler. One time I seen a kid get slapped with scissors. You were timed by the priest. If you say it fast, in the time the priest set, you got a candy.

In class we get French lessons for one hour then English for the rest. Our parents had no say. We were punished if we talked our language. We were forced to learn English and French cultures. Never once did they teach us about our culture. Because of that, in my community now, Gjoa Haven, they call me "White Man." Even now when I go out on land and the people speak and get together, I sit separate. I still talk my language and their dialect but I get treated like that. It hurts but now they are starting to listen. They think I don't know about my culture and it hurts. I try to get involved. I feel like an outcast because of what happened to us — and our culture. Our culture really started to get lost because they wouldn't let us speak our language.

At 12 noon we finish classes and eat lunch. Mostly country food, fish mostly. On feast days or holidays like Christmas we got home-made ice cream. It was good ice cream. After we eat we get to play outside.

We were in class by 1 P.M. sharp. Never miss or cannot be one minute late or one second late. If one was late, everybody was late so we were never late. We would all get punished if one student was late. We were always on time. You have to ask permission to use bathroom outside. School classes went until 3 P.M.

After school we got wood again for about half an hour. Then we had a break where we played outside on swings and merry-go-round. Boys were separated from girls. We couldn't talk to them or look at them even if they were relatives. We were punished and had to go to confession if we looked at girls.

At 5 P.M. we ate supper. Supper was mostly country food like fish. At 6 P.M. we attend church benediction. After benediction we were allowed to play in our playrooms. Then each of us took turns saying rosary. Then say rosary all together. Then we played some more until bedtime at 9 P.M.

On Sunday nights if you were a good boy they showed a film. Silent movies first, then sound movies came.

In summertime there was cabins for boys and for girls above Aklavik.

During trapping season us boys trapped and made lots of money for the church. They used it to buy clothing. I remember one time we did so good at trapping that they bought a movie projector. Even though it was tough on us kids, in a way I think school was good for me because it taught me respect for my faith and church. The hard part was losing the culture and language. My generation could still learn how to speak our language because it was used at home but the children after us had a tougher time because they spent even more time in residential schools where English was the only language allowed.[4]

In the 1950s, the Canadian government became more actively involved in education, opening elementary day schools in most communities. The missions, however, continued to run residential schools, serving students from communities without a day school or those attending high school. The mission schools in Aklavik were moved to Inuvik in 1959. Catholic children from all over the Northwest Territories attended Grollier Hall, while Anglican children attended Stringer Hall.

THE STRINGER HALL EXPERIENCE

An Inuvialuk who attended Stringer Hall but wishes to remain anonymous remembers his experiences:

I can clearly recall my first experience leaving Aklavik for residential school sometime in the late 1960s, when I was a child of about five years. A large group of families were waiting for an airplane at the Aklavik airstrip. When the airplane arrived, the children were ordered into the plane. I had to be pulled from my mother's arms because I did not want to leave her. I fought hard and held onto her for dear life as tears poured down my face. The cries and struggle I put up in refusal to be taken away was no match for the adults who pulled me from my mother's arms. The plane was crammed full of children and I was placed on a young teenage girl's lap. She did her best to comfort me but the tears of loneliness, anger, fright and longing for home and mother, she could not stop as the plane roared to Inuvik.

In Inuvik we were picked up by a bus and taken to Stringer Hall. The residential school looked massive and scary. Two of my brothers and one cousin accompanied me, as we were led up into the junior boys' dormitory. The first thing we were ordered to do was undress and all go into a large shower room. I remember the sadness and crying of some of us younger boys. My older brother told us to stay calm, stop crying and to listen to whatever they told us and we would be

okay. Good advice but he and my cousin ran away from the residential school a week or two later. A little fat old lady dressed in white clothing came into the shower room flicking a towel wetted at one end. She yelled, "Okay, everybody out! Now!" and continued to flick the towel making a cracking sound and scaring the heck out of us younger boys. Once out of the shower we were all provided with a number and hostel clothes which had our number sewn or marked on the inside. These were the clothes we were to wear during our stay in the residential school. We were shown where we would sleep in the dorms and given instruction on wake-up time, sleep time and meal times. We then had to get brush cut haircuts and settle into our residential life. Later on we would attend religious services on a regular basis and go to school in Inuvik.

I remember this as being one of the saddest times of my life. I still have trouble remembering most of my time spent there because it was so traumatic and my mind was at home in Aklavik.[5]

Another sad part of the residential school experience in Inuvik was the fact that Anglican and Catholic friends now found themselves in different schools. Grollier Hall and Stringer Hall were separated by a large utilidor, which held water and sewer pipes above ground. This physical barrier only encouraged fights between Anglicans and Catholics. The same religious differences played out in daily combats on school grounds were repeated in town and in organized sports.

Residential schools were not unique to the Inuvialuit. Through various Christian missions, the Canadian government ran mandatory residential schools for aboriginal children across Canada from the 1850s to the 1970s.[6] The stated goal was the civilization, Christianization and assimilation of Native children. In the words of one historian:

Residential schools were ... important to both missionaries and the government. The boarding schools were often imposing structures, complete with dormitories, classrooms and training facilities. To the missionaries, such schools offered the best hope for the nomadic Indians of the north. Children would be removed from the "backward" influences of family and community and given language, moral, Christian, and vocational training sufficient for full participation in the white world ... It was hoped that the graduates would re-enter their communities as disciples of a new Christian social order, assisting in the social "improvement" of the entire Native population.[7]

The residential schools took their toll. What the Inuvialuit were experiencing would affect them, their families and communities for generations to come. One immediate result was that children did not receive a proper education in their own culture. Parents complained that their children "were taught nothing useful in the schools, and that when they return home they are useless for work in the bush."[8] Having lost their language in favour of English, they could often not even communicate with their own parents. But emotional and even physical abuse left the worst scars.

GROLLIER HALL ABUSE

One of the most disturbing cases of abuse took place in the Grollier Hall residential school between 1959 and 1979. In those years, many young boys were sexually assaulted by men who were their guardians at the school. The pain and suffering of these boys would be carried into their future lives and hurt those they loved.

On June 21, 2002, after reaching an out-of-court settlement, the Government of Canada and the Catholic Church apologized to the victims. "We're sorry for the heavy burden that you have had to carry with you for most of your lives," government representative Shawn Tupper told an audience in Yellowknife, including some of the abuse victims. "We're sorry to you who have had to struggle alone, away from your families and your community. Away from your teachings and your grandparents. Away from your land and your traditions. We're sorry, more than we can possibly say." Bishop Denis Croteau also sent a letter of apology to each abuse victim.

It must be recognized that not all children suffered this kind of abuse. And there were positive benefits to the residential school experience. Children were fed regularly and received health care and an education which might not otherwise have been available. But all were separated from their families and suffered loneliness, grief and cultural loss.

The good news is that healing has begun. In the words of Jean Pochat, who attended the Grollier Hall Healing Circle Conference in Yellowknife, "First justice, then healing. We are on the way." Grollier Hall and Stringer Hall are now just memories. Both schools have been demolished.

The Last Goodbye by **Abraham Anghik Ruben**, 2001
In the artist's words: "I clearly remember when this took place — my mother sitting with my older brother and sister, David and Martha, just before they left for the school in Aklavik. David was five years old at the time and Martha was only a little older …They left in 1955 and we didn't see them again until the latter part of 1958. Those three years had a permanent impact on my brother's life."
PAULATUK, BRAZILIAN SOAPSTONE, PRIVATE COLLECTION, TORONTO

Titus Allen and Danny
Gordon (*standing, left to
right*) with the Shingle Point
whale, 1991

DINO SCHIAVONE, COURTESY

TUSAAYAKSAT, INUVIALUIT

COMMUNICATION SOCIETY

THE SHINGLE POINT WHALE HUNT, 1991

The Inuvialuit have been whale hunters since ancient times.
Beluga whales have always been the favoured species. Bowheads
have been little hunted in recent times, in part because of their
huge size and in part because they were almost obliterated by
commercial American whalers a century ago. Hunts for the bowhead, the largest of Arctic sea mammals, were only fond memories
for Inuvialuit elders, until some Aklavik hunters decided to revive
this traditional practice.

The Inuvialuit desired the hunt for several reasons. First, it
would allow a large group of Inuvialuit to hunt together, as their ancestors
had done in the past. Second, the hunt would allow modern Inuvialuit to
experience an ancient and traditional practice, one their ancestors had been
masters of. And third, the hunt would help Inuvialuit preserve their culture
and provide food for their people through sustainable harvesting and
traditional sharing.

Planning for the bowhead whale hunt began in the late 1980s. It was
fraught with political pressure and legal issues from the start, but almost all
of the resistance came from people living thousands of miles away. As Barry
Zellen reported in the Inuvialuit newspaper *Tusaayaksat*:

Fisheries and Oceans spokesman Burton Ayles has had a lot to say about the
legal issues surrounding the Inuvialuit Bowhead harvest. Because the hunt will
take place in Canadian waters, he says Canada has the legal right to issue a
license to harvest a bowhead. Because the stocks of bowhead whales in the
western Beaufort are healthy and over 7,500 strong, and because the quota
allowed Alaskan Inuit to hunt bowheads is so high (41), Ayles says there is no
real conservation issue involved. Furthermore, "we have an aboriginal right for
the Inuvialuit to harvest a bowhead" enshrined in the constitution and spelled
out in the Inuvialuit Final Agreement. As with many other legal issues, international or federal law does not over-rule the IFA within the settlement region.

Ayles says that the U.S. Department of State has informed their embassies
that the U.S. government has taken a stance opposing the hunt and the issu-
ing of the license, but so far no punitive sanctions have been imposed.

He says that, "we would hope that they would still recognize that the aboriginal right is what's important here."[9]

Despite the protests of the American government and Greenpeace and other environmental groups, the Canadian government issued a bowhead whale licence to the hunters of Aklavik in August of 1991. This demonstrated the strength of the Inuvialuit Final Agreement, which mandates a strong role for the Inuvialuit with regard to the harvesting and co-management of wildlife. It is ironic that opposition to the hunt came from the United States, whose citizens had brought western Arctic whale stocks to the brink of extinction a century earlier.

"We're gonna have a big celebration here," explained hunt captain Danny A. Gordon just before the hunt. "We're gonna have a drum dance, and, you know, things like that. And a big eat every day, so we're gonna have a good day when we get that bowhead."[10]

The hunters were successful. Captain Gordon and Titus Allen harpooned the first bowhead to be taken in Inuvialuit waters in seven decades, and a great celebration was held at Shingle Point. This is how *Tusaayaksat* described the event:

History was made at Shingle Point. On September 4, 1991, the Inuvialuit of Aklavik restored an age-old tradition by harvesting the first Bowhead whale in Canadian waters since the 1920s.

The 37-foot whale was hauled by the hunters and their supporters from between Whiteman Hill and Kinngak, their way illuminated by the shimmering beauty of the Northern Lights.

The next day, with 200 people congregating at Shingle, the whale was butchered, its meat and muktuk cut and dried on the pebbly beach. Just as their forefathers harvested Bowheads, using the combined strength of the whole community to haul the whale out of the sea, and together to prepare the meat and muktuk, Inuvialuit worked together all day long and into the next day.

By the end of the second day, there was little left — the entire whale was used, as it had been traditionally before the white man came and nearly destroyed the Bowhead stocks in pursuit of its baleen and blubber.

While the white man decimated the Bowhead stocks using only a fraction of their meat, wastefully throwing the rest away to rot, the Inuvialuit took only one Bowhead, and used every ounce of it. The meat and muktuk will be shared by all six Inuvialuit communities.

Whale Hunting From an Umiak by Agnes Nanogak and Mona Ohevluk, 1982

HOLMAN, STENCIL, 39.5 × 46 CM (15.5 × 18 INCHES), HI1982-20

If the International Whaling Commission fails to support this harvest and future harvests by Inuvialuit within the Inuvialuit Settlement Region, then it will be clear to the world that the International Whaling Commission has lost its legitimacy. It has no right to dictate how the Inuvialuit should live. And it has no right to criticize the Inuvialuit for living as they always have, before the white man came and made things so difficult — before the white man came and made the water so dirty, the whale stocks so depleted, and the future so uncertain.

This historic Inuvialuit Bowhead harvest restores a proud tradition. The magic and spiritualism felt on the beach at Shingle Point marks the turning point, where Inuvialuit culture and traditions were finally restored, and the Inuvialuit future became a bright and hopeful future.[11]

THE LANGUAGE IN JEOPARDY

The traditional language of the Inuvialuit, Inuvialuktun, has three different dialects, each representing a different language community. Siglitun, or the Siglit dialect, is spoken mainly by people living in Tuktoyaktuk, Paulatuk and Sachs Harbour. According to linguists,[12] it is closest to the original dialect of the Inuvialuit people as it was spoken over a hundred years ago. The Uummarmiut dialect was brought to the Mackenzie Delta from Alaska in the late 19th and early 20th centuries. It is spoken mainly in Aklavik and Inuvik. Finally, the people of Holman speak Kangiryuarmiutun, a central Arctic dialect.

Over the years there has been much intermarriage and movement between communities. Inevitably, this has caused some blurring of dialects. But communication is made easier by the fact that speakers of each dialect can understand the others, although some words and many pronunciations differ. The Inuvialuktun language has suffered greatly over the last century. By 1910, catastrophic disease epidemics had reduced the number of Inuvialuktun speakers to no more than a few hundred. But the survivors retained their language. It would flourish as long as the Inuvialuit continued their traditional lifestyle, on the land and away from European influences.

The early whalers and fur traders had little opportunity or incentive to discourage the use of Inuvialuktun. Social interaction between Europeans and Inuvialuit was still fairly superficial and limited. A rough trade jargon based more on Inuvialuktun than English was sufficient for most needs. As late as 1920, few Inuvialuit spoke much English. The Christian missionaries, who lived more closely with the Inuvialuit, all learned Inuvialuktun.

It was the residential schools that undermined the language, by forcing Inuvialuit students to speak English rather than Inuvialuktun. By the 1950s, most young Inuvialuit were speaking only English, and a generation who had lost their language could not pass it on to their children.

Government and industry continued the work begun by the residential schools. The government, which began to provide health services and social welfare and to administer the new day schools in the 1950s, did all its business in English. With the 1970s' oil boom, many Southerners moved into Inuvialuit territory. The language of employment, again, was English. "Given the inability of teachers, government workers, and industry foremen and representatives to speak Inuvialuktun, functional bilingualism was never a realistic possibility for the Inuvialuit," writes Ronald Lowe. "It was speak English or deliver their lives entirely into others' hands. They made the necessary choice."[13]

Drummers and dancers at the federal day school in Aklavik welcome a visit by the Governor General, 1956

NATIONAL ARCHIVES OF CANADA, PA 114833

The struggle to save the Inuvialuktun language started with the creation of the Committee for Original Peoples Entitlement (COPE) in the 1970s (see page 178). COPE's visionary leaders recognized the need to preserve their culture. In an effort to keep and protect the language, they started the Inuvialuktun Language Commission in May 1981. The commission was made up of speakers of all three dialects. They instituted a language project with four aims: to record, analyze and describe the dialects of Inuvialuktun; to develop Inuvialuktun teaching curricula, materials and a teacher training course; to institute Inuvialuktun language programs in schools and communities; and finally, to monitor and promote the continuing use and learning of Inuvialuktun.

The Inuvialuktun Language Project succeeded in producing dictionaries in all three dialects.[14] An Inuvialuit language curriculum was also developed and language instructors were trained and placed in schools.

In 1987 Mary Lyons, a well-educated professional Inuvialuit woman,

addressed an education conference in Yellowknife. She gave the authorities some strong advice on what must be done to better teach the Inuvialuktun language to young people:

1. Research into learning style using Native people trained by YOU in the universities.
2. Curriculum developed to serve the unique learning style again, done by US with help from YOU in the universities.
3. Training programs for our southern teachers aimed at our needs. This must be done by YOU but with help from US. (We know what we want. You know how to do it.)
4. Money and facilities to do all this.[15]

Leslie Carpenter at a New Year's Eve party, Sachs Harbour, 1958

NWT ARCHIVES, N-1993-002-0108

In 1981 it was estimated that out of 2,800 Inuvialuit, only 515 were fluent in Inuvialuktun, almost none of them under 40 years of age. Twenty years later, there are probably fewer than 200 fluent speakers left. As Lowe explained:

Dictionaries, grammars, teaching curricula, teaching materials, teacher training, adequate funding, community involvement and support — these are the elements whose cumulative force may arrest the decline of a language and even, if deployed in an effective combination, lead to its revitalization. Although it is already too late for Inuvialuktun to become again the first language of the Inuvialuit, it may still provide them, as a firmly established second language, with a cultural stability and access to a cultural heritage that will serve them well in present and future times of change and transition. From the mission schools of the '20s and '30s through the hydrocarbon industrial activities of the '80s, the circumstances arrayed against the survival of Inuvialuktun have been and will continue to be formidable. It remains to be seen whether efforts like those being made by the COPE Inuvialuktun Language Project will prevail against them.[16]

The Inuvialuit are well aware that their language is in danger of disappearing forever, and efforts to save it continue. The Inuvialuit Communication Society (ICS) produces Inuvialuktun programs for television and a bilingual Inuvialuktun/English newspaper called *Tusaayaksat*. All of these efforts help, but they seem like a drop in the bucket compared with the enormous power of the English-dominated media, government and business world. Without new incentives, the Inuvialuktun languages will continue to fade until the last fluent speaker is gone.

THE INUVIALUIT TODAY

The Inuvialuit have gained the knowledge, experience and tools needed to play a meaningful and healthy role in the modern world. While they continue to practise their traditional culture, modern Inuvialuit are much like modern people anywhere. Children attend schools, colleges and universities. Adults work for a living in a variety of trades and professions. They have many excellent role models, including pilots, a doctor, skilled tradespeople, school principals and teachers, engineers, a lawyer, elected officials and senior government administrators, a commissioner of the Northwest Territories, a former premier of the N.W.T., artists, writers, hunters, trappers, businesspeople and elders.

The past hundred and fifty years have proven how adaptable the Inuvialuit and their culture are. Today, the Inuvialuit live in modern houses and eat modern as well as traditional food. They wear modern clothing and have all the modern conveniences enjoyed by other North Americans: cars, trucks, snowmobiles, cell phones, speedboats, the internet, cable television, computers, VCRs and DVD players. They ski, swim and play golf and hockey, while continuing to enjoy traditional pursuits on the land. Visitors to the western Arctic may fly in on an Inuvialuit-owned aircraft, stay at an Inuvialuit-owned hotel and buy groceries from an Inuvialuit business.

At the same time, the ride has sometimes been rough. There is a need to balance positive changes with the challenges that many people face. Substance abuse, suicide and family violence are still serious concerns. By building a strong economic base with a solid educational foundation and a strong sense of community, the Inuvialuit will overcome these problems and continue to adapt to the changes ahead. In the words of one dedicated Inuvialuit leader, Nellie Cournoyea, "The future is positive and filled with new opportunities."[17]

The Northern Games

Inuvialuit elder Abel
Tingmiak demonstrates
the blanket toss

MICHAEL MUIR

The Northern Games are a unique cultural event. "They were passed on from generation to generation," explains Inuvialuit elder Edward Lennie. "Wherever the Eskimo come from, that's where it started."[18] Over time the games have evolved to encompass new experiences, but they have always remained a reflection of the traditional Inuvialuit way of life.

Most of the traditional sports and activities which make up the Northern Games almost disappeared during the first half of the 20th century. Beginning in the late 1960s, they were revived by a group led by Edward Lennie. The first contemporary Northern Games were held in Inuvik in July of 1970.

The Northern Games offer visitors and local people the chance to celebrate skills and strengths rarely seen in other sporting events. One event that demands great muscular strength is the Airplane, originally called the Eagle Carry. The athlete lies face down on the floor with his feet together and his arms spread out like an eagle soaring. He is then lifted up by his wrists and feet and carried about for as long as his strength allows. The One-Foot High Kick is another very challenging sport. The athlete must jump into the air, kick a suspended target and land on the foot with which he kicked. Many athletes can kick well over eight feet (2.5 metres) in the air, the best as high as nine feet (3 metres) or more.

Other events test resistance to pain. One such is the Mouth Pull, played by two men sitting side by side. Each man wraps one arm around the other's head and places a finger in the corner of his opponent's mouth. The competitors then pull each other's mouths as hard as they can until one gives up.

The Good Woman event has become a real crowd-pleaser. The competing women, all in traditional dress, show their skills in a combination of activities including fire-making, tea-boiling, bannock-making, seal-skinning and duck- or goose-plucking. "We thought we'd take our values and see what is a good woman," says Nellie Cournoyea, a founding member of the original Northern Games Association. "A good woman could do many things."[19]

Today the Northern Games are an annual event bringing Inuvialuit from all over the western Arctic together, to compete but also to celebrate. They are truly an inspiration, and help to demonstrate and preserve the rich culture and traditions of the Inuvialuit.

Community Profiles

AKLAVIK

Aklavik means "place of the barren ground grizzly bear" in Inuvialuktun.

LOCATION: At approximately 11 m (36 ft) elevation, Aklavik is located on the banks of Peel Channel in the heart of the Mackenzie Delta. Black spruce, birch, willow and tundra vegetation cover the area, which is interlaced with creeks, rivers and lakes. The beautiful Richardson Mountains are located to the west of Aklavik, and the Beaufort Sea approximately 100 km (60 miles) to the north. Coordinates: 68°13' North, 135°00' West.

CLIMATE: July mean high 18.3°C, low 9.7°C. January mean high –25.5°C, low –33.2°C. Winds predominantly from the west at 10.7 km/h (6.4 mph).

DEMOGRAPHY: Population, 1981: 721; 2001: 632. Average age (2001): 29.7 years. Percentage of population aged 15 and over: 73. Ethnic distribution (1987): 53% Inuvialuit, 29% Dene; 12% Metis, 6% non-aboriginal.

LANGUAGES SPOKEN: Inuvialuktun, Gwich'in, English. Percentage of population with aboriginal language spoken at home: 1.4.

HISTORIC SNAPSHOT: Aklavik was founded by the Pokiak and Greenland families around a small trading post that was established in 1912. A rapid increase in the price of furs from the turn of the century to 1920 helped to accelerate Aklavik's growth as a community. Significant developments include:

    1919   establishment of an Anglican mission
    1922   opening of the western Arctic headquarters of Royal Canadian Mounted Police
    1925   Immaculate Conception Hospital opened by the Roman Catholic Church; Royal Canadian Corps of Signals station opened

1926	All Saints Anglican Hospital built, Roman Catholic mission opens
1929	C.H. "Punch" Dickens lands first airplane in Aklavik; air mail service begins
1931–32	the hunt for the Mad Trapper of Rat River
1939	Dr. Leslie Livingstone arrives to practise medicine and start a small experimental farm that produces wheat, barley and vegetables, as well as dairy products from a small dairy herd
1940–1950s	Aklavik continues to grow and has two hospitals, several churches, a wireless station, trading posts, Anglican and R.C. mission schools, a Royal Canadian Legion, a bakery, post office, sawmill, Native hall and theatre, serving a population of 1,556 people by 1953
1953	the federal government recommends relocation of Aklavik. The present site of Inuvik is chosen and Inuvik, "the model northern Town," is established by 1958.
1958–1960s	much of Aklavik population re-locates to Inuvik but many stay, living up to their motto of "Never Say Die"
1974	Aklavik gains hamlet status
2003	Aklavik continues to flourish as a modern town, but one located far away from the hustle and bustle of Inuvik. It is accessible from Inuvik by air, by boat during the summer and by ice road in the winter.

INUVIK

In Inuvialuktun, Inuvik means "place where people live."

LOCATION: Inuvik is located on a plateau at the edge of the Mackenzie Delta overlooking the East Channel of the Mackenzie River. Mixed black spruce, tamarack, willow and tundra vegetation cover an area of rolling hills at the edge of the tree line. Coordinates: 68°13' North, 135° West.

CLIMATE: July mean high 19.4°C, low 7.8°C. January mean high −24.7°C, low −34.4°C. Light winds in the 10 km/h (6 mph) range.

DEMOGRAPHY: Population, 1981: 3,147; 2001: 2,894. Average age: 27.2 years. Percentage of population aged 15 and over: 70.5. Ethnic distribution: 33% Inuvialuit, 10% Dene; 10% Metis, 47% non-aboriginal.

LANGUAGES SPOKEN: Inuvialuktun, Gwich'in, North Slavey, English. Percentage of population with aboriginal language spoken at home: 1.1.

HISTORIC SNAPSHOT: Inuvik is located in a traditional Inuvialuit trapping area, chosen in the 1950s to replace Aklavik as a regional government centre. Construction began in 1955, and within half a dozen years Inuvik could offer all of the services of a southern Canadian city, including a hospital, churches, government offices, several hotels, a bank, grocery stores and sports facilities.

1970	oil discovered north of Inuvik, creating a boom in oil and gas exploration. Most companies involved open offices in Inuvik.
1979	opening of the Dempster Highway, linking Inuvik to the North American highway system. Oil and gas boom ends.
1984	Inuvialuit Final Agreement signed
1986	the Canadian Armed Forces base in Inuvik closes. Two years later the Inuvik campus of Aurora College is opened using the old Armed Forces facilities.
1992	Gwich'in land claim settled

2000 with an increase in world prices for oil and gas, the oil companies begin to return to the region

2003 Inuvik continues to be a mini-metropolis where various cultures live, work and engage in modern and traditional activities. It is accessible by jet from Edmonton and Yellowknife, and via the Dempster Highway from Whitehorse.

HOLMAN

Holman's Inuvialuktun name is Uluqsaqtuuq, which means "place where they find stones to make ulu. *"*

LOCATION: Holman is located on the northwestern coast of Prince Albert Sound on western Victoria Island, in an area of beautiful rolling tundra. Seal hunting is important in the Holman area, and polar bears, caribou and muskoxen are also to be found. Coordinates: 70°44' North, 117°45' West

CLIMATE: July mean high 11.4°C, low 3.3°C. January mean high −25.7°C, low −32.7°C. Winds east at 18.2 km/h (11 mph).

DEMOGRAPHY: Population, 1981: 300; 2001: 398. Average age: 23.8 years. Percentage of population aged 15 and over: 61.1. Ethnic distribution (1987): 95% Inuvialuit, 5% non-aboriginal.

LANGUAGES SPOKEN: Inuinnaqtun, Inuvialuktun, English. Percentage of population with aboriginal language spoken at home: 10.6.

HISTORIC SNAPSHOT: Holman is a central Arctic town founded in part by Inuvialuit (western Arctic) trappers and traders. In 1984 Holman chose to join the Inuvialuit Settlement Region.

1923 first trading post opened on Prince Albert Sound

1928 post moved to Walker Bay

1939 post moved to King's Bay; Roman Catholic mission opens; community begins to grow

1961 founding of Holman Eskimo Cooperative, outlet for many famous Holman artists including Mary Okheena, Elsie Klengenberg and Helen Kalvak

1962 Anglican church constructed, first resident missionary arrives the following year

1963–64 Government housing built at nearby Queen's Bay

1965–66 community moved to Queen's Bay, the present location

1984 Holman joins the Inuvialuit Settlement Region and gains hamlet status

2003 Today, Holman is a traditional Arctic settlement where many people still engage in hunting, trapping and fishing. It is accessible by air from Inuvik and Yellowknife. Services include a nursing station, school, post office and store.

PAULATUK

Paulatuk (Paulatuuq) means "place of soot or coal" in Inuvialuktun.

LOCATION: Paulatuk is located at the bottom of Darnley Bay on the southern coast of the Beaufort Sea. The area is one of rolling tundra, well stocked with game animals, including brown or grizzly bears, caribou and muskoxen. Nearby lakes and rivers provide excellent trout and char fishing. Coordinates: 69°21' North, 124°04' West.

CLIMATE: July mean high 18.8°C, low 8.3°C. January mean high −24.9°C, low −32.7°C. Winds predominantly from the east at 14 km/h (8 mph).

DEMOGRAPHY: Population, 1981: 181; 2001: 286. Average age of population: 22.6 years. Percentage of population aged 15 and over: 54.5. Ethnic distribution (1987): 96% Inuvialuit, 4% non-aboriginal.

LANGUAGES SPOKEN: Inuvialuktun, English. Percentage of population with aboriginal language spoken at home: unknown.

HISTORIC SNAPSHOT: Paulatuk is located in an area that was little used or occupied during the 19th century. However, ancient Inuit house ruins date back 800 years or more. Some important dates in recent history include:

Early 1920s   first Inuvialuit families begin to settle in the region, lured by its hunting and trapping potential

1927   trading post opened at Letty Harbour

1928   Roman Catholic mission opened at Letty Harbour

1936–37   Catholic mission moves to Paulatuk; opens church-run trading post

1954   mission post closes, community disperses. Many move to Cape Parry, seeking employment in DEW Line construction.

1967   Paulatuk Cooperative Association formed, opens post at Paulatuk; settlement re-established

1968–78   various government services, housing, etc. provided

1987   Paulatuk acquires hamlet status

2003   Paulatuk enjoys many of the modern amenities available in southern Canada, including television, radio, a store, a school, a church and a recreation complex. The residents of this remote community continue to hunt and trap. Many are employed with Parks Canada at nearby Tuktu Nogait Park, with other government departments, or in oil and gas and mining exploration activities. Paulatuk is also the original home of internationally known artists David Piqtuqana Ruben and Abraham Anghik Ruben. Paulatuk is accessible by air from Inuvik.

SACHS HARBOUR

Sachs Harbour is named after the Mary Sachs, *a ship used by Stefansson and colleagues on the Canadian Arctic Expedition of 1913–18.*

LOCATION: Sachs Harbour is located on the north side of the Sachs River on the southwestern coast of Banks Island. It is an area of rugged tundra, looking out over the Arctic Ocean. Banks Island is the most westerly of Canada's Arctic islands, a place of vast beauty. Local wildlife include seals, polar bears, muskoxen (very plentiful) and rare Parry caribou. Coordinates: 71°59' North, 125°14' West.

CLIMATE: July mean high 9.3°C, low 2.5°C. January mean high −26.7°C, low −34.1°C. Winds, predominantly from the southeast at 20 km/h (12 mph).

DEMOGRAPHY: Population, 1981: 101; 2001: 114. Average age of population: 25.1 years. Percentage of population aged 15 and over: 62.9. Ethnic distribution (1987): 89% Inuvialuit, 11% non-aboriginal.

LANGUAGES SPOKEN: Inuvialuktun, English. Percentage of population with aboriginal language spoken at home: 7.4.

HISTORIC SNAPSHOT: Banks Island was little utilized during the 19th century, although ancient house ruins near Sachs Harbour document an Inuit population living in the area as many as 800 years ago.

1918–21	Natkusiak ("Billy Banksland") and partners successfully explore the trapping potential of Banks Island
1928–29	three Inuvialuit families from the Mackenzie Delta travel to Banks Island on their schooners and over-winter, trapping foxes
1930–60	heyday of the Banks Island schooner captains. Inuvialuit families over-winter on Banks Island in various locations, including Sachs Harbour and De Salis Bay, trapping foxes. Each summer they travel by schooner to Aklavik (or occasionally Tuktoyaktuk) to trade, returning in the autumn. The largest and most famous of the schooners was the *North Star*, owned and captained by Inuvialuit Fred Carpenter.
1953	RCMP station opens
1958	Fred Carpenter opens independent trading post
1961	Banks Island population all living at Sachs Harbour; frame houses built, last of the annual schooner trips to Aklavik
1962	Roman Catholic and Anglican missions opened
mid-1970s	anti-fur lobby and international fur embargos destroy trapping industry on the island
2003	Sachs Harbour is a remote Arctic settlement retaining many traditional values and pursuits. A few people still trap on a part-time basis. As well as subsistence hunting, muskoxen are hunted commercially and the meat is marketed throughout the North. Sport hunting of polar bears, catering to a wealthy American audience, is also a valuable source of income, along with employment in the oil and gas industry and with Parks Canada. Sachs Harbour is accessible by air from Inuvik.

TUKTOYAKTUK

Tuktoyaktuk means "looks like a caribou" in Inuvialuktun.

LOCATION: Tuktoyaktuk — or Tuk for short — is located near the mouth of the East Channel of the Mackenzie River, on a peninsula at the edge of the Beaufort Sea. The area is well known for the pingos that stand like large brown ice volcanoes overlooking the town from the south. The Tuk region is one of generally flat, low-lying tundra, dotted with lakes. Coordinates: 69°27' North, 133°02' West.

CLIMATE: July mean high 15.2°C, low 6.0°C. January mean high −25.0°C, low −31.6°C. Winds predominantly from the northwest at 17.4 km/h (10.4 mph).

DEMOGRAPHY: Population, 1981: 722; 2001: 930. Average age: 25.9 years. Percentage of population aged 15 and over: 64.8. Ethnic distribution (1987): 88% Inuvialuit, 2% Dene; 1% Metis, 9% non-aboriginal.

LANGUAGES SPOKEN: Inuvialuktun, English. Percentage of population with aboriginal language spoken at home: 3.2.

HISTORIC SNAPSHOT: Tuktoyaktuk has been a traditional harvesting area of the Inuvialuit for hundreds of years. Before the arrival of Europeans and throughout the 19th century, the nearby settlement of Kitigaaryuit was probably the largest population centre in the western Arctic. The Tuk area provides excellent fishing, whaling and caribou hunting.

Significant developments in and around Tuk over the past hundred and more years include:

1890	arrival of the American whaling fleet in the area
1902	infectious disease epidemics lead to the abandonment of Kitigaaryuit as a permanent settlement
1906	Tuktoyaktuk visited by explorer Stefansson, who describes Ovayuak as "chief." Whaling industry dies.
1920, 1928	fatal epidemics. William Mangilaluk is chief.
1934	trading post opened; Tuk becomes an important harbour serving the western Arctic
1935	arrival of the reindeer herd, providing some wage employment, meat and hides
1937	Anglican and Roman Catholic missions opened
1939	Baillie Island abandoned, much of the population eventually moving to Tuk
1954	Stanton abandoned, much of the population eventually moving to Tuk
1955	Construction work on DEW Line provides limited wage employment
1956	nursing station built
1970	Tuk acquires hamlet status
1970s	arrival of the oil and gas industry proves well-paying but short-term employment
2000	oil and gas companies return
2003	Today Tuk is a vibrant community of Inuvialuit entrepreneurs, hunters and trappers and people working in various occupations. Residents still enjoy traditional activities as well as the modern amenities. If a gas pipeline is built nearby, the community will have a new economic base from which to grow. Tuktoyaktuk is accessible from Inuvik by air, and by ice road during the winter.

Glossary

Dene Self-designation of a group of First Nations ("Indians") speaking a variety of Athapaskan languages, indigenous to the western Canadian Subarctic and adjacent interior Alaska. Important Dene nations include the Gwich'in, Dogrib, Chipewyan and Slavey, among others.

Gwich'in Self-designation of the Dene or Athapaskan-speaking First People ("Indians") living in far northwestern Canada (lower Mackenzie River, northern Yukon) and adjacent regions of interior Alaska. The Gwich'in were the closest Indian neighbours of most Inuvialuit.

Hare (or **Hareskin**) A small Dene nation living in the area north and west of Great Bear Lake. Named for their extensive use of hare or rabbit skin for clothing in ancient times, the Hare lived immediately south of the more eastern Inuvialuit groups.

Inuinnat (plural **Inuinnaq**) Self-designation of the Inuit of the central Canadian Arctic, notably the so-called Copper Inuit of the Victoria Island–Coronation Gulf area.

Inuit The aboriginal inhabitants of Arctic North America, formerly called "Eskimo." The Inuit share a common language and culture (with some regional variations), and have close relatives living in southern coastal Alaska and far eastern Siberia (Aleuts, Yupik-speaking "Eskimo"). *Inuit* is plural; the singular is *Inuk*.

Inupiat Self-designation of Alaskan Inuit.

Inuvialuit Self-designation of Inuit living in the western Canadian Arctic. *Inuvialuit* is plural; the singular is *Inuvialuk*.

Inuvialuktun The language of the Inuvialuit, comprising a closely related group of dialects within the larger Inuit language.

Itqilit The Inuvialuktun (and Inupiat) term for "Indians," specifically the Gwich'in.

Kangiryuarmiut Self-designation of the Inuit (Inuinnat and Inuvialuit) of western Victoria Island, now living in Holman. The community of Holman was founded in part by Inuvialuit (including Alaskan Inuit) fur trappers, and several prominent Holman families trace their ancestry to the western Arctic. The community of Holman chose to join the Inuvialuit Settlement Region in 1984.

Kitigaaryungmiut "People of Kitigaaryuit," one of many Inuvialuit regional groups or societies in the 19th century. The term is now sometimes used to refer generally to the original Inuvialuit population before the arrival of the whalers and the Nunataarmiut.

Kogmullick (or **Kugmalit**, etc.) "Easterner." The term was applied by the Alaskan Inupiat (Nunataarmiut) and American whalers to describe the Inuvialuit, who in turn used it to refer to central Arctic people (Inuinnat).

Nunataarmiut Alaskan Inupiat who moved into the Mackenzie Delta area in the wake of disease epidemics in the late 19th and early 20th centuries.

Siglit (or **Tchiglit**) Ancient self-designation of the Inuvialuit. The precise meaning and application of the word have been lost.

Tan'ngit Europeans, or people of European descent; whites. The word is of Alaskan origin, replacing the original 19th-century term *Kabloonacht*.

Uummarmiut Inuvialuit of Alaskan descent living mainly in the Mackenzie Delta area (Nunataarmiut descendants).

OTHER INUVIALUKTUN TERMS

Angatkuq Shaman.

Ataniq (or **atanik**) Boss, leader.

Iglu (or **igloo**) Literally a house of any sort, sometimes specifically a snow house.

Igluyuaryuk The traditional sod and driftwood house used by most Inuvialuit during the winter.

Kadjigi (or **qadjigi**) The traditional dance or meeting house, used also as a men's house for the repair of tools and equipment, for shamanic performances, etc. The related modern term *katidjvik* describes a community centre or dance hall.

Kaivitjvik The "Polar Nights Festival" marking the winter solstice.

Katak The cold-trap doorway leading into a sod house or igloo.

Kayak The traditional one-man Inuit boat, normally propelled with a double-bladed paddle. In modern Inuvialuktun, the term *kayak* (or *qayaq*) now refers to a canoe, while the traditional kayak is called a *qayavialuk*.

Komatik (or **qamutik**) A simple ladder-like sled, made of a pair of runners and connecting cross-slats, used to haul heavy loads over ice or packed snow. Komatiks are still in common use in the western Arctic, but these days they are usually pulled by snowmobiles rather than dog teams.

Mipku Dry meat.

Mukluk High winter boots, typically made from seal or caribou skin.

Tuutak Lip ornaments or labrets, worn by men.

Ulu The traditional crescent-shaped knife used by Inuit women, still widely employed.

Umiaq The large traditional boat used by most Inuit groups, including the Inuvialuit; the plural is *umiat*. The *umiaq* could be up to 10 metres (33 feet) long and was propelled by oars or paddles, usually by the women.

Umialik Rich man and community leader (literally, an "*umiaq* owner").

Notes

CHAPTER I **Ingilraqpaaluk**
(**A Very Long Time Ago**)

1 Banfield 1974 and Martell et al 1984 describe the wildlife of the western Canadian Arctic, while D. Morrison 2000 describes the traditional fishery.

2 Vol. 5 of *The Handbook of North American Indians* (Damas, ed., 1984) provides an overview of Inuit culture across North America. The article by Woodbury (1984) describes the language.

3 See Mathiassen 1927, Ford 1959, McGhee 1984, McCullough 1989, Arnold and McCullough 1990, Arnold 1994a, D. Morrison 1999. The apparent Inuvialuit silence concerning earlier population in oral tradition comes from Palsson 2001: 301–2.

4 Petitot 1999: 50.

5 Alunik 1998, Peeloolook 1989.

6 Schwarz 1970.

7 Published accounts by Inuvialuit elders include Nuligak 1966, Pokiak 1976, Peeloolook 1989, Anon. 1991, Nuyaviak 1991, Nagy 1994, and Alunik 1998.

8 Franklin 1828, Richardson 1851, Bompas 1871, 1888, Petitot 1878, 1889, 1999, MacFarlane 1891, 1905, Whittaker 1937, and Stefansson 1914, 1971, 1990.

9 McGhee 1974, D. Morrison 1988, 1990, 1997, 2000, and Arnold 1994b.

10 Petitot 1876 first used the word "Siglit" or "Chiglit" in print. Its modern use is described by Lowe 1984a.

11 The different Inuvialuit communities are described in McGhee 1974, D. Morrison 1988, D. Morrison 1990, and D. Morrison and Arnold 1994.

12 Franklin 1828: 100–107.

13 Petitot 1999: 168.

14 Stefansson 1914: 168.

15 Stefansson 1914: 166.

16 Nuligak 1966: Appendix 1.

17 Stefansson 1914: 145, 356.

18 Anon. 1991

19 Franklin 1828: 215–7.

20 The observation that the people of Nuvugaq "dreaded their turbulent countrymen" comes from Richardson 1851: 257–58; the reference to the Avvarmiut at Cape Bathurst is from M'Clure 1969: 96.

21 Petitot 1878: 404.

22 See D. Morrison 1990.

23 Arnold and Hart 1992 and Hart 1997: 28–30 describe traditional houses.

24 Nagy 1994: 90–91.

25 Stefansson 1914: 323.

26 Stefansson 1990: 136.

27 Stefansson 1990: 135–138 provides detailed information about the interior and furnishings of the traditional Inuvialuit house.

28 Of six Inuvialuit winter houses the author has excavated archaeologically, four had interior hearths, a feature rarely recorded in the historic literature.

29 Stefansson 1914: 170 and Nuligak 1966: Appendix III describe *qatdjgit*.

30 Richardson 1851: 257.

31 Whittaker 1937: Fig. 3.

32 Spencer 1959 and Burch 1975, 1980, describe the social organization of the traditional north Alaskan Inupiat.

33 Bompas 1871: 339, Stefansson 1914: 172, Stefansson 1990: 143–44 and Anon. 1991: 11 describe the office and role of the Inuvialuit *umialik*. D. Morrison 1989 presents evidence of a possible coup at Kitigaaryuit.

34 Stefansson 1914: 327, Whittaker 1937: 173 and Nuligak 1966: 14 describe the selection of the beluga hunt leader.

35 Pokiak 1976: 53.

36 Nuligak 1966: 203.

37 Petitot 1999: 89.

38 Stefansson 1914: 161, 339, 363–64 describes Inuvialuit child-rearing.

39 Miertsching 1967: 59.

40 Stefansson 1914: 333 and Nuligak 1966: 194 describe attacks by magic bears.

41 Stefansson 1914: 152.

42 Nuligak 1966: 16–20, Stefansson 1914: 337–38 and Pokiak 1976: 54 also describe the Polar Nights Festival.

43 Petitot 1999: 40.

44 Petitot 1999: 9–10.

45 Stefansson 1914: 139–41, 175–76 and Petitot 1999: 117 describe traditional Inuvialuit clothing.

46 Petitot 1999: 112–13.

47 Pokiak 1976: 52.

48 Nuligak 1966: 14–15.

49 Stefansson 1914: 323.

50 M'Clure 1969: 93.

51 Nuligak 1966: 71.

52 Petitot 1999: 107.

53 Ishmael Alunik, as told to Eddie D. Kolausok.

54 Ishmael Alunik, as told to Eddie D. Kolausok.

55 Pokiak 1976: 53.

56 Richardson 1851: 257.

57 Nuligak 1966: 60–61.

58 Petitot 1999: 13–14.

59 Stefansson 1914: 356.

60 D. Morrison 1991 and McCartney 1988 describe pre-European trade networks.

61 Petitot 1878: 404.

62 Maguire 1988: 212.

63 Simpson 1988: 542–43.

64 Petitot 1878: 512–15.

65 Franklin 1828: 203.

66 Petitot 1878: 404.

67 Franklin 1828: 203.

68 Krech 1979: 105 supplies a population estimate for the Gwich'in.

69 Petitot 1878: 405.

70 Hooper 1853: 273.

71 HBC, B.80/a/8.

72 Petitot 1999: 25.

73 MacFarlane 1891: 32–33.

CHAPTER 3 **The Arrival of Strangers, 1788–1889**

1 Franklin 1828: 130 and Petitot 1999: 19.

2 Simpson 1988: 545. Tan'ngit referred originally to Russians, and seems to derive from a word meaning "to wash or clean," a reference to the regular wash days held at Russian posts.

3 Jenness 1922: 50, 180.

4 D. Morrison 1991.

5 Ray 1975 describes the Russian conquest of Siberia and establishment of the Anyui trading post.

6 Mackenzie 1970: 208.

7 Franklin 1828: 130.

8 Simpson 1988: 542.

9 Both Thomas Simpson (1843: 147) and Franklin (1828: 195) describe the Inuvialuit as non-smokers.

10 Bompas 1888: 49.

11 Petitot 1999: 14–15.

12 Franklin 1828: 91–92, Mackenzie 1970: 192 and Simpson 1843: 103 describe shifting trade patterns in the Mackenzie valley; see also Krech 1979: 106–9.

13 Mackenzie 1970.

14 Wenzel 1823: 79–80.

15 Franklin 1828.

16 Franklin 1828: 195.

17 Franklin 1828: 203.

18 Franklin 1828: 217, 226.

19 Franklin 1828: 99–107.

20 Simpson 1843.

21 Neatby 1958 tells the tale of the Third Franklin Expedition.

22 Published journals from the Franklin search expeditions through Inuvialuit territory include Richardson 1851, Hooper 1853, Armstrong 1857, Miertsching 1967, M'Clure 1969, and Pullen 1979.

23 Miertsching 1967: 57–58.

24 Miertsching 1967: 59–60.

25 Krech 1984: 59.

26 Hooper 1853: 372–73.

27 Stager 1967: 46

28 HBC, B.20/b/31:54, cited in McGhee 1974: 3–4.

29 Cited in Krech 1979: 107.

30 Richardson 1851: 258.

31 HBC, B.200/b/31: 66.

32 MacFarlane 1891: 34.

33 See Stager 1967.

34 Petitot 1999.

35 MacFarlane 1905; see also Lindsay 1993 on the Smithsonian's ambitions in northwestern North America.

36 HBC, B.200/b/35: 75.

37 Cited in Savoie 1970: 140.

38 HBC, B.200/b/35: 94.

39 Cited in Savoie 1970: 136.

40 Early reports of disease are from Petitot (cited in Savoie 1970: 140), Bompas 1871: 333 and the Hudson's Bay Company archives: HBC, B.200/b/38: 22 and HBC, B.200/b/38.

41 Petitot 1999: 101.

42 Petitot 1999: 181.

43 Early missionary ventures are described by Peake 1966, Petitot 1999, Bompas 1871 and Burch 1994.

44 Krech 1979.

45 See D. Morrison 1989.

46 See Hooper 1853: 346–61.

47 Petitot 1999: 55.

48 Petitot 1999: 12.

49 Krech 1979: 109.

50 Wenzel 1823.

51 Yerbury 1977.

52 Cited in Krech 1979: 111.

53 Anon. 1991: 40.

54 Inuvialuit metallurgy is described by Whittaker 1937: 144 and D. Morrison 1988: 49–50.

55 Petitot 1999: 99–101.

56 Verano and Ubelaker 1992 describe the toll of infectious diseases on a continental basis.

57 Stefansson 1914: 307–8, 332.

58 Krech 1978: 713.

59 Krech 1979: 110–11.

CHAPTER 4 **The Winds of Change Blow Hard: The Whaling Era, 1890–1910**

1   HBC, B.200/b/36.

2   Bockstoce 1986: 207–8. Bockstoce 1986 is the authoritative source on the western Arctic whaling industry.

3   Bockstoce 1986: 255–57.

4   Bockstoce 1986: 269–71.

5   Bockstoce 1986: 271.

6   Cook 1926: 41.

7   Bockstoce 1986: 266, Bruemmer 1980: 28.

8   Nuligak 1966: 33.

9   Godsell 1941: 146.

10 Jenness 1964: 14.

11 Nuligak 1966: 31.

12 See Whittaker 1937: 235–40 and Bockstoce 1986: 277 on the "kindergarten captain" and other lurid tales.

13 Cook 1926: 263.

14 Peake 1966: 24.

15 Bodfish 1936: 71.

16 Bockstoce 1986: 276.

17 Bockstoce 1986: 40.

18 Russell 1898: 141–42.

19 Whittaker 1937: 74.

20 Stefansson 1914: 166.

21 Bockstoce 1986: 279 is the source of the Pysha story.

22 Whittaker 1937: 235.

23 Whittaker 1937: 236.

24 Nuligak 1966: 30–31.

25 Stefansson 1990: 101.

26 Krupnik 1994.

27 Peake 1966: 53, 64–66.

28 Whittaker 1937: 225–26.

29 Usher 1971a: 175.

30 Nuligak 1966: 27.

31 On the depopulation of the Brooks Range, see Stefansson 1971: 71–72 and Burch 1972.

32 Anon. 1991: 47.

33 On meat-hunting and the destruction of the caribou in Alaska and in the western Canadian Arctic, see Gubser 1965: 317, Martell et al 1984:

38–43, Nuligak 1966: 27 and Bockstoce 1986: 275. For a more general view of caribou population fluctuations, see also Burch 1972.

34 Stefansson 1914: 173.

35 Nuligak 1966: 93.

36 Anon. 1991: 36.

37 Stefansson 1914: 155.

38 Anon 1991: 41.

39 Stringer's career with the Inuvialuit, and that of his Catholic rival, is told by Peake 1966.

40 Petitot 1999: chapter 12 (on Arviuna).

41 Peake 1966: 29.

42 Peake 1966: 69–70.

43 Peter Thrasher, cited in Nagy 1994: 39.

44 On the conversion and baptism of the Inuvialuit, see Stefansson 1971: 45ff, Nuligak 1966: 62, Whittaker 1937: 68 and Burch 1994.

45 Nuligak 1966: 76–77.

46 Nuligak 1966: 91.

47 Stefansson 1971: 426.

48 Nuligak 1966: 62.

49 Whittaker 1937: 68.

50 Steele 1936: 98–100. A good overview of the early history of the Mounted Police at Herschel Island is presented by W. Morrison 1985.

51 Sutherland n.d.: 21.

52 Cited in Steele 1936: 108.

53 Steele 1936: 105, 113.

54 Sutherland n.d.: 28–29.

55 Sutherland n.d.: 30.

56 Steele 1936: 110–13.

57 Bockstoce 1986: 324–27; see also Bodfish 1936: 229–31.

58 Cited in Bockstoce 1986: 326.

59 Bodfish 1936: 225.

60 W. Morrison 1985: 61.

61 Bockstoce 1986: 335–37.

62 Rasmussen 1942: 49.

CHAPTER 5 **Trappers, Traders and Herders, 1906–**

1 Usher 1971b: 106; Godsell 1946: 260.

2 Godsell 1946: 252.

3 Whittaker 1937: 124 and Rasmussen 1942: 51–53 describe the shift to schooners and their cost.

4 Whittaker 1937: 28.

5 Wolforth 1971: 43.

6 Usher 1971b: 89–110.

7 Usher 1971b: 89–91.

8 Usher 1976a: 21.

9 Honigmann and Honigmann 1970: 30.

10 Wolforth 1971: Fig. 4–2.

11 Honigmann and Honigmann 1970: 42–44.

12 Usher 1976a: 22.

13 Copland 1985: 188–89.

14 Information on Ovayuak and Mangilaluk can be found in Stefansson 1990: 133–150 and Anon. 1991: 11–12.

15 Descriptions of Tuktoyaktuk prior to 1960 are to be found in Ferguson 1961, Mackay 1963 and Abrahamson 1968.

16 The story of Christian "Charlie" Klengenberg is told autobiographically (Klengenberg 1932), and by Stefansson 1990: 47–51 and Condon 1996: 36–39.

17 The story of Kromanak and Tadjuk was told to Nuligak 1966: 44–45.

18 Condon 1996: 43–45.

19 Stefansson 1971: 151.

20 Sources for the story of Natkusiak and the "Blond Eskimo" include Condon 1996: 49, Stefansson 1928 and Jenness 1923.

21 Stefansson 1971 presents his version of events on this controversial expedition.

22 Descriptions of the growth of communities on Banks Island and at Holman are to be found in Usher 1970 and Condon 1996.

23 Cited in Condon 1996: 111.

24 Sources on the history of Paulatuk include Mackay 1958 and Anon. 1994.

25 Sources on the decline of trapping in the Aklavik and Tuktoyaktuk regions during the 1950s and 1960s include Ferguson 1961, Clairmont 1963, Honigmann and Honigmann 1970 and Wolforth 1971.

26 Usher (1970, 1976b) records the history of trapping on Banks Island.

27 Usher 1976b: 208.

28 Wilson 1980: 81.

29 National Film Board of Canada 1989.

30 The section on reindeer herding is taken almost entirely from Elisa Hart's excellent book *Reindeer Days Remembered* (Hart 2001).

31 The anti-fur crusade against northern trapping is described by Coates and Powell 1989: 44–45.

32 *On The Trapline*, Winter 1995/96. The quotation from Rosemary Kuptana is from page 7, in an article entitled "Mission Europe: A Final Effort to Stop a Fur Ban."

CHAPTER 8 **Boom, Bust and Balance:
Life Since 1950**

1 W. Morrison 1998: 152.
2 W. Morrison 1998: 158.
3 W. Morrison 1998: 153.
4 Brown 1998: 28.
5 Hunt 1983: 170.
6 Vince Steen, quoted in Berger, 1988: 227.
7 Berger 1988: 131.
8 W. Morrison 1998: 164–66 provides a brief but useful overview of DEW Line construction.
9 Ishmael Alunik, quoted in Nagy, 1994: 59.
10 Jimmy Jacobson, quoted in Nagy, 1994: 59.
11 *Settlements of the Northwest Territories* 1966: section 48.
12 Ervin 1968: 6–9.
13 The building of Inuvik is described by Ervin 1968, Stoneman-McNichol 1983 and Hamilton 1994: 75–79.
14 Ervin 1968: 2.
15 May 1956, page 4. Issues of the *Aklavik Journal* from 1955 to 1957 have been republished by the editor, Bern Will Brown (1996).
16 Tommy Ross, quoted in Stoneman-McNichol 1983: 8.
17 Stoneman-McNichol 1983: 14.
18 Ervin 1968: 2.
19 Ervin 1968: 5.
20 Ervin 1968: 7.
21 Quoted in Berger 1988: 207.
22 Quoted in Berger 1988: 206.
23 Personal communication to the author.
24 The 1970s oil and gas boom in the western Arctic is chronicled by Coates and Powell 1989: 33–36 and MacLeod 1978.
25 Usher 1973 provides an excellent early history of the Committee for Original People's Entitlement.
26 See Coates and Powell 1989: 102–3 on the Trudeau White Paper.
27 Berger 1977: 224.
28 Ishmael Alunik, quoted in Dickerson 1992: 107.
29 Vince Steen, quoted in Berger 1988: 227–28.
30 Berger 1977: xxvi–vii.
31 See Coates and Powell 1989: 117 on the terms of the IFA.
32 Beaumont 1999.
33 Willimott 2000.
34 *The Western Arctic (Inuvialuit) Claims Settlement Act*, 1984: 1.
35 Willimott 2000: 15.

CHAPTER 9 **Contemporary Inuvialuit Art**

1 Cited in Schrager 1994: *Inuit Art Quarterly*, 1994: 11.
2 Cited in Huston 1997: *Inuit Art Quarterly*, Spring 1997: 31.
3 Brown 1997: *Inuit Art Quarterly*, Spring 1997: 24.
4 *Inuit Art Quarterly*, Fall 1995: 45.
5 *Inuit Art Quarterly*, 2002: 44–45.
6 Abraham Ruben, quoted in catalogue *Abraham Anghik Ruben*: 38.

CHAPTER 10 **The Survival of a Culture**

1 Coates 1985: 124.
2 Coates 1985: 61.
3 Clarke 1922: 23.
4 Personal communication to the author.
5 Personal communication to the author.
6 Miller 1996 provides an excellent overview of the residential school system in Canada.
7 Coates 1985: 126–27.
8 Miller 1996: 166.
9 *Tusaayaksat*, August 28, 1991: 6.
10 *Tusaayaksat*, August 28, 1991: 7.
11 *Tusaayaksat*, September 20, 1991: 1.
12 Lowe 1983: *vii–viii.*
13 Lowe 1984a: *xii.*
14 Lowe 1983, 1984a&b.
15 Lyons 1987: 44.
16 Lowe 1984a: xiv.
17 Willimott 2000: 15.
18 National Film Board of Canada, 1981.
19 National Film Board of Canada, 1981.

Bibliography

Abrahamson, G. 1968. *Tuktoyaktuk–Cape Parry: An Area Economic Survey*. Ottawa: Department of Indian Affairs and Northern Development, Northern Administration Branch.

Alunik, Ishmael. 1998. *Call Me Ishmael: Memories of Ishmael Alunik, Inuvialuit Elder*. Inuvik: Kolausok Ublaaq Enterprises.

Anonymous. 1991. *Inuvialuit Pitqusiit: The Culture of the Inuvialuit*. Northwest Territories Education.

Anonymous. 1994. *Paulatuurmiut Inuusiat: The History of Paulatuuq*. Beaufort Delta Divisional Board of Education.

Armstrong, Alexander. 1857. *A Personal Narrative of the Discovery of the North-West Passage*. London: Hurst and Blackett.

Arnold, Charles. 1994a. "The Importance of Wood in the Early Thule Culture of the Western Canadian Arctic." *Threads of Arctic Prehistory: Papers in Honour of William E. Taylor, Jr*. Ed. D. Morrison and J. L. Pilon. eds. 269–280. Canadian Museum of Civilization Mercury Series, Archaeological Survey of Canada Paper No. 149.

———. 1994b. "Archaeological Investigations on Richards Island." *Bridges Across Time: The NOGAP Archaeology Project*. Ed. J. L. Pilon. 85–94. Canadian Archaeological Assocation, Occasional Paper No. 2.

Arnold, Charles, and Elisa Hart. 1992. "The Mackenzie Inuit Winter House." *Arctic* 45: 199–200.

Arnold, Charles, and Karen McCullough. 1990. "Thule Pioneers in the Canadian Arctic." *Canada's Missing Dimension: Science and History in the Canadian Arctic Islands*. Vol. II. Ed. C. R. Harington. 677–94.

Banfield, A. W. F. 1974. *The Mammals of Canada*. Toronto: University of Toronto Press.

Beaumont, Sue. 1999. *Breaking Trail: Self-Government in the Beaufort-Delta*. Inuvik: Beaufort-Delta Self-Government Negotiations Office.

Berger, Thomas R. 1977. *Northern Frontier, Northern Homeland: The Report of the Mackenzie Valley Pipeline Inquiry*. Vol. 1. Ottawa: Minister of Supply and Services Canada.

———. 1988. *Northern Frontier, Northern Homeland: The Report of the Mackenzie Valley Pipeline Inquiry*. Rev. ed. Vancouver/Toronto: Douglas & McIntyre.

Bockstoce, John. 1986. *Whales, Ice, and Men: The History of Whaling in the Western Arctic*. Seatle: University of Washington Press.

Bodfish, Hartson. 1936. *Chasing the Bowhead*. Cambridge: Harvard University Press.

Bompas, William. 1871. "The Esquimaux of the Mackenzie River." *Church Missionary Intelligencer* 7: 333–41.

———. 1888. *Diocese of Mackenzie River.* London: Society for Promoting Christian Knowledge.

Brown, Bern Will, 1996. *The Aklavik Journal: A Reprint of the Community Newspaper of Aklavik North West Territories, 1955–57.* Colville Lake: Our Lady of the Snows Mission, Bern Will Brown.

———. 1998. *Arctic Journal.* Ottawa: Novalis.

Bruemmer, Fred. 1980. "Herschel! The Big Town." *The Beaver*, Winter: 26–35.

Burch, Ernest S. 1972. "The Caribou/Wild Reindeer as a Human Resource." *American Antiquity* 37: 339–68.

———. 1975. *Eskimo Kinsmen: Changing Family Relationships in Northwest Alaska.* St. Paul: West Publishing Co.

———. 1980. "Traditional Eskimo Societies in Northwest Alaska." *Alaskan Native Culture and History.* Ed. Y. Kotani and W. Workman. 253–304. Senri Ethnological Series, Vol. 4.

———. 1994. "The Inupiat and the Christianization of Arctic Alaska." *Etudes Inuit Studies* 18: 81–108.

Clairmont, Donald. 1963. *Deviance Among Indians and Eskimos in Aklavik, N.W.T.* Ottawa: Northern Coordination and Research Centre, Department of Northern Affairs and National Resources.

Clarke, F. A. 1922–23. "Journal from Capt. F. A. Clarke." Ms., All Saints Anglican Church, Aklavik, N.W.T.

Coates, Kenneth. 1985. *Canada's Colonies: A History of the Yukon and Northwest Territories.* Toronto: James Lorimer.

Coates, Kenneth, and Judith Powell. 1989. *The Modern North: People, Politics and the Rejection of Colonialism.* Toronto: James Lorimer.

Condon, Richard. 1996. *The Northern Copper Inuit: A History.* Toronto: University of Toronto Press.

Cook, John A. 1926. *Pursuing the Whale: A Quarter-Century of Whaling in the Arctic.* London: John Murray.

Copland, A. Dudley. 1985. *Coplalook: Chief Trader, Hudson's Bay Company, 1923–39.* Winnipeg: Watson and Dwyer.

Damas, David, ed. 1984. *Arctic.* Vol. 5 of *The Handbook of North American Indians.* Washington: Smithsonian Institution Press.

Dickerson, Mark. 1992. *Whose North: Political Change, Political Development, and Self-Government in the Northwest Territories.* Vancouver: UBC Press and the Arctic Institute of North America.

Ervin, A. M. 1968. *New Northern Townsmen in Inuvik.* Ottawa: Northern Science Research Group, Department of Indian Affairs and Northern Development.

Ferguson, J. D. 1961. *The Human Ecology and Social and Economic Change in the Community of Tuktoyaktuk, N.W.T.* Ottawa: Northern Coordination and Research Centre, Department of Northern Affairs and National Resources.

Ford, James. 1959. *Eskimo Prehistory in the Vicinity of Point Barrow Alaska.* Anthropological Papers of the American Museum of Natural History, 47(1).

Franklin, John. 1828. *Narrative of a Second Expedition to the Shores of the Polar Sea in the Years 1825, 1826, and 1827.* London: John Murray.

Godsell, Philip. 1941. "Pirate Days in Arctic Waters." *Forest and Outdoors*, May: 145–46, 152–53.

———. 1946. *Arctic Trader: The Account of Twenty Years with the Hudson's Bay Company.* Toronto: Macmillan.

Gubser, Nicholas. 1965. *The Nunamiut Eskimo: Hunters of Caribou.* New Haven: Yale University Press.

Hamilton, John David. 1994. *Arctic Revolution: Social Change in the Northwest Territories 1935–1994.* Toronto: Dundurn.

Hart, Elisa. 1997. *Kitigaaryuit Archaeological Inventory and Mapping Project — 1996.* Inuvik: Inuvialuit Social Development Program.

———. 2001. *Reindeer Days Remembered.* Inuvik: Inuvialuit Cultural Resource Centre.

Honigmann, John, and Irma Honigmann. 1970. *Arctic Townsmen.* Ottawa: Canadian Research Centre for Anthropology, St. Paul University.

Hooper, William H. 1853. *Ten Months Among the Tents of the Tuski.* London: John Murray.

Hudson's Bay Company (HBC). Hudson's Bay Company Archives (microfilm), Public Archives of Canada, Ottawa.

Hunt, Barbara, ed. 1983. *Rebels, Rascals and Royalty: The Colourful North of LACO Hunt.* Yellowknife: Outcrop.

Jenness, Diamond. 1922. *The Life of the Copper Eskimos.* Vol. 12A of *Report of the Canadian Arctic Expedition, 1913–18.* Ottawa.

———. 1923. "The Origin of the Copper Eskimos and their Copper Culture." *Geographical Review* 13(4): 541–50.

————. 1964. *Eskimo Administration: II. Canada.* Arctic Institute of North America, Technical Paper 14.

Klengenberg, Christian. 1932. *Klengenberg of the Arctic.* London: Jonathan Cape.

Krech, Shepard. 1978. "Disease, Starvation and Northern Athapaskan Social Organization." *American Ethnologist* 5: 710–32.

————. 1979. "Interethnic Relations in the Lower Mackenzie River Region." *Arctic Anthropology* 16(2): 102–22.

————. 1984. "'Massacre' of the Inuit." *The Beaver,* Summer: 52–59.

Krupnik, Igor. 1994. "'Siberians' in Alaska: The Siberian Eskimo contribution to Alaskan population recoveries, 1880–1940." *Etudes Inuit Studies* 18: 49–80.

Lindsay, Debra. 1993. *Science in the Subarctic: Trappers, Traders, and the Smithsonian Institution.* Washington: Smithsonian Institution Press.

Lowe, Ronald, 1983. *Kangiryuarmiut Uqauhingita Numiktittitdjutingit: Basic Kangiryuarmiut Eskimo Dictionary.* Inuvik: Committee for Original Peoples Entitlement.

————. 1984a. *Siglit Inuvialuit Uqausiita Kipuktirutait: Basic Siglit Inuvialuit Dictionary.* Inuvik: Committee for Original Peoples Entitlement.

————. 1984b. *Uummarmiut Uqalungiha Mumikhitchiutingit: Basic Uummarmiut Eskimo Dictionary.* Inuvik: Committee for Original Peoples Entitlement.

The Lower Mackenzie Region: An Economic Survey. 1966. Ottawa: Department of Indian Affairs and Northern Development.

Lyons, Mary. 1987. *Committee of Original Peoples Entitlement (COPE) with Special Reference to the COPE Language Project (CLP) in Education, Research, Information Systems and the North.* Ed. W. P. Adams. Ottawa: Association of Canadian Universities for Northern Studies.

McCartney, Allen. 1988. "Late Prehistoric Metal Use in the New World Arctic." *The Late Prehistoric Development of Alaska's Native People.* Ed. R. Shaw, R. Harritt and D. Dumond. 57–80. Alaska Anthropological Association Monograph Series, No. 4.

M'Clure, Robert. 1969. *The Discovery of the North-West Passage.* Ed. S. Osborn. Edmonton: Hurtig.

McCullough, Karen. 1989. *The Ruin Islanders: Early Thule Culture Pioneers in the Eastern High Arctic.* Canadian Museum of Civilization, Mercury Series, Archaeological Survey of Canada Paper 141.

MacFarlane, Roderick. 1891. "On an Expedition Down the Begh-ula or Anderson River." *Canadian Record of Science* 4: 28–53.

————. 1905. "Notes on Mammals Collected and Observed in the Northern Mackenzie River District, Northwest Territories of Canada." *Proceedings of the U.S. National Museum* 28: 673–764.

McGhee, Robert. 1974. *Beluga Hunters: An Archaeological Reconstruction of the History and Culture of the Mackenzie Delta Kittegaryumiut.* Memorial University of Newfoundland, Newfoundland Social and Economic Studies, No. 13.

————. 1984. "Thule Prehistory of Canada." *Arctic.* Vol. 5 of *The Handbook of North American Indians.* Ed. D. Damas. 369–76. Washington: Smithsonian Institution Press.

Mackay, J. Ross. 1958. *The Anderson River Map-Area, N.W.T.* Memoir 5 of the Geographical Branch, Mines and Technical Surveys, Ottawa.

————. 1963. *The Mackenzie Delta Area, N.W.T.* Memoir 8 of the Geographical Branch, Mines and Technical Surveys, Ottawa.

Mackenzie, Alexander. 1970. *The Journals and Letters of Sir Alexander Mackenzie.* Ed. W. Kaye Lamb. Toronto: Macmillan.

MacLeod, William G. 1978. "The Dempster Highway." *Northern Transitions.* Vol 1. Ed. E. B. Peterson and J. Wright. Ottawa: Canadian Arctic Resources Committee.

Maguire, Rochfort. 1988. *The Journal of Rochfort Maguire, 1852–1854.* Ed. J. Bockstoce. London: Hakluyt Society.

Martell, A., D. Dickinson and L. Casselman. 1984. *Wildlife of the Mackenzie Delta Region.* Boreal Institute for Northern Studies, Occasional Publication 15.

Mathiassen, Therkel. 1927. *The Archaeology of the Central Eskimos.* Vol. 4 of *Report of the Fifth Thule Expedition, 1921–24.*

Miertsching, Johann. 1967. *Frozen Ships: The Arctic Diary of Johann Miertsching.* Trans. L. Neatby. Toronto: Macmillan.

Miller, J. R. 1996. *Shingwauk's Vision: A History of Native Residential Schools.* Toronto: University of Toronto Press.

Morrison, David. 1988. *The Kuugaaluk Site and*

the Nuvorugmiut. Canadian Museum of Civilization, Mercury Series, Archaeological Survey of Canada Paper 137.

———. 1989. Rev. of "A Victorian Earl in the Arctic," by Shepard Krech. *Etudes Inuit Studies* 13(1): 138–42.

———. 1990. *Igluyuaryungmiut Prehistory: The Lost Inuit of Franklin Bay.* Canadian Museum of Civilization, Mercury Series, Archaeological Survey of Canada Paper 142.

———. 1991. "The Copper Inuit Soapstone Trade." *Arctic* 44: 239–46.

———. 1997. *Caribou Hunters in the Western Arctic: Zooarchaeology of the Rita-Claire and Bison Skull Sites.* Canadian Museum of Civilization, Mercury Series, Archaeological Survey of Canada Paper 157.

———. 1999. "The Earliest Thule Migration." *Canadian Journal of Archaeology* 22: 139–56.

———. 2000. "Inuvialuit Fishing and the Gutchiak Site." *Arctic Anthropology* 37: 1–42.

Morrison, David, and Charles Arnold. 1994. "The Inuktuiut of the Eskimo Lakes." *Bridges Across Time: The NOGAP Archaeology Project.* Ed. J.L. Pilon. 117–26. Canadian Archaeological Assocation, Occasional Paper No. 2.

Morrison, William. 1985. "The Mounted Police and Canadian Sovereignty in the Western Arctic, 1903–1924." *Collected Papers on the Human History of the Northwest Territories.* 60–81. Prince of Wales Northern Heritage Centre, Occasional Paper 1.

———. 1998. *True North: The Yukon and Northwest Territories: The Illustrated History of Canada.* Toronto: Oxford University Press.

Mowat, Farley. 1952. *People of the Deer.* Boston: Little, Brown.

———. 1959. *The Desperate People.* Boston: Little, Brown.

Nagy, Murielle. 1994. *Yukon North Slope Inuvialuit Oral History.* Heritage Branch, Government of the Yukon, Occasional Papers in Yukon History, No. 1.

National Film Board of Canada. 1989. *Pelts: Politics of the Fur Trade.* Dir., Writ., Ed. Nigel Markham. Prod. Kent Martin. Exec. Prod. Shelagh Mackenzie, Germaine Ying Gee Wong.

Neatby, Leslie. 1958. *In Quest of the North West Passage.* London: Constable.

Nuligak. 1966. *I, Nuligak.* Ed. and trans. Maurice Metayer. Toronto: Peter Martin.

Nuyaviak, Felix. 1991. "Old-tyme reflections of Felix Nuyaviak." *Tusaayaksat,* June: 10.

On the Trapline. Winter 1995/96. Yellowknife: Metis Nation of the Northwest Territories.

Palsson, Gisli. 2001. *Writing on Ice: the Ethnographic Notebooks of Vilhjalmur Stefansson.* Hanover and London: University Press of New England.

Peake, Frank. 1966. *The Bishop Who Ate His Boots.* Toronto: Anglican Church of Canada.

Peeloolook, Kenneth. 1989. "Beginning of the Eskimo People." *Tusaayaksat,* July: 3.

Petitot, Emile. 1876. *Vocabulaire Francais-Esquimau, Dialecte des Tchiglit des Bouches du Mackenzie et de l'Anderson.* Paris: E. Leroux.

———. 1878. "Monograph of the Esquimaux Tchiglit of the Mackenzie and of the Anderson." Trans. Douglas Brymner. *New Dominion Monthly,* October: 403–17, November: 513–25.

———. 1889. *Quinze Ans Sous le Cercle Polaire.* Paris: E. Dentu.

———. 1999. *Among the Chiglit Eskimos.* Trans. Otto Hahn. Edmonton: Canadian Circumpolar Press.

Pokiak, Bertram. 1976. "Tuktoyaktuk Memories." *Inuttituut,* Winter: 50–54.

Pullen, H.F. 1979. *The Pullen Expedition.* Toronto: Arctic History Press.

Rasmussen, Knud. 1942. *The Mackenzie Eskimos.* Vol. X, No. 2 of *Report of the Fifth Thule Expedition, 1921–24.*

Ray, Dorothy. 1975. *The Eskimos of Bering Strait, 1650–1898.* Seattle: University of Washington Press.

Richardson, John. 1851. *Arctic Searching Expedition.* Vol. 1. London: Longmans, Brown, Green, and Longmans.

Russell, Frank. 1898. *Explorations in the Far North.* Des Moines: University of Iowa Press.

Savoie, Donat. 1970. *The Tchiglit Eskimos,* Vol. 1. of *The Amerindians of the Canadian Northwest in the 19th Century, as Seen by Emile Petitot.* Ottawa: Northern Science Research Group, Department of Indian Affairs and Northern Development.

Schwarz, Herbert. 1970. *Elik and Other Stories of the Mackenzie Eskimos.* Toronto: McClelland and Stewart.

Simpson, John. 1988. "Dr. John Simpson's Essay on the Eskimos of Northwestern Alaska."

Appendix 7 in *The Journal of Rochfort Maguire, 1852–1854*, ed. J. Bockstoce. London: Hakluyt Society.

Simpson, Thomas. 1843. *Narrative of the Discoveries on the North Coast of America; Effected by the Officers of the Hudson's Bay Company During the Years 1836–39*. London: R. Bentley.

Spencer, Robert. 1959. *The North Alaskan Eskimo: A Study in Ecology and Society*. Bureau of American Ethnology Bulletin, 171.

Stager, John. 1967. "Fort Anderson." *Geographical Bulletin* 9: 45–56.

Steele, Harwood. 1936. *Policing the Arctic: the Story of the Conquest of the Arctic by the Royal Canadian (formerly North-West) Mounted Police*. Toronto: Ryerson Press.

Stefansson, Vilhjalmur. 1971 (orig. 1913). *My Life with the Eskimo*. New York: Collier.

———. 1914. *The Stefansson-Anderson Arctic Expedition: Preliminary Ethnographic Results*. Anthropological Papers of the American Museum of Natural History, 14(1).

———. 1928. "The 'Blond' Eskimos." *Harper's* 156: 191–98.

———. 1990 (orig. 1922). *Hunters of the Great North*. New York: Paragon House.

Stoneman-McNichol. 1983. *On Blue Ice: The Inuvik Adventure*. Yellowknife: Outcrop.

Sutherland, Forbes. n.d. Letters from Forbes Sutherland to his mother, 1901–1904. McCord Museum, Montreal.

Usher, Peter. 1970. *The Bankslanders: Economy and Ecology of a Frontier Trapping Community*. Ottawa: Northern Science Research Group, Department of Indian Affairs and Northern Development.

———. 1971a. "The Canadian Western Arctic: A Century of Change." *Anthropologica* 13: 169–83.

———. 1971b. *Fur Trade Posts of the Northwest Territories, 1870–1970*. Ottawa: Northern Science Research Group, Department of Indian Affairs and Northern Development.

———. 1973. *The Committee For Original Peoples Entitlement*. Ottawa: COPE.

———. 1976a. "Inuit Land Use in the Western Canadian Arctic." *Inuit Land Use and Occupancy Project*. Vol. 1. Ed. M. Freeman. 21–32. Ottawa: Indian and Northern Affairs.

———. 1976b "The Inuk as Trapper: A Case Study." *Inuit Land Use and Occupancy Project*. Vol. 2. Ed. M. Freeman. 207–16. Ottawa: Indian and Northern Affairs.

Verano, John, and Douglas Ubelaker. 1992. *Disease and Demography in the Americas*. Washington: Smithsonian Institution Press.

Wenzel, W. F. 1823. "Notice of the Attempts to Reach the Sea by Mackenzie's River." *Edinburgh Philosophical Journal* 8: 78–79.

Whittaker, Charles. 1937. *Arctic Eskimo*. London: Seeley, Service & Co.

Willimott, Bonnie, ed. 2000. *Inuvialuit Corporate Group: 2000 Annual Report*. Inuvik: Inuvialuit Regional Corporation.

Wilson, Keith. 1980. *Fur Trade in Canada*. Toronto: Grolier.

Wolforth, John. 1971. *The Evolution and Economy of the Delta Community*. Ottawa: Northern Science Research Group, Department of Indian Affairs and Northern Development.

Woodbury, Anthony. 1984. "Eskimo and Aleut Languages." *Arctic*, Vol. 5 of *Handbook of North American Indians*. Ed. D. Damas. 49–63. Washington: Smithsonian Institution Press.

Yerbury, J. C. 1977. "Duncan Livingstone of the North West Company." *Arctic* 30(3): 187–88.

Index